Studies in Musical Genesis and Struc

General Editor: Lewis Lockwood, Harvard University

Studies in Musical Genesis and Structure

Anna Bolena and the Artistic Maturity of Gaetano Donizetti
Philip Gossett

Beethoven's Diabelli Variations
William Kinderman

Robert Schumann and the Study of Orchestral Composition
Jon W. Finson

Euryanthe and Carl Maria von Weber's Dramaturgy of German Opera
Michael C. Tusa

Beethoven's 'Appassionata' Sonata
Martha Frohlich

Richard Strauss's *Elektra*

BRYAN GILLIAM

CLARENDON PRESS · OXFORD

Oxford University Press, Walton Street, Oxford OX2 6DP
Oxford New York
Athens Auckland Bangkok Bombay
Calcutta Cape Town Dar es Salaam Delhi
Florence Hong Kong Istanbul Karachi
Kuala Lumpur Madras Madrid Melbourne
Mexico City Nairobi Paris Singapore
Taipei Tokyo Toronto
and associated companies in
Berlin Ibadan

Oxford is a trade mark of Oxford University Press

Published in the United States by
Oxford University Press Inc., New York

First published 1991
Reprinted new as paperback 1996

British Library Cataloguing in Publication Data
Data available

Library of Congress Cataloging in Publication Data
Data to follow
ISBN 0-19-816602-8

1 3 5 7 9 10 8 6 4 2

Printed in Great Britain
on acid-free paper by
Biddles Ltd
Guildford and King's Lynn

Editor's Preface

This series provides a number of monographs, each dealing with a single work by an important composer. The main focus of each book is on the compositional process by which the work developed from antecedent stages, so far as these can be determined from the sources. In each case the genesis of the work is connected to an analytical overview of the final version. Each monograph is written by a specialist, and, apart from the general theme of the series, no artificial uniformity is imposed. The individual character of both work and evidence, as well as the author's special critical viewpoint, dictates differences in emphasis and treatment. Thus some studies may stress a combination of sketch evidence and analysis, while others may shift the emphasis to the position of the work within its genre and context. Although no such series could possibly aim at being comprehensive, it will deal with a representative body of important works by composers of stature across the centuries.

By common consent *Elektra* (1909) is the most powerful and original of Richard Strauss's stage works, not excluding *Salome* (1905) and *Der Rosenkavalier* (1911) nor any of his later operas. Quite apart from its extravagance of subject and treatment, *Elektra* is one of the seminal works of twentieth-century opera. For years anyone interested in its background could turn to general works on Strauss; to his marvellous correspondence with Hugo von Hofmannsthal (on whose play of 1903 the opera was based); and to broad-based studies of German opera after Wagner. Now for the first time Bryan Gilliam carefully documents the essential context and development of the work. He establishes its place in the post-Wagnerian mainstream; its focus on demonic themes of domestic violence and psychological perversion; its graphic and powerful music. The book discloses for the first time some of the methods by which the Strauss of 1906–8 achieved 'modernity' and technical brilliance in his most fully realized dramatic work up to this time. Gilliam provides arresting details from Strauss's annotated libretto containing his first musical ideas for the work, and he carries the narrative through to a study of the *Elektra* sketchbooks, the further stages of composition, and a close reading of the final scene of the work from this viewpoint. Gilliam's book reveals the deeper levels below the familiar superficial portrait of a composer who once boasted that he could compose 'everywhere, on walks or journeys, eating or drinking . . . in noisy hotels . . .' and who claimed that 'one of the most important melodies of *Der Rosenkavalier* occurred to me while I was playing a Bavarian card game'.

Forty years ago, Roger Sessions said of *Elektra,* still new and notorious when he was growing up, that Strauss's music 'at that time seemed to carry the development of harmony as far as it could be carried within the limits of the tonal system . . .' and he spoke of the 'harmonic daring and the expressive power which that work embodies' (*The Musical Experience* [Princeton, NJ, 1950], p. 118). Now, when *Elektra* is one of the long-established classics of twentieth-century opera, this study enables us to comprehend better the work and thought that gave rise to it.

Harvard University Lewis Lockwood

Richard Strauss's *Elektra*

BRYAN GILLIAM

CLARENDON PRESS · OXFORD

Oxford University Press, Walton Street, Oxford OX2 6DP
Oxford New York
Athens Auckland Bangkok Bombay
Calcutta Cape Town Dar es Salaam Delhi
Florence Hong Kong Istanbul Karachi
Kuala Lumpur Madras Madrid Melbourne
Mexico City Nairobi Paris Singapore
Taipei Tokyo Toronto
and associated companies in
Berlin Ibadan

Oxford is a trade mark of Oxford University Press

Published in the United States by
Oxford University Press Inc., New York

First published 1991
Reprinted new as paperback 1996

British Library Cataloguing in Publication Data
Data available

Library of Congress Cataloging in Publication Data
Data to follow
ISBN 0-19-816602-8

1 3 5 7 9 10 8 6 4 2

Printed in Great Britain
on acid-free paper by
Biddles Ltd
Guildford and King's Lynn

To
Franz Trenner

Editor's Preface

This series provides a number of monographs, each dealing with a single work by an important composer. The main focus of each book is on the compositional process by which the work developed from antecedent stages, so far as these can be determined from the sources. In each case the genesis of the work is connected to an analytical overview of the final version. Each monograph is written by a specialist, and, apart from the general theme of the series, no artificial uniformity is imposed. The individual character of both work and evidence, as well as the author's special critical viewpoint, dictates differences in emphasis and treatment. Thus some studies may stress a combination of sketch evidence and analysis, while others may shift the emphasis to the position of the work within its genre and context. Although no such series could possibly aim at being comprehensive, it will deal with a representative body of important works by composers of stature across the centuries.

By common consent *Elektra* (1909) is the most powerful and original of Richard Strauss's stage works, not excluding *Salome* (1905) and *Der Rosenkavalier* (1911) nor any of his later operas. Quite apart from its extravagance of subject and treatment, *Elektra* is one of the seminal works of twentieth-century opera. For years anyone interested in its background could turn to general works on Strauss; to his marvellous correspondence with Hugo von Hofmannsthal (on whose play of 1903 the opera was based); and to broad-based studies of German opera after Wagner. Now for the first time Bryan Gilliam carefully documents the essential context and development of the work. He establishes its place in the post-Wagnerian mainstream; its focus on demonic themes of domestic violence and psychological perversion; its graphic and powerful music. The book discloses for the first time some of the methods by which the Strauss of 1906–8 achieved 'modernity' and technical brilliance in his most fully realized dramatic work up to this time. Gilliam provides arresting details from Strauss's annotated libretto containing his first musical ideas for the work, and he carries the narrative through to a study of the *Elektra* sketchbooks, the further stages of composition, and a close reading of the final scene of the work from this viewpoint. Gilliam's book reveals the deeper levels below the familiar superficial portrait of a composer who once boasted that he could compose 'everywhere, on walks or journeys, eating or drinking . . . in noisy hotels . . .' and who claimed that 'one of the most important melodies of *Der Rosenkavalier* occurred to me while I was playing a Bavarian card game'.

Forty years ago, Roger Sessions said of *Elektra,* still new and notorious when he was growing up, that Strauss's music 'at that time seemed to carry the development of harmony as far as it could be carried within the limits of the tonal system . . .' and he spoke of the 'harmonic daring and the expressive power which that work embodies' (*The Musical Experience* [Princeton, NJ, 1950], p. 118). Now, when *Elektra* is one of the long-established classics of twentieth-century opera, this study enables us to comprehend better the work and thought that gave rise to it.

Harvard University Lewis Lockwood

Author's Preface

Elektra, the fourth of fifteen operas by Strauss, is often described in surveys of twentieth-century music as an end of the road, stylistically, for the composer. One might as easily see it as an auspicious beginning, for it marks the start of Strauss's relationship with poet, playwright, and librettist Hugo von Hofmannsthal. *Elektra* is a remarkably modern work, although its stylistic role in early twentieth-century music has not been fully sorted out. Of the various historical interpretations of music in our century, the Schoenbergian paradigm—which sees progress in music in harmonic terms and views musical style as an inevitable, evolutionary process—has probably been the most influential, especially since the end of the Second World War. According to this view, the importance of a work was based principally on whether it was progressive or regressive—a notion based almost entirely on the dichotomy of tonality vs. atonality.

Because of its arresting dissonance and chromaticism, *Elektra* was made part of this evolutionary process towards atonality and, thus, a part of the twentieth-century 'canon'. This line of thought, not surprisingly, recognizes *Elektra* as an early twentieth-century masterpiece, but consigns *Der Rosenkavalier* and the later operas to the unimportant realm of stylistic reversion. But while the ratio of non-diatonic to diatonic or dissonant to consonant material may be higher in *Elektra* than *Der Rosenkavalier*, both are thoroughly tonal works. As this study intends to show, they share more similarities than dissimilarities. One important parallel, which is frequently overlooked, is that both operas exploit a multiplicity of musical styles. Although we may be more aware of manifold styles in *Der Rosenkavalier*, where the models (Mozart, Johann Strauss, Verdi, etc.) are quite clear, the starkly contrasting musical modes of expression in *Elektra* are no less real. Indeed, one senses that what most offended Ernest Newman about *Elektra* were the jarring juxtapositions of brutal dissonance and consonant, lyrical moments of what he termed 'agreeable commonplace'. What he saw was a composer simulating emotion, rather than being emotional. Newman, no doubt, viewed the Strauss of *Elektra* as a composer who felt he could select musical styles as he needed them.

Strauss's seemingly protean treatment of style—whether as irony, parody, or any number of other types of expression—is surely one of his most modern traits. His suggestion that the mind that created *Tristan* was as 'cool as marble' says a lot more about Strauss than Wagner. It suggests a distance between creator and creation, an artistic distance that one would not find in Mahler or Schoenberg, and, not surprisingly, it is an aspect of modernism mostly ignored in the Schoenbergian paradigm. *Elektra*, shorter and more concise than *Der Rosenkavalier*, is composed in what the composer referred to as his 'tragic vein'. But this tragic vein is not monolithic; it is, rather, a succession of contrasting styles. *Elektra*'s powerful and disturbing monologue (scene 2) gives way to the joyous, waltz-like sweep of Chrysothemis' diatonic E-flat-major aria ('Kinder will ich haben'), which in turn leads into the most tense and hyperchromatic scene in the opera: the scene between Elektra and Klytämnestra. Likewise, Elektra's moment of recognition ignites the most turbulent, dissonant orchestral passage in the score only to be followed by her tender, blissful aria in A flat major ('Es rührt sich niemand'). Which sections represent the real Strauss? This study argues that they all do.

Elektra is one of the most important operas of the early twentieth century; it both shocked its audience and solidified Strauss's stature as the leading German opera composer of his day. No operatic work of the time had probed such psychological depths, created such awesome musical climaxes, or exploited such a vast orchestral ensemble. And although, technically, one cannot call *Elektra* a collaboration between Strauss and Hofmannsthal (the composer himself made the textual cuts and very little of the play had to be rewritten), their mutual satisfaction with the opera galvanized their collaborative work for the future. Strauss immediately recognized the importance of this gifted writer and, for better or worse, remained true to him until the end of Hofmannsthal's life.

My interest in *Elektra* began as I was finishing my dissertation on *Daphne*. Unable to locate Strauss's musically annotated copy of that libretto (only a photograph of the last page is extant), I looked at other autograph texts at the Richard-Strauss-Archiv in Garmisch in order to get a sense of what some of these annotated documents looked like. The musical commentary in Strauss's copy of Hofmannsthal's *Elektra* fascinated and puzzled me more than all the others; I then saw the potential for a future long-term project. Shortly thereafter, Lewis Lockwood approached me with the idea of contributing a volume on a Strauss work for his series Studies in Musical Genesis and Structure, and I immediately suggested *Elektra*.[1]

My study is divided into two parts: Chapters 1 to 3, and Chapters 4 to 7. The first three chapters mainly establish the musical-historical context. In Chapter 1 I examine the critical response to *Elektra* just after its première and place the opera within the context of Strauss's career in the first decade of the twentieth century. I also place *Elektra* within the larger framework of German opera at that time. Chapter 2 delves into the work's dramaturgy and discusses the cuts that Strauss made in Hofmannsthal's text. Finally, in Chapter 3 I have constructed a chronology of the evolution of the opera, evaluating creative decisions that Strauss made at crucial

[1] Shortly after my manuscript had gone to press I was pleased to see the Cambridge opera handbook (edited by Derrick Puffett) on *Elektra* appear. It is a collection of essays by various authors, and I trust it will make a fine complement to the present study, which presents *Elektra* from a single perspective.

steps along the way. The compositional timetable is based, in part, on recently published letters as well as unpublished sources gathered in Munich, Garmisch, and Vienna.

The remainder of the book focuses more on the music, beginning with a look at *Elektra*'s tonal structure, which cannot be appreciated fully without understanding Strauss's use of keys to symbolize characters or aspects of the drama. As Chapter 5 shows, some of these keys are sketched in the margins of the text along with other types of musical commentary such as thematic fragments, instrumentation, or style of singing. Chapter 6 concerns the next stage of composition for Strauss: the sketchbooks (both preliminary and fair), which may be found in various parts of the world (Garmisch, Munich, Tokyo, Vienna, and in anonymous private hands). The *Elektra* sketches, in the earliest stages, reveal Strauss's preoccupation with motivic continuity in the orchestra. Strauss's concern for the vocal line is more evident in later preliminary sketches and fair sketches. In the last chapter I analyse the final scene from various perspectives drawn from the preceding chapters. It is part analysis, part sketch study, but it also discusses the dramaturgical problem of dance in the finale and how Strauss chose to delineate different types of dance through symbolic keys, namely E and C major. Sketches for the final scene shed important light on these observations.

Keys that are solely designated by an upper-case letter are in the major; minor keys are designated by an upper-case letter followed by a lower-case 'm' (i.e. C vs. Cm). To avoid unnecessary clutter in sketch transcriptions, I have not corrected many anomalies (rests, accidentals, dots, alignment, etc.) in the text. Where an exact reading of the text is critical, editorial brackets or dotted lines have been supplied.

Unless noted otherwise, all translations are by the author. English quotations from the *Elektra* play, unless otherwise indicated, are taken from Alfred Schwarz's translation in *Hugo von Hofmannsthal: Selected Plays and Libretti*, ed. Michael Hamburger, Bollingen Series 33, No. 3 (New York, 1963).

English excerpts from the libretto are taken from G. M. Holland's and K. Chalmers' translation (DECCA 1986).

This book would not have been possible without the help of many friends and colleagues and to them I am deeply grateful. First, I should like to thank Thomas Hansen (Department of German, Wellesley College), who read every page of this manuscript and whose advice, especially relating to Chapter 2, was invaluable. My colleague, R. Larry Todd (Duke University), was likewise helpful at nearly every stage of this work. This book would obviously not have been possible without the interest of Lewis Lockwood (Harvard University), and I am thankful for his many suggestions. I am pleased to acknowledge the generous support of the Colby College Humanities Research Grant and the Duke University Research Council for their travel grants. Many thanks are also due to the editorial staff of the OUP for their assistance in preparing this volume for publication. For decades now Alice Strauss has devoted her time and energy to building and organizing the Richard-Strauss-Archiv in Garmisch. For each of my many trips to Zoeppritzstrasse over the years, she has never failed to be as helpful and as hospitable as possible. I am also indebted to her for permission to quote excerpts from the *Elektra* sketchbooks at Garmisch as well as Strauss's annotated copy of Hofmannsthal's play. I owe her my deepest gratitude.

At the Bavarian State Library (Munich), I was not only able to examine Strauss manuscripts in the regular catalogue, but—through the help of Robert Münster and Karl Dachs—I was able to go through recently-acquired, uncatalogued Strauss sources. I am also grateful for their permission to cite some examples from a bifolio of *Elektra* sketches at the Bavarian State Library as well as quote some lines from a Strauss letter to Felix Mottl concerning the Munich *Elektra* première. Stephan Kohler of the Richard-Strauss-Institut (Munich) kept me abreast of recent catalogue sales of *Elektra* sketch fragments; I am indebted to him for his generous assistance and expertise. I must also acknowledge Franz Trenner, editor of the *Richard Strauss Werkverzeichnis*. Most Strauss scholars who have gone to Munich for their research have, no doubt, visited the Trenner home and experienced their warm Bavarian hospitality. Trenner has been an important source of information and advice for many years, and he has been a dear friend. Although I could not afford to travel to Tokyo in order to see the *Elektra* sketchbook at the Musashino Academy of Music, they kindly furnished me a microfilm and have generously given me permission to quote some examples. I would also like to thank Jarmila Weissenböck of the Theatre Collection of the Austrian National Library who provided me with the photographs of Strauss's hand-written and musically annotated *Elektra* text. She has also kindly granted permission to quote examples from the *Elektra* sketchbook in the collection. Thanks also to Günter Brosche of the Music Collection of the Austrian National Library for his advice and assistance. I am also grateful to research assistants Donna Lynn and Karen Tiegreen for their invaluable help.

Finally, I would like to thank my wife Vivian, who, despite her busy schedule as a physician and a mother, always allowed me the time I needed in which to write this book. To quote her favourite Strauss Lied: 'Habe Dank!'

Contents

List of Illustrations

Abbreviations

Briefwechsel	Willi Schuh (ed.), *Richard Strauss-Hugo von Hofmannsthal: Briefwechsel*, 5th edn. (Zurich, 1978)
BSt	Bayerische Staatsbibliothek (Munich)
Correspondence	Willi Schuh (ed.), *A Working Friendship: The Correspondence between Richard Strauss and Hugo von Hofmannsthal*, trans. Hanns Hammelmann and Ewald Osers (New York, 1974)
ÖNB	Österreichische Nationalbibliothek, Theatre Collection, Vienna
RSA	Richard-Strauss-Archiv, Garmisch
Tr.	Catalogue numbering system by Franz Trenner in his edition of *Die Skizzenbücher von Richard Strauss aus dem Richard-Strauss-Archiv in Garmisch*, Veröffentlichungen der Richard-Strauss-Gesellschaft, München, vol. i (Tutzing, 1977)

1 Context and Critical Reception

'His new opera, which is to be produced early next year, will probably show whether he is going to realize our best hopes or our worst fears,' predicted Ernest Newman in the final sentence of his 1908 biography of Richard Strauss—just three years after the première of *Salome* and one year before *Elektra*.[1] Newman's hope was that *Salome* would prove to be an aberration, that Strauss would return to the 'high-minded seriousness of *Tod und Verklärung* and *Guntram*'. His fear was that the crude pictorialism and a disposition toward extravagance that he recognized in *Salome* might represent a lasting stylistic change for the composer. Would *Salome* signify a new direction for Strauss, or would it merely be an exceptional *tour de force*? In the first decade of the twentieth century this question was not an easy one to answer.

At the time of *Salome* Strauss was firmly established as a successful composer of tone poems and Lieder, but he remained an enigma as an opera composer. The audience's perplexity about Strauss's musical development in the first decade of the twentieth century stemmed from two related problems. The first one was that his audience perceived no stylistic consistency in his first three operas. Paul Bekker, indeed, viewed Strauss's early operas as a 'series of style experiments'.[2] The second, and much broader, problem is that no one at that time seemed to know in which direction post-Wagnerian German opera was heading. In *Die deutsche Musik der Gegenwart*, published the year of *Elektra*'s première, Robert Louis called Wagner 'the last landmark in the history

[1] Ernest Newman, *Richard Strauss* (London, 1908), 137.

[2] Paul Bekker, *The Changing Opera*, trans. Arthur Mendel (New York, 1935), 261.

of music'.[3] This bewilderment about the state of German opera is reflected in many early *Elektra* reviews. August Spanuth, writing for *Signale für die musikalische Welt*, found it hard to assess the value of *Elektra* given the ambiguous state of German opera after Wagner.

In particular, in relationship to opera in Germany, people [i.e., composers] do not rightly know what they want. Some have copied the Italian *verismo* composers, some have written fairy-tale operas, some have tried various types of themes, but to establish with certainty from what direction our salvation will come is not even discussed.[4]

Spanuth's assertion typifies a prevailing curiosity in early twentieth-century Germany about the direction of opera after Wagner. Bekker addresses the issue in *Wandlungen der Oper* [*The Changing Opera*] (1934), observing that shortly after Wagner's death, 'a genuine fever [in opera composition] breaks out'.[5] Indeed, the list of German opera composers between the year of Wagner's death and the First World War is remarkable. Among the best known of this post-Wagnerian generation are Karl Goldmark (1830–1915), Alexander Ritter (1830–96), August Bungert (1845–1915), Richard Heuberger (1850–1914), Engelbert Humperdinck (1854–1921), and Wilhelm Kienzl (1857–1941).

Strauss (1864–1949) belongs to a slightly younger generation of opera composers, most of whom were active well beyond the First World War. They include Emil von Rezniček (1860–1945), Ludwig Thuille (1861–1907), Friedrich Klose (1862–1942), Felix Weingartner (1863–1942), Eugène d'Albert (1864–1932), Max von Schillings (1868–1933), Siegfried Wagner (1869–1930), Hans Pfitzner (1869–1949), Leo Blech (1871–1939), Alexander von Zemlinsky (1871–1942), Franz Schreker (1878–1934) and Julius Bittner (1879–1939).

[3] Robert Louis, *Die deutsche Musik der Gegenwart* (Munich, 1909), 50.

[4] August Spanuth, 'Nachträge zur *Elektra*', *Signale für die musikalische Welt* [Berlin], 67/5 (1909), 166.

[5] Paul Bekker, *The Changing Opera*, 256.

This outburst of operatic creativity was not only unprecedented in Germany's history, but unmatched by any other country in Europe. Yet the period of activity was equally unmatched in its number of operatic failures. The death of Wagner had, on the one hand, catalysed this 'creative fever', but, on the other hand, prevented any chance for lasting success. Indeed, much of the post-Wagnerian vacuum was filled by mediocre operas, and from the names listed above, only Strauss would emerge as an opera composer of enduring fame. Wagner's influence on the next generation was great, yet those who followed him too closely were doomed to fail. Strauss's first opera, *Guntram* (1894), is an example. The work, with the text written by the composer, is a Wagnerian epigone in both theme and musical language. Its world première in Weimar received a lukewarm reception, while the more important Munich première was an outright failure—the worst in Strauss's career.

Many neo-Wagnerian composers of the time sought to avoid too close a link with Wagner by turning to the *Märchenoper* (fairy-tale opera) with its antecedents in the *Zauberoper* tradition of the late eighteenth and early nineteenth centuries. A major stylistic problem of this later genre is the incongruity between its heavy, polyphonic post-Wagnerian musical language and naïve, child-like subject matter. The frequent inclusion of real or invented German folk tunes only highlighted this incompatibility. Humperdinck was the best-known exponent of the tradition, but there were many others such as Thuille, Ritter, Kienzl, Bittner, S. Wagner, Blech, and Klose. Other genres attracted composers of the time, but none so far-reaching as the *Märchenoper*. Some of these other genres include the sentimental *Volksoper*, following the Lortzing prototype; a German-style verismo, typified by d'Albert's *Tiefland* (1903); and the comic opera of the Cornelius tradition. Few critics were in total agreement as to the particular category into which an opera might fall.

This *Märchenoper* tradition, no doubt, left its mark on Strauss, who not only conducted the world première of

Hänsel und Gretel (1893)—a work that he admired throughout his life—but was a close friend of both Thuille and Ritter. These two composers, along with his father Franz Strauss, were the greatest influences on Strauss during his formative years. After the failure of *Guntram*, Strauss, too, turned towards a *Märchenoper* of sorts with *Feuersnot* (1901), a satirical fairy-tale opera that, in essence, poked fun at the Munich that had rejected *Guntram*.

Is there a German operatic mainstream? That was the central question of the day. Strauss would, no doubt, ultimately embody that mainstream in the first few decades of the new century, but his predominance as an opera composer was not altogether clear before *Elektra*. *Guntram* and *Feuersnot* may have mirrored stylistic movements of their time, but it was only when he broke with these conventions with *Salome*—shunning themes of redemption or German folklore and embracing the spirit of the *fin de siècle*—that he established himself as an opera composer of international stature. Berlin, the bustling capital of the German empire, where Strauss had served as principal conductor of the Court Opera since 1898, provided an ideal cultural atmosphere in which the composer could explore his new artistic direction.

It is not surprising that, in doing so, Strauss should turn his attention away from the masculine world of his tone poems—and *Guntram* and *Feuersnot* for that matter—towards the female psyché. The strong, sensual—even demonic—female figure had become a veritable cult throughout *fin-de-siècle* Europe. In Berlin alone, the first few years of the century had seen the premières of Oscar Wilde's *Salome*, Frank Wedekind's *Erdgeist*, Maxim Gorky's *Nachtaysl*, and Hofmannsthal's *Elektra*. Moreover, turn-of-the-century preoccupation with the *femme fatale* extended well beyond the theatre into the poetry of Richard Dehmel and Peter Altenberg, the writings of Sigmund Freud and Karl Kraus, and the paintings of Gustav Klimt and Egon Schiele.

With *Salome* Strauss found a new, modern voice, and it struck a timely nerve, yet despite the unqualified success of the work he was still considered a maverick as an opera composer. Was the composer a comet racing across the sky, was he merely a phenomenon or a composer whose operas would become an integral part of a German musical tradition? These questions prevailed throughout the first decade of the twentieth century. *Salome* was, no doubt, the most original opera to reach the German stage since Wagner's death. This *succès de scandale*, which both fascinated and disgusted its audience, polarized pro- and anti-Straussian factions throughout Europe and the United States. The opera may have delighted some and revolted others, but it nevertheless established Strauss, at the age of forty-one, as an opera composer to be reckoned with. Critics and general public alike—not knowing what his next stage offering would bring—awaited *Elektra* with great anticipation. That sense of anticipation acquires greater meaning when viewed within the context of the reception of *Salome*.

On 9 December 1905, *Salome* had its world première in Dresden under Ernst von Schuch, who also conducted the first *Feuersnot* in 1901. Berlin would have seemed the likely place for these premières, since Strauss had been principal conductor there for nearly seven years. However, the management of the Court Opera found the text to *Feuersnot* offensive, and it was clear that a Berlin première would run into serious censorship problems. Thus, the composer angrily renounced 'the honor of having *Feuersnot* performed for the first time at the Berlin Opera House, and also the distinction of seeing any of my other stage works presented there'.[6] Strauss was so impressed with Schuch's performance of the work that he rewarded him with the right to conduct first performances of *Salome*, *Elektra*, and *Der Rosenkavalier*, despite the large number of other prominent conductors who vied for those honours.

Both *Guntram* and *Feuersnot* paled in comparison to *Salome*. If *Guntram* was an outright failure—it closed shortly after its

[6] Ernst Krause, *Richard Strauss: The Man and his Work* (Boston, 1969), 51. History has shown that Strauss was true to his word.

première—*Feuersnot* fared only marginally better, with more premières, but remarkably fewer repeat performances. *Salome* was quite a different matter, although it certainly had its share of censorship problems in various cities. Mahler was never able to arrange a performance of it while he was director of the Vienna Court Opera, and the censor's refusal to allow the work to be performed was one of Mahler's greatest disappointments while serving as music director. Within its first year *Salome* was performed in six German cities as well as Graz, Prague, and Milan. The next year saw performances in the United States, Belgium, Switzerland, France, Holland, and Poland. In short, within two years *Salome*'s success was guaranteed.

But Strauss's newly acquired fame as opera composer was a mixed blessing as far as *Elektra* was concerned. On the positive side, Strauss had gained financial independence after *Salome* and certainly a great deal of prestige as an important post-Wagnerian opera composer. He was, indeed, able to sell the *Elektra* score to Fürstner for around 100,000 Marks: an unprecedented sum for any musical work at that time. And it was no longer necessary for him to try to convince opera houses to perform his stage works as he had done with *Guntram*, *Feuersnot*, and—to a lesser extent—*Salome*. By 1909, the situation was quite the other way around. So much so that Strauss could afford to bestow favour upon those who had been loyal to him when times were not as good.

The United States première of *Salome* (22 January 1907) offers a good case in point. Banned at the Metropolitan Opera for twenty-six years after a single performance, it was produced two years later, in French, by Oscar Hammerstein's Manhattan Opera. Strauss saw to it that the Manhattan Opera received exclusive rights to the American première of *Elektra*, much to the chagrin of the Metropolitan, who had hoped to improve their financial situation with an *Elektra* première and subsequent performances. Indeed, by the time of *Elektra*, Strauss had amassed enough influence to have a four-day Strauss opera festival—*Elektra*, *Feuersnot*, *Salome*, and a repeat of *Elektra*—written into the contract for the Dresden première.

The event received international publicity, and some called Dresden Strauss's Bayreuth. English music critic Alfred Kalisch remarked that one 'met' *Elektra* all over the city: 'The shopping windows were full of *Elektra* boots, spoons, and beer mugs'.[7] Despite all of the publicity, details about the work and its rehearsals were kept secret. An annoyed press was not allowed to attend rehearsals, nor were piano-vocal scores available before the first performance. Some critics wondered aloud in their reviews whether these restrictions were designed to ensure a better performance or to heighten a sense of expectation. Not only did these strict controls anger many in the press, but they contributed to numerous, often bizarre, rumours that circulated throughout the city. Kalisch recounted one story 'that the farmyards and slaughter-houses had been ransacked for livestock to figure in the sacrificial procession'.[8]

But the external events that helped to sensationalize the première of *Elektra* had a decidedly negative effect as well. Distractions of rumour, gratuitous predictions, and other irrelevant commentary—which grew at an exponential rate during the week preceding the première—coloured much of the criticism. Misguided expectations led many opera-goers to feel a sense of disappointment after the première. The aftershocks of the *Salome* première of three years earlier still resonated throughout Dresden; the public wondered what new sensation they might expect. It would have been difficult for an opera to have outdone *Salome*'s colourful première, and *Elektra* no doubt failed to outshine her flashier sister, yet critical reaction to the première and early performances of *Elektra* was as strong as it was mixed. Both Dresden performances (25 and 28 January 1909) of *Elektra* had been sold out well in advance; people had come from all

[7] Alfred Kalisch, 'Impressions of Strauss's *Elektra*', *Zeitschrift der Internationalen Musikgesellschaft*, 7 (1909), 198.
[8] Ibid.

over the world more out of curiosity than anything else. Bekker was surely not alone when he lamented that seldom had the reception of a work had so little to do with its artistic worth as with the case of *Elektra*.[9]

Elektra criticism took various forms. There was, of course, the plethora of reviews in various newspapers and music journals. But within the year of the première there appeared two full-length articles as well: one in the *Riemann Festschrift*, by Carl Mennicke, and the other (in three instalments) by Paul Bekker in the *Neue Musik-Zeitung*.[10] The London première of *Elektra* (19 February 1910), not unlike Dresden's, was also the centre of massive publicity, and it was so successful that the Covent Garden season was extended to accommodate extra performances. The London *Elektra* also caused a heated exchange of open letters between Newman and George Bernard Shaw that spanned six weeks in *The Nation*. Sir Thomas Beecham, who conducted the première, surely had that protracted polemic in mind when he declared that the general 'journalistic fever' inspired by that performance was rivalled only by the death of King Edward VII later that year.[11]

The *Elektra* reviews not only reveal a polarization of opinion about Strauss as a twentieth-century composer, but also point to the confusion about the present state of German opera and where it should be going. Some critics saw the Strauss of *Elektra* as a cunning charlatan; others believed him to be a genius who embodied a new era in German music; only a few found middle ground. The following overview of criticism—stemming mostly from the world première—surveys both sides of the issue.

[9] Paul Bekker, '*Elektra* Studie', *Neue Musik-Zeitung*, 14 (1909), [293].

[10] Carl Mennicke, 'Über Richard Strauss' *Elektra*', *Riemann-Festschrift: Gesammelte Studien* (Leipzig, 1909). Bekker's article, '*Elektra* Studie', appeared in Nos. 14, 16, and 18 of the *Neue Musik-Zeitung*.

[11] Sir Thomas Beecham, *A Mingled Chime* (London, 1944), 146.

Elektra Reception

Elektra made a powerful impression; no critic—pro or con—would deny that observation, but that is about all they could agree upon. Most of the points raised by critics, regardless of their sympathies, fall under one or two broad rubrics: (i) Strauss's choice of text (for better or for worse) and (ii) the issue of industry vs. inspiration in the composer's latest opera.

Negative critics saw Strauss's choice of text as further indication of the composer's decline in the early twentieth century. A recurring question among a majority of these critics was how the composer of *Macbeth*, *Tod und Verklärung*, and *Also Sprach Zarathustra* could also be attracted to a perversion of Sophocles. They viewed Hofmannsthal's text as problematic for a number of reasons, but the most vociferous criticism was aimed at the play's inherent violence and preoccupation with themes of hysteria and insanity. A number of other shortcomings were perceived as well, especially the fact that the libretto lacked any empathetic character or love element. Spanuth observed that without such an element the opera audience could only take a half-hearted, at best, literary interest in the text.[12] F. A. Geissler, writing for *Die Musik*, found the text overwhelmingly unmusical and undramatic because of its distorted emphasis on insanity: Elektra exemplifies revenge madness, Chrysothemis embodies the insanity of denial and escape, while Klytämnestra represents the insanity of a tortured conscience.[13] For Mennicke, Hofmannsthal's greatest transgression against Sophocles—even more than the violence—was the lowering of godly characters to the purely human level. By removing the tension between gods and mortals, Hofmannsthal reduced the drama to a mere family scandal.[14]

[12] Spanuth, 'Nachträge', 166.
[13] F. A. Geissler, '*Elektra*, von Richard Strauss', *Die Musik*, 8/10 (1909), 244.
[14] Mennicke, 'Strauss' *Elektra*', 506.

Admirers of *Elektra* were divided on the issue of text; some savoured the power and expression of Hofmannsthal's play, while others believed the opera to be great despite its text. Two critics who marvelled at Hofmannsthal's modern treatment of Sophocles were Oskar Bie and Bekker. An author and music critic from Berlin, Bie was an enthusiastic advocate of contemporary music and, indeed, gave a public lecture on 'Modern Music and Richard Strauss' in Dresden a day before the première. Bie does not deny the violence of the play, and he freely admits that the work is devoid of love or empathy. Recognizing that this atypical libretto requires a special composer, Bie implies that only someone as forward-looking as Strauss could set such a text. He explains: 'The coolness of antiquity delights [Strauss's] technical spirit, the force of the cyclopean world inspires him to ideas that always lie at the boundaries of music'.[15]

Bekker, whose three-part review appeared after he had seen the Dresden and Berlin premières of *Elektra*, would not quarrel with Geissler's remarks that the opera was undramatic—indeed, to Bekker's thinking, *Elektra*'s strength stems from the fact that it is not a drama, but rather a compelling series of sharply-delineated character studies. Hofmannsthal's Freudian version of Sophocles represents a stunning departure from the original, but, as Bekker emphasizes, not because it is an immoral play that corrupted the Greek.

> The fundamental difference between the original and the newer rendering lies not in the elimination of Sophocles' prevailing idea of a gloomy fate, which arises from the motive of revenge and compels the people in its spell. With Hofmannsthal, by comparison, the tragedy of events is based, in the first place, on the characters of the individual people.[16]

[15] Oskar Bie, '*Elektra*', *Die neue Rundschau* [Berlin], 4 (1909), 591.
[16] Bekker, '*Elektra* Studie', 14, p. 295.

Bekker dismissed the notion of the Greek world being purer than Hofmannsthal's as a fallacy stemming from a prudish, contemporary ignorance of the Greeks.

The dichotomy of *Könner* vs. *Künstler*, of skilful artisan vs. artist, is a topic to be found in nearly every review of *Elektra*. Negative critics intended *Könner* as a pejorative description; it had been used against Strauss in the past and would continue to be used for years to come. This dichotomy raises a host of related issues such as calculation versus creativity, skill as opposed to inspiration, a composer's identification with his subject matter, his choice and treatment of that subject matter, and the like. Strauss's greatest detractors would freely admit that his musical skill—especially his orchestrational abilities and leitmotivic technique—rivalled any living composer, but those abilities alone—they would add—do not necessarily make a good opera composer. Newman saw most of *Elektra* as 'merely frigid intellectual speculation simulating a white heat of emotion . . . [Strauss] drives furious at us, with all of his enormous technique; but at heart he is cold, for all the whipping and spurring.'[17]

Otto Röse and Julius Prüwer put together a lengthy motivic guide that was published shortly before the *Elektra* première; we recall that the score was not published before the première.[18] Richard Sternfeld was not alone when he observed that Strauss's preoccupation with motivic writing undermined any chance of sharp vocal characterizations.[19] Mennicke, who lauded Strauss's remarkable thematic unity in *Elektra*, none the less maintained that the composer's

[17] Ernest Newman, 'Minority Report', *The Nation* (26 Mar. 1910), repr. in *The Bodley Head Bernard Shaw: Shaw's Music*, iii, ed. Dan H. Laurence (London, 1981), 613.

[18] Otto Röse and Julius Prüwer, *Richard Strauss: Elektra. Ein Musikführer durch das Werk* (Berlin, 1909). Another, and less ambitious, thematic guide by Georg Gräner appeared that year: *Elektra: Tragödie in einem Aufzuge von Hugo von Hofmannsthal und Richard Strauss*. Schlesinger'sche Musik-Bibliothek Opernführer Nr. 122 (Berlin, 1909). Schirmer published the first thematic guide in English: Ernest Hutcheson, *Elektra by Richard Strauss: A Guide to the Opera* (New York, 1910).

[19] Richard Sternfeld, '*Elektra*', *März*, 8 (1909), 138–9.

painstaking effort was nothing more than an attempt to solve the incongruity between libretto and music; the motivic network, in essence, bypassed Hofmannsthal's words.[20] Wilhelm Altmann dismissed the score as a 'witches sabbath' of short-breathed leitmotifs made to seem more profound by their orchestration.[21]

A perceived overreliance on the orchestra by Strauss is another example of the victory of calculation over inspiration in *Elektra*, according to sceptics. Mennicke complained that not only had the orchestra made the words unintelligible, but, much worse, Strauss saw to it that it was no longer necessary to understand them. The voice, which he termed the 'soul of the operatic action', became a means—a new addition to the orchestral line—rather than an end.[22] Newman viewed Strauss's exploitation of the orchestra as the composer's greatest shortcoming in the period surrounding *Elektra*. 'His orchestra doth protest too much,' he observed, adding that even in the few years leading up to *Elektra* Strauss had been trying to 'carry through' sloppy vocal writing 'by means of orchestral bravado'.[23]

Graphic details evoked by the orchestra, as well as Strauss's willingness to create ugly, violent, even trivial music for various expressive reasons, revolted some and annoyed many. Even Kalisch, one of Strauss's earliest advocates outside Germany, found certain orchestral sound effects in Klytämnestra's procession 'almost an insult to the ear'.[24] Karl Storck ascribed these tendencies to what he terms Strauss's 'journalistic nature'. His term was intended to describe a composer concerned entirely with the present day, and he saw Strauss as a composer who responds to the needs and exploits the means of the present—seeking success at any price. He is a composer not motivated from within, but

[20] Mennicke, 'Strauss' *Elektra*', 511–12.

[21] Wilhelm Altmann, '*Elektra* von Richard Strauss', *Velhagen und Klasings Monatshefte*, 23/8 (1909), 575.

[22] Mennicke, 'Strauss' *Elektra*', 510–11.

[23] *Shaw's Music*, iii. 598, 611.

[24] Kalisch, 'Impressions', 200.

externally inspired, exploiting the trends and sensations of the day.[25]

The problem of 'external inspiration' summons a broader issue, one that vexed Strauss's detractors for years: Strauss's approach to his art. The composer's matter-of-fact approach to his musical subjects caused much controversy in the early twentieth century. It is the essence behind the dichotomy of *Könner* vs. *Künstler*. An artist's identification with his subject matter was an integral aspect of post-romanticism, yet it was a role that Strauss rejected as a mature composer. Thus, although he may have embraced a late-romantic musical language, he created a modern, self-imposed distance between himself and his art. Of the various comparisons made between Strauss and Wagner in these *Elektra* reviews, Strauss's detachment from his art vs. Wagner's identification recurs with the greatest frequency. According to Sternfeld: 'Wagner could only become inspired by subjects that fulfilled his clairvoyant genius and that urged him to composition. Strauss can be attracted to the most varied types of subjects providing they serve to encourage his abilities'.[26]

Supporters of *Elektra* would not gainsay most of the conclusions outlined above—the technical brilliance, the pervasive motivic network, and the strong reliance on the orchestra as vehicle for expression—but these elements represented not an end, but a means to creating an opera of unprecedented power, a work that probes psychological realms like no other opera of its time. Many, such as Bekker, marvelled at Strauss's ability to juxtapose contrasting moods and states of mind within a short span of time (such as Elektra's monologue or her scene with Klytämnestra), yet still preserve a sense of an organic whole.[27] In short, admirers of *Elektra* saw Strauss's bold musical language as a complement to the spoken language of Hofmannsthal's modern treatment

[25] Karl Storck, 'Richard Strauss' *Elektra*', *Der Türmer* [Stuttgart], 11/6 (1909), 878–9.

[26] Sternfeld, '*Elektra*', 140.

[27] Bekker, '*Elektra* Studie', 14, p. 297.

of Sophocles; in it they saw great promise for the music of a new century.

Bie also dubs Strauss a *Könner*, but in the best sense of the term, for it is his 'inimitable technique' that sets him apart from most of the lack-lustre composers of his day and puts him at the head of what Bie perceives as the avant-garde.[28] Bekker, too, believed that *Elektra*, with its originality, dramatic profundity, and concentration, had not only surpassed any opera that Strauss had written thus far, but 'all that other musicians of the present have attempted'.[29] Kalisch also believed *Elektra* superior to *Salome*, which betrays a greater element of uncertainty, as if Strauss 'elaborated his style as he went on'.[30]

Heinrich Platzenbecker asserted that, despite some of the overwrought dissonances and graphic musical depictions such as falling axes, dripping blood, and the like, *Elektra* bears evidence that Strauss had become an important music dramatist:

> In *Salome* he searches for a new path, in *Elektra* he expands it. The daughter of Herodias is only a means for the colourful dramaturgy of the orchestra, for the symphonic tragedy. In *Elektra* Strauss projects a new, self-chosen style. And for that reason here the orchestra must—despite the great, polyphonic painting, despite the occasional obtrusive and brutal tonal language—subordinate itself to the whole.[31]

But, as Bie would remind us, it is still the orchestra that carries the essential drama; the symphonic-motivic unity gives power and coherence to the work. Kalisch not only admired that motivic unity, but savoured the force of the well-paced musical climaxes that culminate in the final scene, which he found impossible to describe 'without seeming to exaggerate'.

[28] Bie, '*Elektra*', 591.

[29] Bekker, '*Elektra* Studie', 18, 391.

[30] Kalisch, 'Impressions', 198–9.

[31] Heinrich Platzenbecker, 'Uraufführung der *Elektra* und Rich[ard] Strauss-Woche in Dresden', *Neue Musik-Zeitung*, 10 (1909), 206.

Not only is there colossal skill in the way in which all previous threads are woven into one, not only is there great art in the way in which the climax grows and the orchestral colour gradually changes from darkness to the bright light of noonday; but the result is achieved without sacrifice of euphony or beauty, and the whole conception of the scene betrays the creative power which is certainly without rival in the present day.[32]

In 1909, the future of German opera was far from certain. Hovering above this critical discourse about *Elektra* loomed the shadow of Wagner—the omnipresent benchmark of comparison. Unlike *Elektra*'s supporters, negative critics never compared Strauss to his contemporaries such as Kienzl, d'Albert, Schillings, or others, but rather to the older master. Was Strauss never held accountable to his own generation—or the Goldmark generation for that matter—because, beyond their negative rhetoric, they recognized Strauss as a composer greater than his contemporaries, or because his detractors viewed Wagner as the last clear milestone? Probably both.

Nearly all the negative critics tried to avoid being labelled a philistine of the anti-Wagnerian ilk; they were well aware that the broad rubrics of their complaints (an overexploitation of the orchestra, predominance of the motivic over the lyrical, excessive chromaticism and dissonance, etc.) had been used against Wagner a couple of generations earlier. Newman, who admired most of Strauss's tone poems and *Guntram*, was most defensive about the issue, and he addressed the matter in the very opening of his *Elektra* review.

[The pro-*Elektra* critics] cannot possibly like a great part of what they hear, but at the back of their heads is the thought that, as Wagner was abused by the critics of his own day for the extravagances that time has shown to be no extravagances at all, so time may show that Strauss was right in *his* extravagances, and that the critics who objected to them were wrong.[33]

32 Kalisch, 'Impressions', 201–2.
33 *Shaw's Music*, iii. 595.

Newman typifies many of the critics who tried to persuade their readers that they were not attacking Strauss for the same reason that others had earlier attacked Wagner, but that Strauss was an unworthy heir of Wagner's legacy. Unsure and unsettled about the operatic present or future, they looked to the past for their sense of orientation. *Elektra*'s supporters, on the other hand, saw great hope for the future.

Positive or negative opinions notwithstanding, by the time of *Elektra* Strauss had become the best-known living German opera composer. And although some critics considered *Elektra* a stronger work than *Salome*, the general public, early on, showed greater enthusiasm for the latter. Strauss, himself, termed the *Elektra* première a *succès d'estime*.[34] Yet on the strength of the composer's reputation and large profits made by opera houses that produced *Salome*, *Elektra* was staged in Munich, Frankfurt, Berlin, Hamburg, Düsseldorf, Vienna, Graz, and Milan within the first year alone. The next year saw many first performances outside Germany: New York, The Hague, London, Budapest, Prague, and Brussels. But success is determined, to a large extent, by repeat performances, and on that score *Elektra* was outdone by *Salome* in the early twentieth century. *Salome* continues to be easier to produce; the title role is less vocally and physically taxing than Elektra. Circumstances were further complicated by the fact that *Elektra* was directly followed by *Der Rosenkavalier* (1911), which soon became his most popular opera. Between the two World Wars *Elektra* increased in popularity.

Elektra may have realized Newman's worst fears in 1910, but nearly three decades later, he took another backward glance to evaluate the present—this time not at Wagner, but at Strauss himself—and confessed a dramatic change of heart about the work in a column for the London *Sunday Times*. In the article, written shortly after a May 1938 revival of the opera, he urges the public ('if it has any intelligence at all') to

[34] Richard Strauss, *Recollections and Reflections*, ed. Willi Schuh, trans. L. J. Lawrence (London, 1953), 156.

rush out and see *Elektra* before it is too late.[35] Thus, by 1942, after having lived to see a changing tide of opinion, Strauss was able to declare that, after an uncertain start, 'many now consider *Elektra* the acme of my work'.[36]

[35] Vera Newman, *Ernest Newman: A Memoir by His Wife* (London, 1963), 173.
[36] *Recollections*, 156.

2 From Play to Libretto

Hofmannsthal's *Elektra* premièred on 4 October 1903 in Berlin, approximately five years before Strauss finished composing the operatic version. Although the opera marks the beginning of Strauss's and Hofmannsthal's long-standing artistic relationship, the libretto, for the most part, represents little or no collaboration at all. Letters between poet and composer, as well as Strauss's own copy of Hofmannsthal's play, show Strauss to be the major figure behind *Elektra*'s transformation from play to libretto, and that transformation essentially entailed cutting Hofmannsthal's text down to what Strauss considered a more manageable size as an opera libretto. Hofmannsthal's only significant contribution to the libretto was the additional text for Elektra's aria in the Recognition Scene and the text for the duet between Elektra and Chrysothemis in the final scene.

Strauss already had had the experience of transforming a play into a libretto with the composition of *Salome*. As early as spring 1902 Strauss planned to base an opera on Oscar Wilde's play, but he was not satisfied with Anton Lindner's translation and versifications of the opening portions. Soon enough Strauss decided to set the play itself (translated by Hedwig Lachmann) to music, although he made some significant cuts and alterations in the text. In 1903 the composer, who had been in Berlin since 1898, saw a performance of Wilde's stage play, *Salome*, at Max Reinhardt's *Kleines Theater* with Gertrude Eysoldt in the title role. Strauss, who was already in the midst of early sketching, was no doubt affected by her stunning performance and Reinhardt's imaginative direction, and the opera was completed by summer 1905. That autumn Strauss once again saw Eysoldt on the Berlin stage, but this time in the title role of

Reinhardt's production of Hofmannsthal's *Elektra*. Her stage performance was a primary catalyst in his decision to set Hofmannsthal's play to music.

One may draw numerous parallels between *Salome* and *Elektra*. No doubt the similarities Strauss perceived between the two plays influenced his desire to compose *Elektra*. The composer saw both of these Reinhardt productions within a relatively short span of time in Berlin. Both works feature a powerful female protagonist, and both culminate in dance. Neither play required extensive rewriting to become a libretto, despite numerous cuts Strauss made in both works. Yet, although Reinhardt's directing and Eysoldt's acting linked the two plays in Strauss's experience, these two works are distinctly different in content and dramaturgy.

Wilde's play is a decadent, *fin-de-siècle tour de force*: an effective, yet unsettling combination of oriental exoticism and sexual depravity. Hofmannsthal's work is a modern interpretation of an ancient Greek myth. Salome's dance, though vital to the plot, is essentially erotic diversion; Elektra's dance is a culminating celebration absolutely welded to the structure of the play. To be sure, both characters are consumed by an *idée fixe*, both are pushed to psychological extremes, and both are ultimately undone by their own neurotic fixations. But Elektra's death is the result of her triumphant, cathartic ritual, while in Salome's death, one senses that she collapses beneath the weight of an oppressive air of decay as much as the shields of Herod's guards.

Thus, paradoxically, the similarities that Strauss perceived between the two works both ignited his interest in composing *Elektra* and yet caused hesitation. Strauss expressed reluctance to move right ahead with the *Elektra* project, preferring to postpone composing the opera until he had 'moved much farther away from the *Salome* style'.[1] But the playwright, who probably feared that postponement might lead to

[1] *Correspondence*, 3.

permanent derailment, stressed the differences between the two plays in a letter to Strauss (27 April 1906).[2] He reminded the composer of the 'rapid rising sequence of events relating to Orestes and his deed which leads up to victory and purification', and remarked that the sequence would be more powerful in music than the purely written word. Furthermore, such a sequential build-up is not to be found in *Salome*. Hofmannsthal's persistence during the spring of 1906 paid off, for Strauss ultimately decided to go ahead with *Elektra*.

The Context of *Elektra* in Hofmannsthal's Career

The late 1890s marked a turning point in Hofmannsthal's career as a writer, a time when he turned away from lyric poetry, seeking new forms of literary expression. It is remarkable that one should speak of a turning point in the 1890s, since the early lyric phrase had begun in 1891, when the poet was a mere seventeen years of age. But Hofmannsthal was a phenomenon above the normal prodigy. A precocious youth fluent in many languages, with a deep sensitivity to art and literature and a remarkable facility as a writer, he went well beyond that stereotype. His lyric poetry evinced a profound maturity that seemingly could only be based upon years of experience. When Hofmannsthal was introduced to Viennese literary society at the Café Griensteidl—at the age of seventeen—literary figures such as Hermann Bahr, Richard Beer-Hofmann, and Arthur Schnitzler accepted him not as an amazing talent, but as a literary equal.

Stefan George, another writer who had met Hofmannsthal at the Café Griensteidl, looked to the young Hofmannsthal as a peer and encouraged him to become a part of his symbolist circle. But Hofmannsthal felt uncomfortable with George's solipsistic style of aestheticism, fully at odds with the

[2] *Correspondence*, 4. Hofmannsthal later (18 Sept. 1919) described *Elektra* as a 'mere variation' of *Salome*. See *Correspondence*, 331.

younger poet's world view. As a poet and as a playwright, Hofmannsthal sought to forge connections between art and experience, between the individual and civilization. His ultimate rejection of poetry stemmed in part from a danger that he perceived in much of the contemporary poetry: the danger of art being cut off from society. No doubt Hofmannsthal viewed the symbolist poetry of George as an unhealthy, dead-end road. To his thinking, a poem must at once be distanced from life, yet also have its roots planted in the tangible realm of experience. 'Experience has to be purified by art,' observed one critic of Hofmannsthal.[3] It was, indeed, this very belief that contributed to the poet's ultimate rejection of lyric poetry and his embrace of theatre.

Hofmannsthal's *Letter of Lord Chandos* (1901–2) both commemorates this change in artistic direction and serves as a manifesto of his scepticism about language.[4] In this imaginary letter from Lord Chandos to Francis Bacon, he expresses his distrust of words as the sole bearer of expressive or emotional content, and he confesses his feeling of isolation as a writer and as an individual. If language is the product of consensus, of generalization, it is, therefore, meaningless in the world of individuation. Hofmannsthal's scepticism was not a sudden crisis that had surfaced at the turn of the century, but was an evolving phenomenon foreshadowed by earlier works. If anything, the *Chandos Letter* represents a resolution of that crisis.

In his letter, Lord Chandos expresses his distrust of narcissism in its purest form, of words cut off from human experience. He writes of the 'whirlpools of language . . . [that] lead into myself' (p. 140) and remarks that he has become estranged from his earlier work, written at a time

[3] Hans Reiss, 'Hugo von Hofmannsthal', *The Writer's Task from Nietzsche to Brecht* (Totowa, N.J., 1978), 55.

[4] Hofmannsthal, 'Ein Brief', *Prosa II*, ed. Herbert Steiner, Hugo von Hofmannsthal: Gesammelte Werke in Einzelausgaben (Frankfurt a.M., 1951). For the English translation see: *Selected Prose*, trans. Mary Hottinger and Tania and James Stern, Bollingen Series 33, no. 1 (New York, 1952). All subsequent page references in the text refer to the English translation.

when words that penetrated the subject matter flowed freely. Yet in his present state of mind 'rhetoric . . . is not sufficient to penetrate into the core of things' (p. 130). Words alone fall short of explaining human action; they float about isolated and disconnected. 'The abstract terms of which the tongue must avail itself', complains Lord Chandos, 'crumbled in my mouth like mouldy fungi'. (pp. 133–4) He has reached a level of thought more immediate than words. The problem lies in the outward manifestation of that inner thought: '. . . the language in which I might be able not only to write, but to think is neither Latin nor English, neither Italian nor Spanish, but a language none of whose words is known to me' (pp. 140–1).

Hofmannsthal found the new language he was seeking in the discourse of the theatre, which, for him, embodied a fusion of the arts: acting, gesture, ritual, myth, scene design, and, ultimately, music. This synthesis of the arts was not quite identical to Wagner's vision of a *Gesamtkunstwerk*, which Hofmannsthal found too heavily weighted in the direction of music. His essay, *On Pantomime* (1911), stresses the fundamental importance of gesture as an expressive tool. 'A pure gesture is a pure thought,' he remarked, 'in pure gestures the true personality comes to light.'[5] Human speech lacks such purity, it can only generalize rather than reveal pure thought. The dichotomy between language and gesture—between word and deed—is a central theme in Hofmannsthal's *Elektra*, and he makes a specific reference to this dichotomy towards the end of the brief scene between Elektra and Aegisthus. Her stepfather asks whether or not the visitors can report that Orestes is dead in such a way that there will be no doubt. Elektra replies: 'O my lord, they

[5] 'Eine reine Gebärde ist wie ein reiner Gedanke, von dem auch das augenblickliche Geistreiche, das begrenzte Individuelle, das fratzenhafte Charakteristische abgestreift ist. In reinen Gedanken tritt die Persönlichkeit vermöge ihrer Hoheit und Kraft hervor, nicht eben allen sogleich fasslich. So tritt in reinen Gebärden die wahre Persönlichkeit ans Licht und über die Massen reichlich wird der scheinbare Verzicht auf Individualität aufgewogen.' See 'Über Pantomime' in *Prosa III*, 46–50.

report it not merely with words, no, but with actual tokens which cannot be doubted.'. (p. 73)

Thus, through the theatre Hofmannsthal sought to move away from the preciosity of the polished word to a language that could embody the perfect gestural idea. Admirers of his poetry were bewildered by his move from this subtle, personal genre to the extroverted, public art of the stage. From this perspective we see Hofmannsthal's first published letter to Strauss (17 November 1900) in a sharper light. Here he asks the composer whether or not he might be interested in setting music to his ballet scenario *Der Triumph der Zeit* (*The Triumph of Time*). Strauss declined the offer, though he would later set other dance scenarios by Hofmannsthal such as *Josephslegende*, parts of *Bürger als Edelmann*, and the reworkings of *The Ruins of Athens* and *The Creatures of Prometheus*.

Elektra is the first major product of Hofmannsthal's new artistic direction. In this fresh, new work for the stage he searches for alternatives to the poetic world of his youth—a world that had become irrelevant to him by the turn of the century. With *Elektra* the speculative issues raised in the *Chandos Letter* become concrete, and the play is an important part of a cluster of classical subjects by Hofmannsthal at the turn of the century. His short adaptation of Euripides' *Alcestis* was written in 1893, followed by *Elektra*, *Oedipus und die Sphinx* (1905), and *Oedipus Rex* (1906).[6] He had also sketched some incomplete mythological dramas as well: *Leda und der Schwan* (1900–4), *Jupiter und Semele* (1901), and *Pentheus* (1904). His concentration on myth at this time is directly connected with his quest for a new language in the realm of drama; the attraction to classical subjects was another part of his search for a connection between art and life, between the individual and society. That link was found in the fusion of word, gesture, and ritual provided by myth. The vehicle would be the theatre and the guidance of the innovative

[6] *Oedipus und die Sphinx* was produced by Reinhardt in 1906.

Max Reinhardt. Myth offered Hofmannsthal a ready-made structure, with all its ethical and social concerns. His *Ariadne auf Naxos* (1912) and *Die ägyptische Helena* (1928) attest to his concern with mythological subjects throughout his life.

Elektra on the Stage: Language, Image, and Gesture

Hofmannsthal once likened *Elektra* to a 'taut chain of heavy, massive iron links'.[7] The play is remarkably concise; its concentration of action and structural clarity, combined with stark imagery, make for a powerful stage work. Gesture serves as Hofmannsthal's fundamental expressive tool, and its force is felt in all seven scenes, which are symmetrically arranged. Tension steadily rises as each scene segués into the next with increasing momentum. The only notable break in that tension is the arrival of Orestes, which is highlighted by a brief period of self-reflection as Elektra looks back to her childhood. Thereafter the playwright wastes little time in going from her lyrical moment to the murders of Klytämnestra and Aegisthus.

The outer form of this one-act play is a monumental arch spanning from the introduction to the finale. The symmetrical arrangement of scene and characters no doubt appealed to Strauss. As we shall later see, his cuts strengthen our perception of Hofmannsthal's inherent balance (see Figure 2.1).

The keystone to this arch is the confrontation between Elektra and Klytämnestra; this dramatic midpoint represents the moment of greatest psychological conflict in the work. If the dialectic of word and deed has only previously been hinted at, it reaches fruition in the lengthy dialogue of this fourth scene. Midway through the scene Klytämnestra

[7] *Correspondence*, 410.

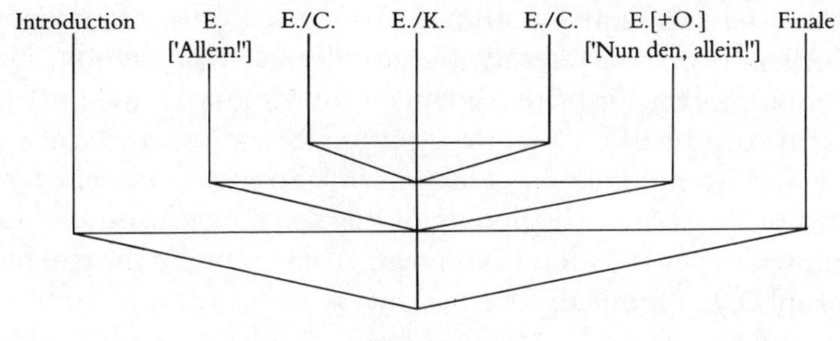

FIG. 2.1

distances herself from the act of killing; she feels estranged from the act of murder against her husband:

Klytämnestra

Deeds! We and deeds! What odd words! For am I still the same who has done the deed? . . . Now it was before, and then it was past—in between I did nothing.

Elektra

No, the work that lay between the axe had done alone.

Klytämnestra

How you thrust in words.

Elektra

Not so skilled nor so fast as you the strokes of an axe.

(pp. 33, 34)

This scene is flanked by dialogues between Elektra and her sister Chrysothemis. The first dialogue is largely a vehicle for Chrysothemis, in which she declares her vitalistic wish for 'a woman's destiny' ('ein Weiberschicksal'). She refuses to dwell in the past and wants no part of any vengeance for her father's murder. In the second dialogue of the two sisters—following the mid-point of the play—Elektra entreats Chrysothemis to help her with the murder of their mother and Aegisthus now that she has learned of Orestes' apparent death. Elektra's opening monologue (sc. 2) and the Recognition Scene (sc. 6), where Orestes arrives and reveals his identity to his sister, are equally strongly connected. Her monologue ('Allein!') not only recalls the murder of Agamemnon, but prophesies the ultimate atonement for his murder ('Dein Tag wird kommen!'). The Recognition Scene is in essence a second monologue for Elektra, and Strauss's cuts enhance this quality. At the beginning of this scene Elektra once again expresses her isolation ('Nun den, allein!') and by the end her prophecy is fulfilled; Orestes exits with his tutor to commit the two murders.[8]

Reduction to bare essentials is a major aspect of Hofmannsthal's reworking of Sophocles' original. In his version, Hofmannsthal eliminates the Greek chorus altogether and significantly reduces the role of Orestes' servant. In December 1907, while Strauss was well into the composition of the opera, Hofmannsthal apparently even suggested eliminating the role of Aegisthus entirely.[9] To counterbalance textual brevity he relies heavily on image and gesture. More powerful than the Greek model, Hofmannsthal's imagery is strengthened by its boldness, starkness, and pervasiveness.

The recurring allusions to animals, in stage directions and the dramatic language itself, provide an important metaphor for understanding Elektra's dehumanization. Hofmannsthal's Elektra is a lonely, isolated individual, robbed of the Greek chorus that gave her classical prototype a firm social footing. At the outset servants portray Elektra as howling for her father; they liken her to a wild cat and a dog. Elektra, in turn, calls them flies, for, both metaphorically and socially, she is consigned to vermin. The third servant states that Elektra 'stretched her fingers like claws at us and screamed . . . I'm feeding a vulture in my body' (p. 7). Klytämnestra distances herself from her exiled son by reducing him to animal status. She claims to Elektra: 'they say [Orestes] . . . lies in the yard

[8] Strauss's preoccupation with Elektra during the Recognition Scene might not have been so different from Hofmannsthal's original intent. In a letter (6 Oct. 1904) to Eberhard Freiherrn von Bodenhausen-Degener, Hofmannsthal confessed that the entire play might have been purer without the character Orestes. See *Hugo von Hofmannsthal: Briefe 1900–09* (Vienna, 1937), 170.

[9] *Correspondence*, 12.

with dogs, and cannot distinguish man from beast' (p. 36). Her fantasy is temporarily fulfilled by the false report that Orestes has been killed by his own horses.

The recurring animal imagery not only objectifies the relationship between Elektra and her mother in their confrontation scene, but intentionally confuses the distinction between hunter and quarry. Haunted by nightmares, Klytämnestra envisions long-beaked demons sucking her blood and believes that only when the right beast has been slaughtered, when the proper blood has flowed, will her dreams cease. Elektra compares herself to a hound on her mother's traces as she reveals that Klytämnestra, herself, is the sacrificial beast: 'What must bleed? Your own neck must bleed when the hunter has moved in for the kill! He will knife his game: but only on the run! Who'd slaughter a victim in sleep!' (p. 38). Indeed, as Orestes goes into the palace to murder Klytämnestra, Hofmannsthal directs that 'Elektra [stands] alone, in terrible suspense. She runs to and fro in a single straight line in front of the door, with lowered head, like a captive animal in its cage' (p. 70).

Hofmannsthal once lamented to Strauss that the public dwelt too much on the frequency of the word 'blood' (he uses the word no less than eight times in Elektra's monologue alone), yet the image does play a fundamental role in the drama.[10] Graphic references to this homologous symbol abound, for example, in Elektra's opening scene, where it serves a threefold purpose—as a reference to Agamemnon's violent death, to the sacrificial blood that will avenge that death, and to the blood relation between Agamemnon and his children.

Gesture is a fundamental expressive component throughout the play. Sacrificial rituals, processions, torch-bearing, and, most important, dance are as integral to this drama as any line from the text. The attention to theatricality is certainly in keeping with Hofmannsthal's dramatic theory. 'In action, in

[10] *Correspondence*, 98.

deeds the enigmas of language are resolved,' Hofmannsthal observed sometime after *Elektra*.[11] The playwright composes no final monologue for Elektra after her father's murder has been avenged; rather, her triumph is summarized in dance—a dionysiac victory celebration that, on a more psychological level, signals Elektra's dissolution of the Self. Up until this moment Elektra has separated herself from the group, but now that the deed has been done, her personality is negated—or submerged—via the social gesture of the round dance; she moves into the realm and destiny of mere mortals. She entreats all to join her in the dithyrambic celebration, and she will die after this cathartic ritual. 'Be silent and dance. All must approach! Here join behind me! I bear the burden of happiness, and I dance before you. For him who is as happy as we, it behooves him to do only this: to be silent and dance!' (p. 77).

Certain undeniable psychological elements in Hofmannsthal's modern treatment distinctly separate it from the ancient world. Scholars have addressed the issue of Freudian elements in *Elektra*, and from many of these studies we not only know that he read Breuer's and Freud's *Studies in Hysteria*, as well as the latter's *Interpretation of Dreams*, but was preoccupied with these issues at the time of *Elektra*.[12] Hofmannsthal and Freud are, no doubt, alike in their use of myth to explain certain psychological constellations.

It has been stressed how memory is the central theme in this work. Lorna Martens points out how Hofmannsthal draws a parallel between the resolution of guilt through retribution of classic Greek myth and the resolution of repressed memory through psychoanalytic cure. We recall that Hofmannsthal described *Elektra* to Strauss as a mixture of dark and light; darkness, no doubt, symbolizes the realm of the subconscious.[13] The well, the central image on stage at

[11] Hamburger, Introduction to *Hofmannsthal: Selected Plays and Libretti*, ed. Hamburger, Bollingen Series 33, No. 3 (New York, 1963), [xli].

[12] Most of these studies are cited in Lorna Martens, "The Theme of the Repressed Memory in Hofmannsthal's *Elektra*," *German Quarterly* 60 (1987), no. 1.

[13] *Correspondence*, 4.

the outset of the play, is our entrance into that subconscious. He refers to other dark regions in the play such as the palace, Agamemnon's grave, and the womb, which Elektra compares to 'the dark door through which I crept into the light of the world' (p. 24). The well also serves as an archetypical female symbol; only women gather around it in the opening scene as they gossip about Elektra. Devoid of overt sexuality, Elektra will not approach it. In the stage directions Hofmannsthal specifies: 'Elektra comes running [toward the well] from the hallway [and] . . . bounds back like an animal into its hiding place, one arm before her face' (p. 5). We shall later see that, by his choice of cuts, Strauss seeks to underplay Elektra's warped sense of sexuality, a dramatic element that was important to Sophocles' version as well. Sophocles makes it clear that Clytemnestra's greatest transgression, in Electra's eyes, was the fact that she now shared Agamemnon's bed with the accomplice.

Agamemnon's murder took place in the dark palace. The torches of Orestes and his servant probe that same darkness as Sophocles' retribution or Hofmannsthal's psychoanalytic cure is undertaken. Aegisthus, indeed, demands light ('Is there no one to light my way?') as he enters the palace, and Elektra willingly complies. In much of the dialogue between mother and daughter, Elektra probes and questions, much in the manner of an analyst. Indeed, at one point Klytämnestra declares: 'she speaks like a physician!' (p. 24).

Klytämnestra (after a pause)

I do not have good nights. Have you no remedy for dreams?

Elektra (moving closer)

Do you dream, Mother?

Klytämnestra

Have you no other words to comfort me? Loosen your tongue. Yes, yes I dream. As one gets older one dreams. Yet it can be dispelled. Why are you standing there in the dark? (p. 27)

If any one character of Hofmannsthal's play best exemplifies the difference between the worlds of Sophocles and Hofmannsthal it is surely Klytämnestra. The Viennese playwright portrays her as a decadent despot, covered with talismans, haunted by nightmares and hallucinations, and unable to come to terms with her deed; by her own admission she knows only what happened before and after. Her bizarre nightmares and her wish to rid herself of them form the centre-piece of her dialogue with Elektra. Strauss was fascinated by Klytämnestra and composed some of the most complex music of the score for this scene.

Clytemnestra's dream, in Sophocles' treatment, plays a comparatively minor role in the play. She neither wears talismans nor makes daily sacrifices to purge herself of nightmares. Sophocles' Clytemnestra feels justified in her action, which, after all, was to avenge the death of her first daughter, Iphigenia, by Agamemnon's hand—an element of the story missing in Hofmannsthal's version. Furthermore, Sophocles' Clytemnestra is a character not tormented by dreams of Orestes and was truly saddened by the news of his death. The hysterical, hollow-eyed Klytämnestra of Hofmannsthal's play, on the other hand, seems a fit subject for one of Freud's famous case studies.

Reinhardt, Hofmannsthal, and Strauss

Elektra represents not only Hofmannsthal's first significant move in the direction of theatre, but also his first collaboration with Max Reinhardt, the most innovative stage director of the period. Reinhardt's imaginative direction had also, no doubt, inspired Strauss, who readily admitted that it was only after seeing the play that he realized what a great opera *Elektra* might be. His influence on the careers of Strauss and Hofmannsthal is significant, but his role as artistic stimulus for Hofmannsthal was more far-reaching, for Reinhardt profoundly affected his development as a playwright. *Elektra* would be only the first of nineteen of their stage collaborations, which, of course, included some of the major works in twentieth-century opera. The value that Strauss applied to Reinhardt's skills is exemplified by his insistence on Reinhardt for the *Rosenkavalier* première in Dresden, despite the serious political problems that resulted from the composer's insistence.[14] In appreciation for his assistance composer and librettist dedicated their next opera, *Ariadne auf Naxos*, to him.

Reinhardt came to Berlin in 1894 (four years before Strauss's arrival at the Court Opera), as an actor at the *Deutsches Theater* under Otto Brahm, but he soon began directing and formed an experimental cabaret (*Schall und Rauch* [Sound and Smoke]) of his own in 1901. A year later this theatre became the *Kleines Theater*, where Wilde's *Salome* premièred on 15 November of that year. *Elektra*, which first appeared in October of the next season, was, in part, the product of conversations Hofmannsthal had had with Reinhardt as early as 1901, in Berlin.[15]

A reminiscence (17 July 1904) by Hofmannsthal, as well as an undated letter by him to Brahm, indicate that both Reinhardt and Eysoldt were directly connected with the genesis of *Elektra*. In the letter (autumn 1903?) he reports that he has just finished *Elektra*, written in direct regard to the actress Gertrude Eysoldt.[16] In his reminiscence Hofmannsthal states that he had been thinking about Sophocles' *Electra* as early as 1901, and, before composing the play in earnest, he had originally thought of another actress in Reinhardt's theatre, Adele Sandrock—an actress who, according to one contemporary, possessed a 'powerful temperament' and

[14] Strauss, 'Reminiscences of the First Performances of My Operas', *Recollections and Reflections*, ed. Willi Schuh, trans. L. J. Lawrence (London, 1953), 157–8.

[15] See Hugo von Hofmannsthal, *Aufzeichnungen*, Gesammelte Werke in Einzelausgaben, ed. Herbert Steiner (Frankfurt a.M., 1959), 131–2.

[16] See above and *Briefe 1900–09*, 124–5.

could rise 'to a tragic zenith in moments of passionate emotion'.[17]

I [originally] thought of Sandrock for *Elektra.* At the beginning of May 1903 I saw Eysoldt in *The Lower Depths* and then at breakfast. At this same breakfast I promised Reinhardt an *Elektra* for his theater and for Eysoldt to undertake [the title role].[18]

Strauss's decision to set *Elektra* to music marks the beginning of his association with Hofmannsthal—one of the most fruitful artistic relationships of the twentieth century. Their collaboration, which spanned nearly a quarter of a century, has been a subject for music historians and Germanists alike, and it has been interpreted in various ways. George Marek paints Hofmannsthal as an opportunist, latching on to the more famous international artist to further his own career.[19] He explains the poet's interest in the *Elektra* project by observing that 'through Strauss, Hofmannsthal was able to augment his income considerably. He was paid a good royalty [for *Elektra*].'[20] His suggestion ignores the context of Hofmannsthal's initial approach to Strauss, his search for new forms of expression around the time of the *Chandos Letter.* If he needed Strauss, it was not for career advancement (he came from a monied, *haute bourgeois* background), but rather to explore a new artistic direction.

Others have suggested that Hofmannsthal introduced a negative element into Strauss's development as an opera composer, that through his choice of libretti the poet somehow steered the composer away from the cutting edge of modern music. 'Strauss had yielded supremacy to his reactionary co-author,' asserts William Mann in his study of the Strauss operas.[21] Mann seems to imply that Strauss was

[17] Willi Handl, 'The Artists of the Deutsches Theater', *Max Reinhardt and his Theater*, ed. Oliver Sayler (New York, 1924), 110.

[18] *Aufzeichnungen*, 131–2.

[19] George Marek, *Richard Strauss: The Life of a Non-Hero* (New York, 1967).

[20] Marek, *Strauss*, 178–9.

[21] William Mann, *Richard Strauss: A Critical Study of the Operas* (London, 1964), 167.

once a member of the avant-garde, and that opinion is sustained in many historical surveys of twentieth-century music. The composer of *Salome* and *Elektra* is, thus, viewed as a progressive force in German music, who relinquished that position with the composition of *Der Rosenkavalier*.

This prevalent view presupposes a steady development, or evolution, of style in a sort of Darwinian mould culminating with *Elektra*. As Chapter One has shown, no contemporary critic ever perceived such a view. Strauss's letters to his librettists throughout his career show his constant wish for contrasting operatic subjects. The stylistic differences between *Elektra* and *Der Rosenkavalier* are sharp indeed, but are they any sharper than those between *Feuersnot* and *Salome*, or *Die Frau ohne Schatten* and *Intermezzo*? It was, we recall, the lack of apparent contrast between *Salome* and *Elektra* that gave Strauss early misgivings about setting Hofmannsthal's play right away.

Adorno gets to the heart of the problem when he observes: 'To do justice to Strauss means to reject the patronizing historical observation which asserts that at the start of the century he was ahead of his contemporaries.'[22] Indeed, in his essay, 'Is There an Avant-Garde in Music?', written two years before *Elektra*, Strauss dissociates himself from the label *progressive*.

> Now, I find it impossible to call a man a reactionary, just because he prefers Beethoven's *Eroica* to a feeble modern symphonic poem or because he says he would prefer to see the *Freischütz* twelve times in succession, rather than some worthless modern opera. To this extent I am a reactionary myself.[23]

To trace a stylistic evolution in Strauss's music in the same manner as one might in the life work of Arnold Schoenberg is not only fallacious, but ignores the variety of subject matter in the works leading up to *Elektra*. Indeed, Strauss's

[22] Theodor Adorno, 'Richard Strauss, Born June 11, 1864', trans. Samuel and Shierry Weber, *Perspectives of New Music*, 4/1 (1965), 14–32; 4/2 (1966), 113–29.
[23] *Recollections*, 15–16.

catholic tastes in both programmes and libretto subjects must have offended Schoenberg's sensibilities. In responding to these various subjects, Strauss felt a need for stylistic flexibility; the given musical style must meet the expressive demand. He would surely argue that it would be inappropriate to give the Marschallin music in the style of Klytämnestra. To paraphrase a well-known Schoenberg quotation, Strauss probably viewed style more as a question of *können* rather than *müssen*.

Hence, *Symphonia Domestica* and *Salome*, although adjacent works, are worlds apart in both content and musical language. Moreover, within *Elektra* alone there are various strata of musical style ranging from the chromatic realm of Klytämnestra to the simpler diatonic world of Chrysothemis. *Der Rosenkavalier*, therefore, represents no fundamental turning backward after having come so far with *Elektra*, for the earlier work cannot be said to be a culmination of any steady evolution. It is, rather, one of many examples of the composer's need for stylistic contrast in his operatic output.

Much, too, has been made of contrasts in personality between Hofmannsthal and Strauss, and there were profound differences between the sensitive Viennese and the robust Bavarian. But Hans Mayer goes too far when he states that their entire artistic bond was an example of a 'profound misunderstanding'.[24] Strauss was self-assured, sanguine, pragmatic, and down-to-earth, even to the point of being downright blunt at times. Hofmannsthal was, by comparison, insecure, moody, and occasionally prone to envisioning plans that were impractical for the stage. Mayer, to be sure, draws convincing contrasts between these two men, especially in their relationship to their art (Strauss's celebration of technique vs. Hofmannsthal's distrust of technique). Yet he overstates Hofmannsthal's musical ignorance as much as he does Strauss's literary shortcomings in an effort to illustrate

[24] Hans Mayer, 'Hugo von Hofmannsthal und Richard Strauss', *Sinn und Form*, 13 (1961), 893.

their apparent inability to understand each other, and Mayer is not alone in this regard. On the contrary, the twenty-three years of their published correspondence show that, for the most part, they understood each other's differences fairly well and exploited those differences to good advantage.

Face-to-face meetings between Strauss and Hofmannsthal were rare events in the span of their relationship; the bulk of their work is, thus, documented in the correspondence. Some writers have attributed their lack of personal contact to Hofmannsthal's aversion to Strauss's personality, others cite his dislike of the composer's wife, Pauline de Ahna. These observations, true or false, fail to address the more important issue of the writer's need for distance and solitude as a working method; he required it well before he began collaborating with Strauss. Moreover, Hofmannsthal stressed to Strauss himself his need for an impersonal relationship with the composer.[25] Therefore, aside from superficial anecdotes, little is gained by positing an animosity between these two artists who complemented each other in an important way.

Strauss's Cuts in Hofmannsthal's Drama

Strauss, no doubt, relished the tautness and structural symmetry of Hofmannsthal's *Elektra*, which he sought to make even more concise with some cuts of his own. The composer made these cuts in his copy of Hofmannsthal's play (fifth edition, 1904), probably in early 1906.[26] This document, which is at the RSA, shows a confident composer with a firm grasp of the musico-dramatic shape for the future opera. His cuts are specific, decisive, and, with but a handful of exceptions, they represent his final decision. These cuts fall into two basic categories, although sometimes the categories

[25] *Correspondence*, 342–3. [26] *Corrersponderce*, 3.

overlap. The first comprises cuts designed specifically to telescope stage action. Reasons behind this first type are twofold: (1) to streamline and condense for specific musical reasons, and (2) to heighten or speed up the action where Strauss felt it lagged. Strauss knew instinctively how important it was to reduce a text to its essentials in order to produce a good opera text. Later on in his career he had to remind librettist Joseph Gregor of this fact time and time again during their work on *Daphne*. Citing Wagner as a model he wrote: 'Bear in mind: "Elsa's Dream", an aria that is 3 pages of a piano-vocal score = 12 lines [of text]!'[27]

The second type of deletion reflects the composer's desire to reduce or even simplify manifold psychological strata explored by Hofmannsthal. This is especially true in the Klytämnestra-Elektra scene as well as the scenes with Chrysothemis. In doing so Strauss simplifies Elektra's mother and sister; he makes the former more horrible and the latter an even more obvious *alter ego* for the asexual Elektra. The composer also plays down sexual references in Hofmannsthal's play, especially references to Klytämnestra's sexual relationship with Aegisthus and Elektra's own view of sexuality. One wonders whether the composer's various bad experiences with censors *vis-à-vis Salome* influenced any of his decisions in these matters, which seem, for modern sensibility, inconsequential.

Strauss reduced Hofmannsthal's play by approximately one third to create his opera text. Where do most of these cuts lie and what are their proportions? Strauss left the first scene, as well as the murder and final scenes, essentially unchanged. Elektra's opening monologue is preserved almost in its entirety; only some 4–5 lines are excised. Most of Strauss's cuts encompass Elektra's first encounter with Chrysothemis, her scene with Klytämnestra, the second scene with Chrysothemis, and her scene with Orestes. The Cook-Servants Scene, which follows the news of Orestes'

[27] *Richard Strauss und Joseph Gregor: Briefwechsel (1934–1949)*, ed. Roland Tenschert (Salzburg, 1955), 51.

alleged death, is short as it is in the original (*c.*40 lines). As noted earlier, Strauss eliminates the cook altogether and pares this scene down to a mere fifteen lines.

Most severely reduced is the first scene between Elektra and Chrysothemis, where he eliminates about 50 per cent of the text. Strauss undoubtedly envisioned this scene chiefly as a lyrical outpouring for Elektra's sister, highlighted by her exclamation 'Kinder will ich haben!' By tailoring the revised scene so exclusively around Chrysothemis, a character so preoccupied with the present, Strauss creates a strong counterbalance to Elektra's previous monologue, which dwelt only in the past or the future. In the process, however, Strauss not only eliminates a good portion of Elektra's dialogue, but important underlying psychological elements as well.

The opening of their scene concerns the issue of memory, a central theme in the play, and which Strauss chose to delete at this point in the drama:

Elektra

Forget? What! Am I a beast? Forget?
The brute beast falls asleep, the half-devoured
prey still dangling from the lip, the brute forgets
and begins to chew while death already sits
on it and throttles it; the beast forgets
what crept out of its body, and stills its hunger
with its own child—I am no beast, *I cannot forget*!
(p. 18)

Elektra is as much the embodiment of memory as she is the personification of revenge. To her thinking, her mother's crime was not just the deed, but the fact that she repressed that deed. Elektra is the self-appointed cure for her mother's hysterical nightmares, which result from that repressed memory. In another vital section of this scene, which Strauss also cut, Elektra tells her sister that she has sent Klytämnestra the recurring nightmare of Orestes' return and describes it in detail:

Elektra

I sent it to her. From out of my breast
I visited this dream upon her! I lie
and hear steps of him who looks for her.
I hear him walk through the rooms, I hear him
raise the curtain from the bed: screaming
she escapes, but he is after her:
the hunt is on, down the stairs
through the vaults, vaults upon vaults.
It is much darker than night, much quieter
and darker than the grave, she pants and staggers
in the darkness, but he is after her
he waves the torch in his left, in his right the axe.
And I am like a dog upon her heels:
if she tries to run into a cave, I leap
at her from the side, thus we drive her on
until a wall blocks everything, and there,
in the deepest darkness, yet I see him well,
a shade, and yet limbs and yet the white
of one eye, there sits our father:
he does not heed it and yet it must be done:
in front of his feet we press her down,
and the axe falls!

(pp. 20, 21)

One can see in Orestes' chase into the darkness—with torch and axe—a metaphor for the psychoanalyst's search into the patient's subconscious, where he 'penetrates into ever-darker areas'.[28]

Strauss cut some 40 per cent of the confrontation scene between Klytämnestra and Elektra—the moment of greatest psychological intensity in the drama. The composer responded to the electricity of this scene, but his interpretation differed slightly from the playwright's. What appealed to Strauss was the scene's steadily increasing tension, and his cuts heighten this build-up. He telescopes the scene into three basic parts: (1) Klytämnestra's complaint about her recurring nightmares

[28] Martens, 'Repressed Memory', 46.

and her need for Elektra to find her a cure; (2) a dialogue where Elektra speaks in riddles, enigmatically leading her mother along; (3) Elektra's ultimate 'prescription'. This symmetry is well designed for an operatic climax: monologue (Klytämnestra)—dialogue (Klytämnestra and Elektra)—monologue (Elektra). Thus, as Klytämnestra's part diminishes, Elektra's role steadily increases, reaching its climax when she declares that her mother's neck must be sacrificed.

Intensity is added to the operatic version of her monologue by the brief addition of text that is a compressed version of the speech from the previous scene, where Elektra tells Chrysothemis that she has sent Klytämnestra her dreams. In Strauss's reworking the third person becomes the second person; Elektra tells her mother directly that she has sent her these nightmares:

Elektra

Down the steps and through the vaults,
through vault after vault goes the chase—
And I! I! I! I! I! who sent him to you,
I am like a hound on your heels.
If you would creep into a hole, I'll spring at you
from the side, and so we drive you on—
until a wall shuts off everything, and there
in the deepest darkness, yet I see him well,
a shade—yet there are limbs and the white
of an eye—there sits my father:
he pays no heed, and yet it must be done.
We drive you to his feet.

In an effort to accelerate the pace, to move more quickly to the moment in Elektra's vision where the axe falls, Strauss cut a good third of her text in this last part of the scene. The text in italics represents Strauss's omissions.

Elektra

And I stand next to you:
you cannot turn your eyes away from me,
for you are tortured with convulsive desire

to read one word upon my silent face,
you roll your eyes, you want to think
of anything, grinning you want to lure the gods
down from the cloudy skies of the night:
the gods are having supper! As at the time
when you slaughtered my father, they sit
at supper and are deaf to choking throats!
Only a half-mad god, Laughter, he staggers
in by the door: he thinks you are dallying
with Aegisthus at loving time; but
instantly he notes his error, laughs
his shrill laugh and is gone at once.
Then you also have enough. Your gall trickles
bitter drops into your heart, expiring
you want to recollect one word, to utter
only one word, any word, instead of
the tear of blood which even the beast
is not denied in death: but I stand there
before you, and then you read with a fixed
eye the monstrous word that is written
upon my face; for my face is mingled
of my father's features and of yours,
and so with my standing there in silence
I have utterly destroyed your last word;
hanged is your soul in the noose twisted
by yourself, the axe now whistles through the air,
and I stand there and see you die at last!
Then you will never dream again, then I need
dream no longer, and he who then is still
alive can shout with joy over his life!

(pp. 39, 40)

The build-up to this speech and its culmination contribute to one of the most stirring moments in the score. Strauss sets up this climax with the combination of a bold textual addition from the previous scene and an equally effective cut at the end, while sacrificing psychological depth and motivational complexity in order to achieve these musical goals.

Strauss eliminates 20 per cent of the second scene with Chrysothemis, and his reworking of the scene is noteworthy.

Even in the play, Elektra dominates scene 5 as she tries to seduce Chrysothemis into taking part in the murders. By cutting and rearranging the text, Strauss fashions this scene as one large monologue for Elektra with short outbursts by Chrysothemis. The most sensual language of the play is contained in this quasi-incestuous scene, as Elektra flatters her sister with words praising her beauty and strength:

Elektra

How strong you are!
The virgin nights have made you strong.
Your hips, how slender and lithe they are!
You can twist yourself through every crevice,
pull yourself through a window! Let me feel
your arms: how cool and strong they are!
As you struggle against me, I feel what arms
they are. You could crush whatever you clasp
in your arms. You could press me, or a man,
★*against your cool firm breasts* with your arms
and one would suffocate!

(p. 49)

★ Cut.

The interplay between physical strength and sensual beauty has far-reaching implications for Hofmannsthal's play. In a broader sense it suggests Elektra's inability to distinguish between the act of sex and the act of murder, and in most cases Strauss tries to expunge this element from the play in his libretto, as he did in the example above as well as in Elektra's first scene with Chrysothemis:

Elektra

Choked breathing, faugh! and the death-rattle
of strangled men, there's nothing else here
in all these rooms. *No, leave alone the door*
behind which you hear a groan: for they're not always
killing, sometimes they are alone together!

(p. 15)

Likewise, Strauss makes a small, localized cut in Elektra's last major speech in the second scene with Chrysothemis, when she likens her sister to the angel of death, who straddles the victim that 'looks up at you, forced to look up at your slender body . . . as shipwrecked sailors look up at the cliffs before they die' (p. 52). The omission of that phrase is surely for no other reason than to suppress a sexual element that is vital to the scene. Imagery of death and sexuality is a theme dating back to ancient times, but in *Elektra* the firmly established dialectic of *eros* and *thanatos* assumes a new context in the Freudian world of Vienna *c.*1900.

In Elektra's scene with Orestes, the composer reduces the brother's role to its bare essentials until the moment she recognizes him. All in all, Strauss shortens this scene by approximately 40 per cent. The highlight of this scene (and perhaps the entire opera) is the soliloquy that follows the moment of recognition—a modern reinterpretation of the classic Aristotelian anagnorisis. Here the swiftly-paced action comes to a halt, and, in a rare instance, Strauss asks the poet for more text:

> In *Elektra*, page 77 [Strauss's copy], I need a great moment of repose after Electra's first shout: 'Orest!'
>
> I shall fit in a delicately vibrant orchestral interlude while Electra gazes upon Orestes, now safely restored to her. I can make her repeat the stammered words: 'Orest, Orest, Orest!' several times; of the remainder only the words: 'Es rührt sich niemand!' and 'O lass Deine Augen mich sehen!' fit into this mood. Couldn't you insert here a few beautiful verses until (as Orestes is about to embrace her gently) I switch over to the sombre mood, starting with the words: 'Nein, Du sollst mich nicht berühren . . .' etc.?[29]

Hofmannsthal's added lines, along with 'Es rührt sich niemand. O lass Deine Augen mich sehen!', form a slow, lyrical, closed aria for Elektra at the outset of her long soliloquy:

[29] *Correspondence*, 16.

Elektra

Orestes!
Orestes! Orestes! Orestes!
No one is stirring! Oh let my eyes
gaze at you, a vision in a dream, a vision
granted to me, fairer than any dream!
Noble, ineffable, sublime features,
oh stay by me! Do not melt
into air, do not vanish from my sight.
Even if now I have to die,
and you have revealed yourself to me
and come to fetch me, then I will die
happier than I have lived! Orestes! Orestes! Orestes!

Elektra's part in this scene is, in the main, distilled into this extended monologue—a conflation of two speeches from the scene. In both speeches Elektra ultimately explains her loss of sexuality, which she sacrificed to her father. 'When I rejoiced in my own body,' she asks Orestes, 'do you think his sighs did not reach, his groans did not press up to my bed? . . . he sent me hate, hollow-eyed hate as a bridegroom' (p. 64). That is Strauss's sole reference to the central issue of the scene: that in living only for revenge Elektra sacrificed—indeed replaced—her sexuality for hate. Any other allusions are cut, even Elektra's ensuing metaphor for her 'hollow-eyed bridegroom':

Elektra

And I had to let the monster,
who breathes like a viper, come over me
into my sleepless bed, who forced me to know
all that goes on between man and woman.

(p. 64)

Later in the next speech (also cut) she confesses:

I have sacrificed
my shame, as if I had fallen into the hands
of bandits who have torn from my body
even the last garment! I am not

without my wedding night as virgins are,
I have felt the agony of childbirth
and have brought nothing into the world . . .

(p. 66)

After Elektra's moment of introspection, Strauss seeks to move to the murders as swiftly as possible, and he must eliminate more dialogue in order to do it. Hofmannsthal's original intention was that Elektra must, first, convince her brother to go ahead with the deed:

Elektra

You will do it!

Orest

Yes, yes. If only I did not
have to look first in my mother's eyes.

Elektra

Then look at me, what she has made of me.

(p. 65)

In the libretto, Orestes' mind is already made up; these lines—among others—were deleted.

The remainder of the play (i.e. the murders and the celebration of the deed) is not only uncut, but, rather, augmented with extra text by Hofmannsthal. It is here, at the end of the drama, that we see two distinctly different visions for the finale. For Hofmannsthal, the expressive power of the ending was in its abruptness, which for Strauss was simply too short for an operatic finale. The moment in question is towards the very end of the play, between Chrystothemis' lines: 'Don't you hear, they carry him, they carry him on their hands . . .' and Elektra's 'Be silent and dance. All must approach!'

It is possible that they discussed this part of the scene during their meeting of late December 1907. Strauss reminds Hofmannsthal that he needs 'those small additions to *Elektra*' in a letter of 20 February 1908; the poet's reply is not extant.

None the less, we know that Strauss received them, for on 6 July 1908 he writes Hofmannsthal: 'Enclosed herewith your final verses which I am asking you to extend as much as possible, as a *simultaneous* duet between Elektra and Chrysothemis. Nothing new, just the same contents, repeated and working towards a climax'.[30]

These verses are indeed nothing new, and, purely from the standpoint of the play, they are a needless, even harmful, impediment to the swift dramatic pace at this moment:

Elektra

We are with the gods.

With enthusiasm

Our bodies are transfixed by the golden sword
of the gods, but all their glory is not too much for us!

Chrysothemis

All faces are transformed,
In each eye, upon each cheek,
the happy tears we see
All weep for joy. Do you not hear?

<table>
<tr><th>Elektra</th><th>Chrysothemis</th></tr>
<tr><td>I have sown shadows
and now reap joy upon joy.
I was a black corpse among the living,
and at this hour I am the fire of life
and my flame burns up the darkness
of the world. My face must be whiter than
the pale-glowing face of the moon.</td><td>The gods are good! Good!
A life begins for you and me.</td></tr>
<tr><td>If someone should see me, he must die
or faint with joy. Do you see my face?
Do you see the light that emanates from me?</td><td>It is the gods in their infinite
goodness who have granted it to us.
Who has always loved us?
Who has always loved us?</td></tr>
</table>

Chrysothemis

Now our brother is here and love
flows over us like oil and myrrh, love
is everything! Who can live without love?

[30] *Correspondence*, 18.

Elektra	*Chrysothemis*
Ah! Love kills! but no one can go through life without knowing love!	Elektra! I must go to my brother!

Chrysothemis runs out

Strauss's request for more text after the dénouement goes against the grain of Hofmannsthal's original intent. At this moment gesture should override text; action should triumph over word. Before the deed Elektra incessantly talks of her father's murder; her constant recounting of it, however, never brings her the necessary catharsis, which can only occur after the fall of the axe. A lengthy monologue following this critical point would be superfluous from Hofmannsthal's viewpoint. 'Be silent and dance!' she exclaims at this moment of purgation. Additional text dilutes this tension between word and deed that has been mounting throughout the drama.

But this argument ignores the issue of music altogether. The musical tension that culminates in Elektra's dance and moves fairly swiftly to the end is one of the most remarkable musico-dramatic moments in the score. As many critics at the première pointed out, the words to the final duet between sisters were mostly inaudible anyway. What Strauss intended at the point just after the murder of Aegisthus was a symphonic finale for the opera, which might explain the cryptic annotation ('Musik!') that the composer jotted in the upper left-hand margin of text (which begins this final section) followed by a long vertical arrow drawn down that margin (Fig. 2.2).

Strauss's finale is a *tour de force*: an intricate motivic culmination unrivalled by any of his previous operas or even tone poems, for that matter. We shall look at this passage, along with Hofmannsthal's textual additions, in greater detail in the final chapter. The musical shape for this section was, no doubt, in his mind before he received those additions, for words play an indirect role at this juncture; they are needed only to fill out his symphonic conception. Thus, Strauss asks Hofmannsthal for 'nothing new' in content, only that the

Musik!

CHRYSOTHEMIS:

Elektra! Schwester! komm mit uns! so komm
mit uns! es ist der Bruder drin im Haus!
es ist Orest, der es getan hat!
(Stimmengewirr, Getümmel draußen.)
Komm!
Er steht im Vorsaal, alle sind um ihn,
sie küssen seine Füße, alle, die
Aegisth im Herzen haßten, haben sich
geworfen auf die andern, überall
in allen Höfen liegen Tote, alle,
die leben, sind mit Blut bespritzt und haben
selbst Wunden, und doch strahlen alle, alle
umarmen sich –
(Draußen wachsender Lärm, die Frauen sind hinausgelaufen, Chrysothemis allein, von draußen fällt Licht herein.)
und jauchzen, tausend Fackeln
sind angezündet. Hörst du nicht, so hörst du
denn nicht?

FIG. 2.2 Hofmannsthal, *Elektra*, 5th edn. (RSA)

words repeat the established mood and rise to a climax. He had already made a similar request for more text following the 'orchestral interlude' of the Recognition Scene.

Was Strauss fully sensitive to the multiple levels of psychological symbolism and motivation in *Elektra*? Perhaps not. Yet the fact that he chose to omit important strata of the drama in his reworking of Hofmannsthal's *Elektra* need not imply that his opera is any the weaker for it. On the contrary, the shift of emphasis in certain areas contributes to the success of the altered work. Strauss, the seasoned conductor and practical man of the operatic stage, had an uncanny instinct for what would work and what would not work as music theatre. He had already composed three operas and knew better than Hofmannsthal the perils of using too much text in music for the stage.

Strauss surely felt that certain psychological implications would not be picked up by the opera audience, that it was necessary to simplify the dramaturgy; he was, no doubt, correct. One might even argue that some of those nuances made their way to the orchestra pit rather than the stage. Future collaborations between Strauss and Hofmannsthal show how the former's down-to-earth sense of the theatre was a vital complement to the latter's often complicated and ambitious theatrical ideas. In Strauss's own words, what appealed to him in the *Elektra* play was its 'unity of structure' and 'the force of its climaxes'.[31] He made the most of these two elements in his libretto and, ultimately, in his score.

[31] *Recollections*, 155.

3 Elektra *Chronology*

More than eight decades separate us from the première of *Elektra* in 1909, yet since then we have learned little more about how the opera evolved. *Elektra* not only fully established Strauss as the most prominent German opera composer of his time, but also marked the beginning of the most important artistic collaboration of his life. It is, therefore, curious that documentation pertaining to important events surrounding *Elektra*'s genesis have remained so obscure. The aim of this chapter, thus, is to establish a reliable chronology of the opera's evolution, an account based upon published letters by Strauss and Hofmannsthal, unpublished letters from Strauss to his family and friends, the composer's diaries, and other hitherto unexamined sources.

In an essay of 1942 entitled 'Reminiscences of the First Performance of My Operas', Strauss states that he decided to set *Elektra* to music after he saw the play; he does not say when he witnessed that performance.

> When I first saw Hofmannsthal's inspired play in the *Deutsches Theater* with Gertrude Eysoldt, I immediately recognised, of course, what a magnificent operatic libretto it might be (after the alteration I made in the Orestes scene it has actually become one) and, just as previously with *Salome*, I appreciated the tremendous increase in musical tension to the very end.[1]

Thus, a fundamental task in determining the chronology of the opera is to establish when Strauss saw the play.

We know that Strauss and Hofmannsthal met before the composer had seen the play. They first met on 23 March 1899

[1] Richard Strauss, *Recollections and Reflections*, ed. Willi Schuh, trans. L. J. Lawrence (London, 1953), 154.

in Berlin at the home of the writer Richard Dehmel, and they met again in 1900 in Paris. In fact, the first letter of their published correspondence (11 November 1900) is a letter from the poet in which he reminds Strauss of their Paris meeting and the discussion of a possible ballet scenario (*Der Triumph der Zeit*), which he had nearly completed. Thirteen days later, after receiving no reply, Hofmannsthal again asks the composer whether he is interested in the project; Strauss declines, saying he is preoccupied with a ballet project of his own, *Kythere*, which was never finished.

By the time of the next letter (7 March 1906) Strauss had evidently seen the play and had discussed the idea of an *Elektra* opera with Hofmannsthal, who writes: 'How goes it with you and *Elektra*? It is, I must say, the hope of no mean pleasure which you have so unexpectedly aroused in me. Will you let me know in a very few lines whether this hope may remain alive or is to be buried?'[2] Strauss replies four days later, stating that he is 'as keen as ever on *Elektra*' and reports that he has indeed gone ahead and made cuts in the text for his own private use.[3] Upon this slim documentation a significant portion of the Strauss literature has based its various conclusions about the onset of Strauss's work with *Elektra* and the beginning of the artistic association between Strauss and Hofmannsthal. Moreover, these various—and undocumented—accounts of the opera's origins, ranging from possible to implausible, have contributed to a certain amount of confusion about the inception of the opera.

Ernst Krause states that 'shortly before the completion of *Salome* (20 July 1905), a friend drew [Strauss's] attention to . . . [Hofmannsthal's] *Elektra*,' and at the beginning of 1906 he supposedly attended the play for the first time.[4] Krause does not identify the friend nor does he support his claim with any source. Most researchers generally conform

[2] *Correspondence*, 2–3.

[3] Ibid.

[4] Ernst Krause, *Richard Strauss: The Man and his Work*, (Boston, 1969),

to Krause's time frame, yet they differ with certain details.[5] William Mann asserts that 'early in 1906 Strauss got in touch with Hofmannsthal and asked permission to set *Elektra*,'[6] while Norman Del Mar declares that three months after the *Salome* première (9 December 1905) Hofmannsthal heard of Strauss's interest and wrote the composer [letter of 7 March 1906?] to 'find out for himself how the land lay'.[7] Ironically, both Mann and Del Mar seem to have based their conclusions on the same sketchy evidence in the Strauss–Hofmannsthal correspondence.

More puzzling, however, are inferences made by George Marek and Michael Kennedy concerning the genesis of the libretto, which they claim was the product of Hofmannsthal's reworking of the play. Marek asserts that Strauss 'approached Hofmannsthal and asked whether the poet would be willing to turn the play into an operatic text'.[8] Kennedy suggests that 'Hofmannsthal completed the task in 1905.'[9] These undocumented statements are all the more puzzling because they are flatly contradicted even by the published Strauss–Hofmannsthal letters, not to mention unpublished sources. Not only does the above-mentioned letter by Strauss (11 March 1906) make it clear that the composer himself made the cuts in *Elektra* for his own use, but three months later (9 June 1906) Hofmannsthal acknowledges that the *Elektra* 'libretto' was the product of editing on the part of the composer. In discussing the issues of royalties with Strauss, the playwright suggests:

I, as well as my publisher, will renounce in favour of your music publisher all our rights in the libretto for *Elektra* as shortened by

[5] Joseph Gregor, *Richard Strauss: Der Meister der Oper* (Munich, 1939); Norman Del Mar, *Richard Strauss: A Critical Commentary on his Life and Work*, 3 vols. (London, 1962–72); George Marek, *Richard Strauss: The Life of a Non-Hero* (New York, 1967); Michael Kennedy, *Richard Strauss*, The Master Musician Series (London, 1976); Kennedy, 'Richard Strauss', *Turn of the Century Masters* from The New Grove Composer Biography Series (New York, 1985); William Mann, *Richard Strauss: A Critical Study of the Operas* (London, 1964); and Franz Trenner, *Richard Strauss: Dokumente seines Lebens und Schaffens* (Munich, 1954).

[6] Mann, *Critical Study*, 69.

[7] Del Mar, *Critical Commentary*, i, 289.

[8] Marek, *Life of a Non-Hero*, 180.

[9] Kennedy, *Richard Strauss*, 45.

you and thus distinguished from the play, in return for a royalty in the German as well as in all foreign editions of this libretto to be settled between the publishers.[10]

Perhaps the most puzzling account, however, is offered by Suzanne Bales, who, in her doctoral work on Hofmannsthal's *Elektra*, implies that Strauss first saw *Elektra* on 17 November 1906.[11] She cites no source, but Helmut Fiechtner, in some *Elektra* programme notes, also mentions that 'Strauss saw the [*Elektra*] staging by Max Reinhardt on 17 November 1906: It inspired him to [compose] his opera.'[12] The latter statement is not necessarily untrue, for Fiechtner does not say that he saw it for the first time in November of that year. By that time Strauss had started composing the first scene of the opera. In short, a good deal of confusion about the origins of Strauss's *Elektra* has amassed over the decades.

Strauss's Initial Interest in the *Elektra* Play

Strauss almost certainly knew of the world première of Hofmannsthal's *Elektra* in Berlin and its ensuing performances. He had been in Berlin first as conductor of the Court Opera from 1898–1908 and then as General Music Director from 1908–18. The play premièred on 30 October 1903 at the *Kleines Theater* and enjoyed a run until 28 June 1905: a total of ninety performances.[13] The production was revived for

[10] *Correspondence*, 6.

[11] Suzanne Bales, 'Elektra: From Hofmannsthal to Strauss', Ph.D. Diss. (Stanford University, 1984), 76, 92.

[12] 'Diese Inszenierung von Max Reinhardt sah Richard Strauss am 17.11.1906: sie inspirierte ihn zu seiner Oper.' These programme notes by Fiechtner (copyrighted 1960) were used by the Zurich Opera for the 1983–4 season of the *Opera-Mobile* in the Tonhalle. Bales cites some Fiechtner *Elektra* notes that appeared in the programme book of the Bavarian State Opera (1976–7 season), although the author has not seen them.

[13] Heinrich Huesmann, *Welttheater Reinhardt* (Munich, 1983), 207. Stage design was by Max Kruse; costumes were designed by Lovis Corinth, who later designed the cover for the piano-vocal score and libretto of the opera. The main cast for the première was as follows: Gertrude Eysoldt (Elektra), Rosa Bertens (Klytämnestra), Lucie Höflich (Chrysothemis), Adolf Edgar Licho (Orest), and Josef Klein (Ägisth).

only three performances at the *Deutsches Theater*: from 21 October to 7 November 1905 (we do not know the date of that second performance). On 17 November 1906, this production was again revived at the *Kammerspiele*—a branch of the *Deutsches Theater*—for a series of five performances; a final run of six performances was mounted there beginning on 15 December 1908 (see Table 3.1).[14]

TABLE 3.1 Berlin productions of Hofmannsthal's *Elektra* (1903–1909)

Dates	Theatre	Producer	Performances
30 Oct. 1903–28 June 1905	Kleines Theater	Reinhardt	90
21 Oct.–7 Nov. 1905	Deutsches Theater	Reinhardt	3
17 Nov. 1906–4 Jan. 1908	Kammerspiele	Reinhardt	5
15 Dec. 1908–22 Mar. 1909	Kammerspiele	Reinhardt	6

But in his 1942 *Elektra* reminiscence, Strauss states that he saw Gertrude Eysoldt in the title role in the *Deutsches Theater*, which limits the possible dates for Strauss attending to three performances: 21 October and 7 November 1905, or the unknown date in between (see Table 3.1). A further unpublished document corroborates that the evening at the *Deutsches Theater* was firmly etched in the composer's memory. In a belated eightieth-birthday greeting (7 July 1944) from Eysoldt, the actress recalls the play's première:

Honored Master Richard Strauss!

Your birthday is celebrated. The great bestowers and receivers within the realm of sound are celebrated. And all of the [birthday] givers display their thanks to you from the heart. Among these givers I would not want to be missed: the first Elektra in the play of Hoffmannsthal [*sic*] and the first Salome of Wilde. Many years have

[14] The *Kammerspiele des Deutschen Theaters* was founded by Max Reinhardt in 1906 and opened in November of that year with a Reinhardt production of Henrik Ibsen's *Ghosts*.

gone by since the first performance of Elektra in the *Kleines Theater* in Berlin. . . .[15]

Eysoldt neglects to mention when Strauss attended her performance, but Strauss wrote a memorandum at the bottom of the last page of the letter: 'Berlin, Deutsches Theater. Schumannstr[asse]'. Furthermore, an entry in Strauss's engagement calendar suggests the unlikelihood that the composer attended the 21 October performance. That evening he was scheduled to conduct Peter Cornelius's *Barbier von Bagdad*, thus trimming down the possibilities to two dates.[16]

Letters from Strauss to librettists Hofmannsthal, Stefan Zweig, and Joseph Gregor show that from *Elektra* onward Strauss typically began thinking about new opera projects by the time he was well into orchestrating the previous opera.[17] The reason that Strauss had not actively sought ideas for new opera projects while he orchestrated *Salome* was in part due to the unique circumstances of *Salome*'s scoring. He finished the full score on 20 June 1905, but had not yet composed the famous dance, which—with great effort—was completed exactly two months later. The death of his father, Franz Strauss, on 31 May of that year also preoccupied the composer in those ensuing months.

We still do not know when Strauss told Hofmannsthal of his interest in setting *Elektra*. He may have expressed his

[15] Letter from Gertrude Eysoldt to Strauss, 7 July 1944, RSA. 'Verehrter Meister Richard Strauss! Ihr Geburtstag wird gefeiert. Der grosse Schenkende und Empfangliche im Reich der Töne wird gefeiert. Und alle Beschenkten legen Ihnen ihren Dank aus Herz. Unter diesen Beschenktern möchte ich doch nicht fehlen: die erste Elektra im Schauspiel von Hoffmannsthal [*sic*] und die erste Salome von Wilde. Viele Jahre sind dahingegangen seit der ersten Aufführung der Elektra im kleinen Theater in Berlin.' [. . .]

[16] RSA; I have not been able to confirm whether or not Strauss actually conducted the Cornelius work, but it seems likely that he did. The composer revived *Der Barbier von Bagdad* with a new production for the 1905–6 season; 21 October opened that new production. Moreover, in his *Schreibkalender*, Strauss typically drew a line through a work that he, for whatever reason, did not conduct.

[17] *Richard Strauss–Stefan Zweig: Briefwechsel*, ed. Willi Schuh (Frankfurt a.M., 1957) and *Richard Strauss und Joseph Gregor: Briefwechsel (1934–1949)*, ed. Roland Tenschert (Salzburg, 1955).

intentions through a no longer extant letter of November or December 1905, or January 1906. He might have just as easily communicated his plan by telephone or by way of a mutual friend. One thing is for certain: Hofmannsthal was in Berlin by 2 February 1906 for the première of his *Oedipus und die Sphinx*, produced by Reinhardt at the *Deutsches Theater.*[18] Günther Erken suggests that they met that day and discussed the possibility of an *Elektra* opera.[19] This possible meeting would readily explain the apparent lacuna at the beginning of their *Elektra* correspondence. It is plausible that Hofmannsthal heard nothing further from Strauss after the February meeting and, on 7 March, wanted to know whether he was still interested in the project.

Strauss's reply (11 March) seems contradictory. On the one hand, he 'is as keen as ever' on *Elektra*, so keen that he has trimmed the text for use as a libretto. Yet on the other hand, he also expresses reluctance to go ahead with the project right away: '[I would] do better to wait a few years before approaching *Elektra*, until I have myself moved much farther away from the *Salome* style.'[20] Hofmannsthal's well-known reply (27 April) seeks to dramatize the differences between the two plays: *Salome* is a torrid mixture of purple and violet; *Elektra* is a mixture of dark and bright.[21] But, ironically, it was the similarities—not the contrasts—between the two works that had attracted Strauss to Hofmannsthal's work in the first place.

The playwright, perhaps somewhat self-servingly, stressed differences between the two operas in an effort to keep Strauss on track with the project. The composer mentioned numerous alternatives at the time: *Semiramis*, *Saul und David*, *Dantons Tod*, *Die Tochter der Luft*, and others. Thus, Hofmannsthal suggested that they talk about the problem in person, in Vienna on 9 or 10 May 1906, since Strauss would

[18] Huesmann, *Welttheater Reinhardt*, 293.

[19] Günther Erken, 'Hofmannsthal Chronik: Beitrag zu einer Biographie' (unpublished, *c.*1963). Willi Schuh Estate.

[20] *Correspondence*, 3.

[21] *Correspondence*, 4.

be passing through the Austrian capital on his way to Graz to conduct the Austrian première of *Salome.*[22] Due to a change of schedule, the two were only able to meet for about an hour on the 8th, but this short meeting was evidently critical, for Hofmannsthal finally persuaded Strauss to go ahead with *Elektra.*[23] Less than a month later (5 June) Strauss wrote from his summer residence in Marquartstein, 'I would like to begin work on *Elektra*!'[24]

Timetable of Composition

Strauss worked on *Elektra* from 1906 to 1908.[25] Evidence to chronicle progress on the opera is far sparser than with *Salome*, where the composer dated most of his sketches as well as the Particell. His correspondence with Hofmannsthal also tells us little about his composing. Indeed, throughout his life, Strauss appears to have been reluctant to offer any specific information about his composing to his librettists, friends, or acquaintances. Rather, in letters to librettists, he discusses possible opera themes, requests textual clarification, or makes dramaturgical suggestions. Time and time again the correspondence indicates that once matters relating to the text have been worked out, a significant pause in correspondence often occurs; at this point Strauss has begun composing.

When did Strauss begin composing *Elektra*? Although he declared his intent to begin work on the opera on 5 June 1906, he had already undertaken some preliminary work months earlier. On 11 March 1906 he told Hofmannsthal that he had cut down the text for his own use, and he had

[22] Strauss conducted *Salome* on 16, 18, and 20 May; the performance on the 16th was the Austrian première. Gustav Mahler, who was unable to get the work approved by the censors of the Vienna Court Opera, attended the performance on the 18th.

[23] *Briefwechsel*, 21. This letter and the next one (n. 24) did not appear in Schuh's first or second editions (1952 and 1955, respectively), nor do they appear in the English translation, which was based on Schuh's first edition.

[24] *Briefwechsel*, 21.

[25] See Elektra Chronicle in Appendix I.

probably assessed the basic shape by then. The composer's ability to size up musico-dramatic possibilities after only a couple of readings amazed many who knew him, including Zweig and Gregor.[26] Strauss's fifth-edition copy of Hofmannsthal's play shows musical annotations in the margins made simultaneously with many of his cuts.[27] The significance of that marginal musical commentary will be discussed in the next chapter.

But it was not until his June arrival at Marquartstein, the small village in upper Bavaria where he regularly spent his vacations between 1890 and 1908 and composed some of his most important works, that he began sketching *Elektra* in earnest.[28] By mid-June he informs Hofmannsthal that he is 'making heavy weather' of the first scene,[29] and just a month later he reports to his friend, Willy Levin, to whom the opera is dedicated, that he has finished the second scene.[30] How far he progressed beyond scene 2 in 1906 is unclear, although he informs his mother (7 August 1906) that he is 'working diligently' on the opera.[31] By December Strauss felt that he had composed enough of *Elektra* to perform portions of it for Hofmannsthal in Berlin.[32]

In 1907 work on the opera slowed down considerably, owing largely to two basic factors. First, Strauss's guest-conducting duties burgeoned with the ever-increasing popularity of *Salome*. Second, he was unable to spend a peaceful, uninterrupted summer at Marquartstein, where he had been able to compose every summer with little outside interruption since the time of *Guntram*. During the first half of June

[26] Gregor, *Der Meister der Oper*, pp. 246–7 and Stefan Zweig, *The World of Yesterday* (Lincoln, Nebr., 1964), pp. 368–9.

[27] RSA.

[28] Stephan Kohler, 'Richard Strauss in Marquartstein: Eine Chronik', *Richard-Strauss Blätter*, 2 (Dec. 1979), 29–50.

[29] *Correspondence*, p. 7.

[30] BSt: Ana 330, I, Levin, No. 1.

[31] BSt: Ana 330, I, Strauss, No. 567.

[32] 'Gestern spielte und sang mir Richard Strauss einige Teile aus der *Elektra* und mir machte das Gedicht in dieser Form (obwohl er natürlich elend singt) eine grosse Freude, viel mehr als von Schauspielern gesprochen.' *Hugo von Hofmannsthal–Helene von Nostitz: Briefwechsel*, ed. O. Nostitz (Frankfurt, 1965), 29.

Strauss had extensive conducting engagements in Holland, including the Rotterdam music festival, where he conducted his *Burleske*, *Don Juan*, *Tod und Verklärung*, *Sturmlied*, and *Heldenleben*. On 13 June he took a cure at Bad Nauheim, but was occupied with composing the *Parademarsch für Cavallerie* (one of a number of marches written for the German Kaiser), which he finished on the 19th. He managed to take a vacation from mid-July to 11 August, but undertook an extensive conducting tour during the second half of that month.

Strauss's hectic summer puts his letter to Ernst von Schuch (24 August 1907) in sharper relief: 'I don't want to exert myself too much with conducting this winter [in Berlin] and would like to work steadily on *Elektra*.'[33] A sentence from a letter to his wife, Pauline de Ahna, on 13 September reveals precisely how far the sketching of the opera had gone: '*Elektra* [has] progressed to page sixty of the [text]book.'[34] Page sixty of Strauss's edition is approximately midway through scene 5: Elektra's second encounter with Chrysothemis, shortly before the Recognition Scene. Ten days later he writes Schuch: 'I shall play for you *Elektra*, which has progressed quite far.'[35] By the end of September or the beginning of October, Strauss had sketched the work up to the beginning of the Recognition Scene.

With the Recognition Scene, Strauss reached a creative impasse, and on 7 October he decided to delay further sketching and begin scoring the work, which was a relatively routine task for the composer.[36] Part of the his creative block can be attributed to his busy autumn schedule at the Court Opera (he typically conducted approximately sixty operas per season at this time), but that is far from the whole story. The more serious problem stemmed from the similarities that

[33] Friedrich von Schuch, *Richard Strauss, Ernst von Schuch, und Dresdens Oper* (Leipzig, 1953), 80.

[34] RSA: '*Elektra* bis Seite 60 Buch gediehen'. Letter of 13 Sept. 1907 to the composer's wife.

[35] Friedrich von Schuch, *Richard Strauss*, 81.

[36] 'The Composer Speaks: Richard Strauss', in *Book of Modern Composers*, ed. David Ewen (New York, 1942), 55.

Strauss still perceived between *Salome* and *Elektra*, notwithstanding Hofmannsthal's encouragement. In his *Elektra* memoir Strauss explains that in both works he 'appreciated the tremendous increase in musical tension to the very end: In *Elektra*, after the recognition scene, which could only be completely realized in music, the release in dance—in *Salome*, after the dance . . . the dreadful apotheosis of the end.' He continues that, with *Elektra*, he at first 'doubted whether [he] should have the power to exhaust this subject also'.[37] At this moment in the drama, Strauss probably lacked the creative strength to continue and therefore chose to back off temporarily. He did not resume sketching the Recognition Scene until some nine months later.

In his *Schreibkalender* Strauss kept a sporadic account of his progress in scoring the opera by recording the page number of the most recent page scored on a particular day. A comparison of these recorded page numbers with the autograph score tells us fairly precisely how he progressed with the orchestration (see Table 3.2).

Aside from his regular Berlin duties Strauss enjoyed a relatively calm October in 1907, and he found ample opportunity to score in his spare time. The next month was more hectic. He toured most of November as guest conductor; it was highlighted by a trip through Holland from 11 to 21 November, when he conducted *Salome* in Amsterdam, The Hague, Utrecht, and Rotterdam. Still, on 17 November he wrote to his wife that he was staying at Mengelberg's home and was orchestrating *Elektra* at the conductor's desk.[38] Table 3.2 shows that he had completed the first two scenes by the first week of December and was able to work on the score without much interruption through the rest of the month and the first three weeks of January. By 19 January he was nearly finished with the fourth scene, but numerous conducting tours in Italy, Poland, Austria, France, and Germany slowed his work considerably in the spring of

[37] *Recollections*, 154–5.
[38] See Elektra Chronicle, Appendix I.

TABLE 3.2 *Elektra* chronology: a documentary timetable

Date	Sketching	Particell	Scoring
1906		[Documents entirely lacking for 1906–7]	
5 June	States intent to begin *Elektra*		
16 June	Works on scene 1		
16 July	Scene 2 finished		
1907			
13 Sept.	Sketches to middle of scene 5		
7 Oct.			Begins scene 1
7 Dec.			Finishes scene 2
14 Dec.			Up to beginning of Chrysothemis' final speech (scene 3)
25 Dec.			Up to Klytämnestra's entrance (scene 4)
1908			
19 Jan.			Up to Elektra's final speech (scene 4)
12 Mar.			Midway through instrumental interlude following scene 4
18 Mar.			Through Chrysothemis' entrance 'Orest ist tot!' (scene 5)
4 Apr.			Finishes first half of scene 5
21 June	Begins Recognition Scene (scene 6)		
*c.*6 July	Finishes scene 6		
13 July		Finishes scene 6	
14 July			Begins scene 6
*c.*20 Aug.	Finishes sketching the opera		
11 Sept.		Finishes Particell	
22 Sept.			Finishes score

1908. He had only scored half-way through scene 5 by early April.

The Strauss–Hofmannsthal letters of 1908 reflect the composer's preoccupation with dramaturgical problems in the final scenes of the opera. The single letter by Strauss of 22 December 1907 is so late in that year that it should be considered part of this latter period of correspondence. Indeed, part of Strauss's reluctance to continue composing in October 1907 was, perhaps, the result of his inability to apprehend important aspects of the dramaturgy towards the end of the play. Hofmannsthal visited the composer in Berlin in late December 1907, at which time Strauss probably voiced some of his hesitations. Hofmannsthal evidently suggested cutting Aegisthus entirely from the opera, although by 22 December Strauss had some second thoughts:

> As for our recent conversation about *Elektra*, I believe that we can't leave out Aegisthus altogether. He is definitely part of the plot and must be killed with the rest, preferably before the eyes of the audience. If it isn't possible to get him into the house earlier, so that he is slain immediately after Clytemnestra, then we'll leave the next scene as it now stands—but maybe you'll think it over.[39]

Hofmannsthal replies (3 January 1908) that they should cut the Serving Maids' Scene, seguéing to Aegisthus' murder just after the murder of Klytämnestra.[40] Hofmannsthal visited Strauss again on 26 February, and the composer played *Elektra* for him; the two probably discussed the end of the play once again.[41]

Spring 1908 was a busy period for Strauss, who—besides his regular Berlin duties—toured as guest conductor, continued to score *Elektra*, and was also in the process of undertaking business negotiations with publishers for the nearly-completed opera. The composer approached both Schott and Fürstner, and, on 22 April, he accepted the latter's offer of 100,000 marks for the rights to publish the score.[42] Shortly before

[39] *Correspondence*, 12.

[40] Ibid.

[41] RSA: Strauss records this visit in his *Schreibkalender*.

[42] RSA.

20 June, Strauss submitted the completed portion of the orchestral score (i.e. up to the Recognition Scene) to the publisher.[43]

Strauss did not return to composing the remainder of *Elektra* until 21 June.[44] In May he took the Berlin Philharmonic on an extensive European tour, and in early June he moved into his newly-completed summer residence in Garmisch, which was financed by the royalties from *Salome*.[45] Thus, as the summer began Strauss commenced work on the Recognition Scene, but his musical plan—which included a lyrical solo for Elektra ('Es rührt sich niemand')—did not entirely conform to Hofmannsthal's play at that moment in the drama. He, therefore, asked the playwright for additional text to fill out 'a great moment of repose after Elektra's first shout: "Orest!".' Strauss requested the additional text on 22 June and Hofmannsthal sent it to him three days later; it is, technically speaking, Hofmannsthal's first work as librettist for the composer.

In that same letter of 22 June Strauss also admitted that he still did not understand the scenic layout for the two murders that follow the Recognition Scene. No passage from any other *Elektra* letter better illustrates the composer's blunt, down-to-earth approach to the theatre than his query about that scene:

I still don't understand the scenic action at the end. Surely, Orestes is *in* the house. Surely, the front door in the middle is shut. Chrysothemis and the serving maids hurried off on p. 88 [just before Aegisthus' murder] *into the house on the left*. On page 91 [just

[43] Hans Schneider, ed., *Richard Strauss: Manuskripte und Briefe*, Catalogue No. 194 (part 1), 37.

[44] *Correspondence*, 16.

[45] Strauss often told the anecdote about *Salome* royalties paying for his Garmisch villa, and it is quoted in numerous sources. He finally wrote down the story in 1942 [see 'Reminiscences of the First Performance of My Operas' in *Recollections and Reflections*, 152]: '[Kaiser] William the Second once said to his intendant: "I am sorry Strauss composed this *Salome*. I really like the fellow, but this will do him a lot of damage." The damage enabled me to build the villa in Garmisch.' Evidence of royalty income from Strauss's *Schreibkalendar* supports the composer's claim.

after Aegisthus' murder] they are 'rushing out madly.' Out of where? The left or through the middle?

Page 93 [the penultimate page]: Chrysothemis comes running out. Out of which way? Through the courtyard gate on the right? What for? Surely, Orestes is in the centre of the house! Why does Chrysothemis run back in on p. 94? Why is she at the end beating at the front door? Surely because it is barred? Do please answer these questions of mine in detail. I have never been quite clear about the scenario since reading it through.[46]

Hofmannsthal responded to Strauss's blunt questions by drawing a plan for the stage.

Strauss finished sketching the Recognition Scene by 6 July and shifted his attention on the exchange between Elektra and her sister at the end of the opera. The composer once again required more text to fill out his musical plan: 'Enclosed herewith your final verses, which I am asking you to extend as much as possible, to a *simultaneous* duet between Electra and Chrysothemis. Nothing new, just the same contents repeated and working towards a climax.'[47] On the 8th, he predicted that the opera would be finished by September.[48] Five days later Strauss finished the Recognition Scene in Particell and began orchestrating that portion the next day.[49]

When did Strauss finish sketching the opera? By 16 August he was probably concerned with sketching the final scene. On that date Hofmannsthal writes to Strauss: 'It pleases me from the heart that you are happily further along in the work and are satisfied. Now I wish you strength and joy for the close, which will be more meaningful and more powerful in your work than in the poem'.[50] Strauss finished composing (i.e. sketching) the opera by 20 August, according to a letter

[46] *Correspondence*, p. 16. I have restored a sentence omitted in the English translation ('Why does Chrysothemis run back in on p. 94?'). See *Briefwechsel*, 37.

[47] *Correspondence*, 18.

[48] BSt: Ana 330, I, Strauss, no. 632.

[49] RSA (*Schreibkalender*): 'Scene zwischen Elektra und Orest fertig. | Klavierskizze *Elektra* fertig bis zum Eintritt des Pflegers.' (13 July 1908) 'Fortsetzung der *Elektra*partitur von Seite 218 [6 bars after reh. 111a] ab.' (14 July 1908)

[50] *Briefwechsel*, 46 (author's translation). The English translation in the *Correspondence* (p. 22) falls short of the exact meaning.

to his friend Levin; it is the only other known letter pertaining to the progress of *Elektra* from that month.[51] Therefore, by late summer 1908 Strauss focused on finishing the Particell and scoring the work. On 11 September, he wrote to Schuch, who would conduct the première in Dresden on 25 January 1909, that he had completed the Particell: '*Elektra* is finished and the close is quite juicy.'[52] Eleven days later, the day that he scored and dated the last page of the orchestral score, Strauss sent the remainder of the manuscript to Fürstner, along with a one-page covering letter: 'Hurrah! Just finished. Herewith the end of the score.'[53] A summary of Strauss's compositional schedule appears in Table 3.2.

With typical assiduousness and business sense, Strauss was not only already making arrangements for the Dresden première and other early performances, but also making sure that *Feuersnot* and *Salome* were to be included with as many of these first performances as possible. The enormous success of *Salome* had given Strauss leverage with the world's major opera houses. We recall he had amassed enough influence to have a four-day Strauss opera festival (*Elektra*, *Feuersnot*, *Salome*, and a repeat of *Elektra*) in conjunction with the Dresden première. And he was in constant touch with a number of conductors as well, suggesting singers and other important details. A letter to his colleague Felix Mottl in Munich—written a day before he finished the full score—is exemplary. In it he goes over details for the Munich première scheduled for 14 February 1909:

Two thirds of the piano-vocal score *are* finished and ready (for example also Dresden, Vienna, Frankfurt) to be sent to begin the rehearsals for the three major roles [Elektra, Klytämnestra, and Chrysothemis]. The rest of the piano-vocal score (which can easily be studied in 14 days) follows around mid-November. Score and orchestral parts will be finished certainly in December. The

[51] Schneider, *Manuskripte und Briefe*, Catalogue No. 194, 38.
[52] Von Schuch, *Richard Strauss*, 82.
[53] Schneider, *Manuskripte und Briefe*, Catalogue No. 194, 38.

Dresden production will be possible for 24 January at the latest. In regard to the casting requirements, I have also requested Herr Intendantzrat Tollner to convey my urgent request that the role of Elektra—which requires a tragic actress of the first rank—be sung by Frl. [Zdenka] Fassbender in the first cast. According to all that I have heard about her Isolde and Brünnhilde, she appears to be the most suitable.[54]

Strauss, of course, wished to ensure that *Elektra* would be properly launched. He was obviously eager for it to spread across Europe and the world with the same speed and enthusiasm that *Salome* had enjoyed. The wide-ranging list of *Elektra* performances within the first couple of years is remarkable, but the opera would not immediately inspire the same heated enthusiasm as its predecessor. Moreover, the composer's desire to help co-ordinate and arrange *Elektra* first performances—and, when possible, arrange performances of *Feursnot* and *Salome* around those premières—was a major reason behind his decision to take a one-year sabbatical from his Berlin duties. But it was not the sole reason. Balancing regular conducting duties in Berlin (and ever-increasing demands as guest conductor) with work on *Elektra* proved to be more than the composer could handle at times, especially during that busy summer of 1907.

Also, well before his one-year leave, Strauss had already begun to explore various future projects with Hofmannsthal (they had finally settled on *Der Rosenkavalier* by April 1909), and he needed time to compose without the bustle of the Berlin Court Opera. *Salome* and *Elektra* had taught him the difficuties of composing a stage work while trying to manage an opera house and guest-conducting career at the same time; the genesis of his next opera would be different. Strauss returned to the Court Opera for the 1909–10 season, and the highlight of his return was a performance of *Elektra* on 13

[54] BSt: From the Willi Krienitz Collection, which (at the time this went to press) was still uncatalogued. I wish to thank Robert Münster and Karl Dachs for permitting me to look at this collection.

October with the composer conducting the work for the first time.

Compared to *Elektra*, the composition of *Salome* had been a somewhat steadier endeavour. But the composer's busy schedule does not fully explain his slower pace with the later opera, for Strauss was already one of Europe's busiest musicians at the time of *Salome*. A retrospective glance over the genesis of *Elektra* reveals that the composer's initial reluctance was not without grounds. He believed that *Elektra* required, once again, the tragic musical vein that he felt he had nearly depleted with *Salome*, and, at first, he doubted whether he had the creative power to see it through. That doubt resurfaced when he was confronted with the Recognition Scene and the finale of the opera. We recall Hofmannsthal wishing his collaborator 'strength and joy for the end [of *Elektra*]' in August 1908. Thus, paradoxically, the similarities that Strauss perceived between the two works ignited his interest in composing *Elektra*, yet caused moments of hesitation as well. Hindsight shows that those moments of reluctance were instinctively correct, for the Recognition Scene is the most moving moment in the work and the finale is certainly the most powerful ending he wrote for any opera.

Therefore, although Strauss was tentative about *Elektra* at certain stages of the work, the result was an opera far bolder and, according to many contemporary critics, more stylistically uniform than its predecessor. One might even argue *because* of that hesitation. Early on *Elektra* could not overcome the popularity of her flashier sister, but Strauss lived to see a changing tide of opinion. Ultimately, Strauss would have preferred a lighter operatic subject immediately following *Salome*. But the playwright held his ground, and the industrious Strauss, who by June 1906 was anxious to begin composing a new stage work over the summer, finally gave in. That lighter subject was deferred. It ultimately took the shape of what we now know as *Der Rosenkavalier*.

4 Elektra: *Summary of Tonal Structure*

Hofmannsthal's *Elektra* made a profound impression on Strauss when he saw it in the autumn of 1905. We recall from Chapter 2 how the impact of the work was strong enough to reverse his original desire not to compose another tragic opera directly after *Salome*. Strauss instinctively realized that the play—in both structure and dramaturgy—contained all the necessary elements for a powerful opera. The broad symphonic implications inherent in Hofmannsthal's arch structure were readily apparent to the composer, and Strauss's tonal plan for the work responds directly to these implications. The terse introduction with the serving maids sets the atmosphere, while Elektra's opening establishes the expository material: she recalls her father's murder and foresees the ultimate atonement. Her inner rage is sharply developed in a revealing exchange with her mother, Klytämnestra, and, in a quasi-recapitulation, Elektra's premonitions are fulfilled.

But before we examine the composer's tonal plan for *Elektra* it is first essential to understand some important aspects of his tonal thinking, especially the associative role of keys in his music. Extra-musical associations with keys, whether in a tone poem or an opera, comprise a central element in Strauss's formal thinking when composing.[1] In a sketch for *Symphonia Domestica* [Tr. 10, fol. 3], for example, he writes above the staff: 'The mother's worries: will the child represent the father (F major) or (B major) the mother?'

[1] Adorno also observed this technique in Strauss, although he viewed it negatively, believing that it undermined any strong autonomous sense of form: 'Not infrequently what results is harmonizing and modulating which in terms of the form is planless and which can only be controlled extra-musically through tonal symbolism.' See Theodor Adorno, 'Richard Strauss. Born June 11, 1864', trans. Samuel and Shierry Weber, *Perspectives of New Music*, 4 (1965), 30.

This tritone relationship between father and mother symbolizes the often stormy relationship between Richard and Pauline, and it plays an important structural role in the tone poem.[2]

Tonal Symbolism in Strauss's Music

More than a half-century ago, Edmund Wachten proposed an ambitious table of *Strauss'schen Tonartenbestimmigen* for both operatic and stage music.[3] Although his system, fraught with omissions and inconsistencies, betrays the dangers of a mechanistic application of programmatic tags to particular keys, he was not altogether incorrect in his assumptions. Kurt Overhoff, in *Die Elektra Partitur von Richard Strauss*, provides a table of keys and their meanings as they relate specifically to the opera.[4] Overhoff, too, is sometimes prone to a dogmatic approach, but this should not obscure the fact that, in Strauss's music, certain keys do carry fairly consistent extra-musical associations. Moreover, for Strauss, these keys often anticipate themes that share significant similarities.

For example, Strauss typically uses E major to express dionysian, passionate, or even erotic sensations in music, hence the use of E as tonal centre for *Don Juan*. But its connection with the sensual is more far-reaching, for Strauss chooses E major as a tonal frame of reference for the ardent, young Octavian in *Der Rosenkavalier*; the passionate side of the husband in *Symphonia Domestica*; the stormy, invisible love-making scenes in the instrumental introductions to Acts I and III of *Der Rosenkavalier* and *Arabella*, respectively; the bacchic chorus 'Gib Dionysos' of *Daphne*; and, of course, Elektra's dionysian, cathartic dance that commences after the murder of Aegisthus. Example 4.1 illustrates some of

[2] The child's tonality (D) falls midway between these two keys.

[3] Edmund Wachten, 'Das Formproblem in der Sinfonischen Dichtungen von Richard Strauss', Ph.D. Diss. (University of Berlin, 1933).

[4] Kurt Overhoff, *Die Elektra-Partitur von Richard Strauss* (Salzburg, 1978), [8].

these E major themes, which share a rapid, upward surge. Theme 1*a* ascends a minor tenth in four bars, 1*b* encompasses an octave and a major sixth in the span of merely two bars, 1*c* covers two octaves in four bars, 1*d* leaps two octaves and a major third in just two bars, and 1*e* vaults upward an octave and perfect fifth in the same number of bars.

Ex. 4.1

Strauss delineates most of the characters in *Elektra* by certain recurring keys: D minor, for example, depicts Orestes, E flat major symbolizes Chrysothemis, and F major represents Aegisthus. Indeed, Strauss's tonal and thematic setting for Aegisthus matches, and perhaps goes beyond, Hofmannsthal's effeminate portrayal of a craven who is one of 'two women' and who 'only realizes heroic deeds in bed'. Not only does the composer set him in the jocular key of *Till Eulenspiegel*, but always in the first inversion. His sudden, tongue-in-cheek shifts to F whenever Aegisthus is mentioned—especially startling within the context of a complex, chromatic passage—further trivialize the hapless character (Ex. 4.2).

Ex. 4.2

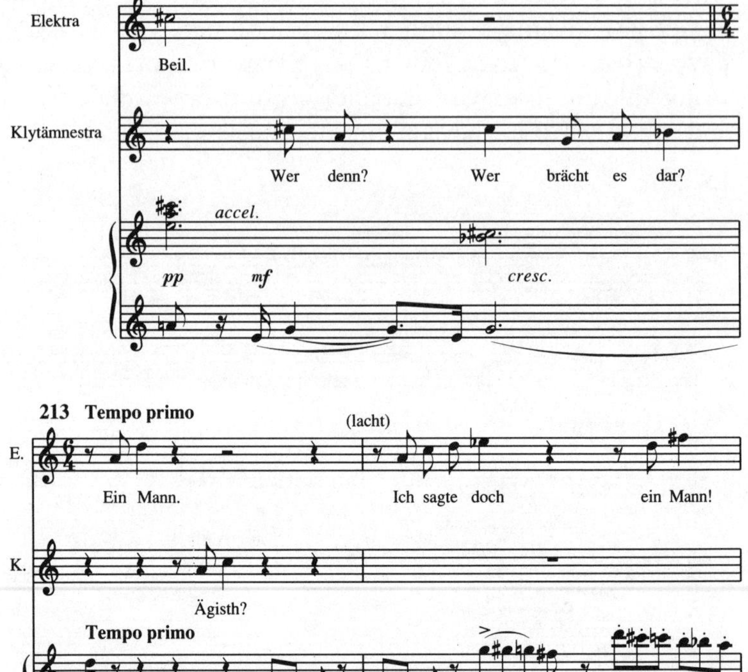

Klytämnestra is not as sharply delineated as most of the other characters. Strauss visualizes her in F sharp major and casts her in no less than three different themes, presenting them in succession when Elektra calls her sister 'Tochter meiner Mutter, Tochter Klytämnestras' (see Exx. 4.3 and 4.4), although the last one (Ex. 4.3*c*), which is as sinuous as it is chromatic, seems to defy more than confirm F sharp.

Elektra, who takes part in every scene of the opera save the introduction, has no key of her own, a significant omission for Strauss. In sacrificing her self-identity, Elektra has also sacrificed any sense of the present; she lives either vicariously

Ex. 4.3

through Agamemnon in the past or, with the hope of Orestes' return, for the future. Her lack of an associative key is synonymous with her lack of identity. Only the so-called 'Elektra chord' (a polytonal combination of E major and D flat major) acts as a harmonic point of reference for the title role, yet Strauss never referred to the chord as 'Elektra' in any known sketch (see Ex. 4.5 and p. 179).

Ex. 4.4 Tr. 18, fol. 48v

There are keys that carry more general connotations as well. We have, for example, already mentioned the importance of E major with reference to Elektra's bacchic finale. A flat major evokes childhood memories, such as when Elektra asks her father: 'zeig dich deinem Kind' in her opening monologue. Strauss makes a sudden shift to A flat during the Klytämnestra scene when Elektra makes the forbidden reference to her brother ('Lässt du den Bruder nicht nach Hause, Mutter?'), and, of course, Elektra's lyrical, reflective 'Es rührt sich niemand'—just after she recognizes her brother—is also set in A flat. B flat minor signifies Elektra's solitude, while its parallel major represents Elektra as a royal daughter. E flat minor, at first glance, does not seem to play a prominent role in the opera, but it is integral to the composer's dramatic plan. It is first introduced midway through the opera as Chrysothemis rushes onstage with the news of Orestes' alleged death, but it ultimately signifies not Orestes' but Elektra's death. With a hushed suddenness, a sustained E-flat-minor chord (along with the stage directions, 'Elektra falls lifeless') ends the animated revelry of her victory dance.

The most crucial expressive harmonic relationship in the opera, however, is the one between C minor and C major. Although structurally they form the same key by this time in post-romantic music, Strauss carefully differentiates these two modalities on the surface level. The former represents the murdered Agamemnon and its parallel major dramatizes the ultimate atonement for that murder. The tension between C minor and C major exists, in one guise or another, in nearly every scene of the opera and is not resolved until the final bars of the work, when it comes to a startling culmination as Chrysothemis beats on the palace door shouting: 'Orest!'

It is paradoxical that *Elektra*, an opera utterly dependent upon tonality as an expressive element, should be considered by some as a work testing the limits of tonality. A not uncommon textbook view of *fin-de-siècle* Strauss sees *Salome* and *Elektra* as sister operas that brought the composer to the brink of atonality only to step back with *Der Rosenkavalier*.[5] Although the ratio of non-diatonic to diatonic material is higher in *Elektra* than in *Der Rosenkavalier* or, say, *Arabella*, his basic approach to tonality is consistent in all three works. The temporary lack of clear tonal centre as Klytämnestra reveals her nightmarish world to her daughter is no more, or less, important than Chrysothemis' life-affirming, diatonic declaration of her desire for a normal life. Both are important tools in Strauss's stylistic workshop.

[5] See, for example, Charles Rosen, *Arnold Schoenberg* (Princeton, NJ, 1975): 'The operas *Salome* and *Elektra* that he wrote in 1905 and 1908 are daring in their extreme chromaticism and in their representation of pathological states, but after *Elektra* Strauss quickly retreated into eighteenth-century pastiche and the delicious Viennese pastry of *Der Rosenkavalier*.' (p. 16) Later, Rosen even asks: 'What had frightened Strauss? It was as if his experiments in chromaticism had led him unknowingly into a brutal world at odds with his more comfortable, solid nature.' (p. 17)

Nearly a quarter of a century ago, Glenn Gould commented on Strauss's approach to tonality.

> Through all of Strauss's works there runs one prevalent ambition, the desire to find new ways in which the vocabulary of key-signature tonality can be augmented without at the same time being allowed to deteriorate into a state of chromatic immobility.[6]

Gould's observation points to an important difference between Strauss and Wagner, whose chromatic language Strauss probably knew better than anyone else. For Wagner, chromaticism and dissonance function at a deeper level than for Strauss. Beneath the surface dissonance and chromaticism of the younger composer remain clear, steadfast tonal underpinnings. Much of the difference between these two composers can be understood by Strauss's approach to the cadence. Strauss continually depended upon the clarifying, affirming power of the cadential gesture. In his music it is often heightened—sometimes exaggerated—as if to counter-balance the extensive chromaticism that preceded it. Despite occasional surface ambiguity, Strauss often exploits cadence to clarify, intensify, and confirm the symmetrical tonal blocks in *Elektra*.

There is another aspect of Strauss's chromatic language that he clearly inherited from Wagner and others: the breakdown of the distinction between major and minor at the structural level. Rather than twenty-four keys (twelve major and twelve minor) there are, rather, twelve chromatic keys in tonal operation. Schoenberg pointed out this phenomenon as early as his *Harmonielehre* (1911), and, more recently, Robert Bailey has explored the issue more rigorously, applying it to formal analyses of Wagner, as well as Mahler and Strauss. Bailey sums up this important issue in late nineteenth-century tonality in his analysis of the *Tristan* prelude to Act I.

> The terms *major* and *minor* remain useful, of course, but only for the purpose of identifying the qualities of particular triads. When we

[6] Glenn Gould, 'Strauss and the Electronic Future', *Saturday Review*, 30 May 1964, 59.

want to identify the tonality of large sections . . . it is best simply to refer to the key by itself and to avoid specifying mode, precisely because the 'chromatic' or mixed major-minor mode is so often utilized. By extension, the sense that a passage from a piece . . . is in the major mode or in the minor mode is usually no more than an illusion, created by restricting the particular inflection of the *tonic triad* during the passage or movement in question to its major or minor form.[7]

As we shall see, modal distinctions are none the less vital to Strauss's expressive aims in *Elektra*, but operate closer to the surface.

Elektra: Overall Harmonic Structure

Before we delve into Strauss's harmonic structure we should first survey, in sequence, the essential dramatic components of Hofmannsthal's play:

1. Introduction: Serving maids both set the atmosphere for the entire play and provide a vivid portrait of Elektra before her opening scene.
2. Elektra's Monologue: Elektra relates the essential events of the past and foresees Orestes' return. He will avenge Agamemnon's murder by killing his mother and stepfather.
3. Elektra–Chrysothemis Dialogue: Chrysothemis tells her sister that Klytämnestra and Aegisthus plan to throw her in a tower, and she also confesses her desire to bear children.
4. Elektra–Klytämnestra Dialogue: Confrontation between mother and daughter. Klytämnestra complains of nightmares; Elektra suggests that the only proper sacrifice that will end her dreams is her own mother's neck. Orestes must perform the ritual. Chrysothemis

[7] Robert Bailey, 'An Analytical Study of the Sketches and Drafts', *Wagner: Prelude and Transfiguration from Tristan und Isolde*, Norton Critical Scores (New York, 1985), 116.

rushes onstage with the false news of Orestes' death. [Cook-Servants Scene: A young servant rushes off on horseback to tell Aegisthus the news of Orestes' death.]

5. Elektra–Chrysothemis Dialogue: Elektra entreats her sister to join her in the murder of their mother and Aegisthus; Chrysothemis refuses.
6. Recognition Scene: Elektra resolves to do it alone. Orestes enters in disguise, and after a brief exchange she recognizes him as her brother. She strengthens his resolve to commit the murders. Moments after he exits Klytämnestra's screams are heard from above. Elektra, who remains onstage, urges Orestes to strike the death blow.

   [Elektra–Aegisthus Dialogue: Aegisthus enters and demands light so that he may go inside the palace; Elektra complies. He exits and is also murdered.]
7. Final Scene: Chrysothemis rushes onstage, both rejoice that Agamemnon's death has been avenged. Elektra dances a wild victory dance and soon falls lifeless. Chrysothemis beats on the palace door shouting for Orestes.

Two of the above scenes, the Cook–Servants and Elektra–Aegisthus, are short and extraneous to the fundamental structure of the play. We recall from Chapter 2 that Hofmannsthal had even suggested that they could be cut for the opera version.[8] If we set both of these minor scenes aside, Hofmannsthal's symmetrical plan of seven structural scenes becomes readily apparent, as shown in Fig. 4.1.

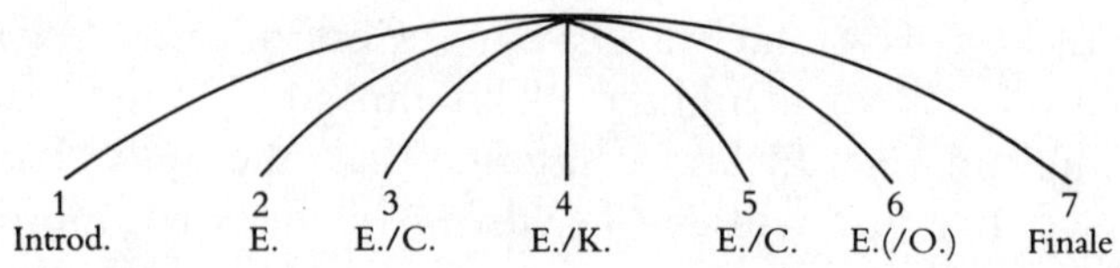

FIG. 4.1

[8] See Chapter 2, p. 26.

Strauss's symmetrical musical design is directly generated by Hofmannsthal's scenic layout (see Fig. 4.2).

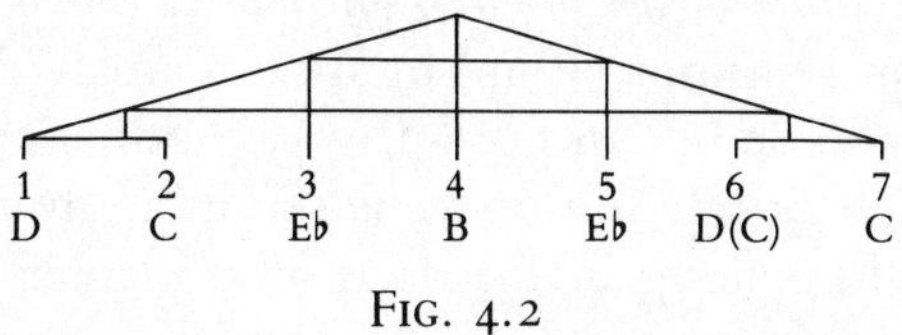

FIG. 4.2

The two minor episodes both relate to Aegisthus—in the first the servant rushes off to tell him of Orestes' death and in the second Aegisthus returns to the palace after having heard the news. They are set in his key of F major, although the second one establishes E flat major as a strong secondary key.

The keystone to Strauss–Hofmannsthal's arch is the turbulent Elektra–Klytämnestra scene, which contains the most chromatic foreground of any scene in the opera, although the harmonic frame is clearly B. Within lengthy stretches of seemingly suspended tonality, keys from earlier scenes resurface, are shed in new light, and then dissolve. But the most noteworthy aspect of scene 4, as it relates to Strauss's structural plan, is the fact that it is a semitone from the opera's tonal centre of C.

The two scenes involving Elektra and Chrysothemis flank this keystone, and although both of these scenes are in E flat, they differ in dramatic and harmonic content. The first Elektra–Chrysothemis scene centres around Chrysothemis' lyrical outpouring, 'Ich hab's wie Feuer in der Brust.' Here Chrysothemis declares her desire for a 'Weiberschicksal', to bear children, etc. Her vitalistic urge is suggested by the diatonic treatment of E flat major. The second Elektra–Chrysothemis scene is cast as a dialogue, although it is clearly Elektra's scene. Here the dramaturgy is more confrontational, and, although it, too, is set in E flat, the key structure of this scene is more complex.

Symmetrical relationships between the outer pairs of structural scenes in the opera (scenes 1, 2 and 6, 7) are more complex than the others; these proportional connections can be assessed in three ways:

1. *The repetition of the progression from D minor to C major.* The scenes in D minor (1 and 6) are obviously different yet they are parallel in one important way: both are preparatory in nature. The first D minor scene serves as an introduction to Elektra's foretelling of the deed of atonement, while the second D minor section prepares us for the actual execution of that deed.

2. *The C minor to C major modal transfiguration.* In scene 2 this process, which symbolizes murder and atonement, is played out in Elektra's mind; the events she outlines are only visionary. The C minor/major complex is temporarily suppressed (with brief flashes in ensuing scenes) and finally erupts when her vision becomes reality.

3. *Outer- and inner-arch relationships.* There are compelling relationships between parts 1 and 7, and 2 and 6. The oppressive atmosphere that is established in scene 1, and which pervades most of the play, is finally purged by scene 7. We see an important connection between the second and penultimate scenes as well. The aria in the latter so-called Recognition Scene is in certain ways a second—and more revealing—monologue for Elektra.

Evidence suggests that once Strauss assessed the dramaturgical implications of the text he began devising his tonal strategy.[9] His method of tonal planning—as evinced by marginal annotations in the *Elektra* text and jottings in preliminary sketchbooks—will be addressed in the next chapter. What follows is a brief summary of harmonic structure in each scene. Exploring the tonal underpinnings of

[9] See, for example, Willi Schuh, 'Hugo von Hofmannsthal und Richard Strauss: Legende und Wirklichkeit', *Umgang mit Musik* (Zurich, 1970), 173–202; Charlotte Erwin, 'Richard Strauss's Presketch Planning for *Ariadne auf Naxos*', *The Musical Quarterly*, 67 (1981), 348–65; Bryan Gilliam, 'Strauss's Preliminary Opera Sketches: Thematic Fragments and Symphonic Continuity', *19th-Century Music*, 9 (1986), 176–88.

each scene—and ultimately relating it to the opera as a whole—sheds light on the essence of Strauss's musico-dramatic ideas.

Serving-Maids' Scene (Scene 1)

After a swift upbeat of two semiquavers a full-orchestral D-minor chord erupts like a volcano. It is the only solidly-affirmed D-minor chord in the scene; all ensuing references to D in this seemingly tonally suspended scene act like momentary aftershocks. Strauss accomplishes two tasks in the opening three bars. First, the unison orchestral presentation of the Agamemnon motive conjures up the image of the dead king with arresting speed and directness. Second, the sustained D-minor chord in the opening bars sets the necessary atmosphere of death and decay that pervades the scene and, in a broader sense, the entire work.

This scene has the quality of ensemble recitative—a textual and harmonic preparation for Elektra's massive monologue. The overseer and serving maids do not recount the past in their animated dialogue; they focus on Elektra herself, consigning her to animal status in their varied descriptions of the king's daughter. Only one servant dares to contradict the others, and she is beaten for it at the end of the scene. These women, including the defiant serving maid, offer a composite portrait of Agamemnon's daughter, who rushes on to the stage as they leave.

There is a subtle, yet effective, harmonic preparation for Elektra's monologue in this introductory scene, although most of the scene is not tonally functional. Much of this sense of suspended tonality results from Strauss's use of the time-honoured *recitativo secco*. Adorno likened Strauss's use of recitative to a 'centrifugal force' away from tonality despite the composer's tonal orientation.[10] More recently, Anthony

[10] Adorno, 'Richard Strauss', 113–14. 'The extreme example in music of a centrifugal phenomenon—that dissociation into individual sounds which symbolizes the contingency, the idolic aspect of an empirical life no longer held

Newcomb pointed out the use of this older technique with a progressive aim in Wagner's music.[11] None the less, D—whether in the guise of minor or major—is the tonal frame for the scene with the emphatic Agamemnon motive at the outset and an exaggerated, traditional cadential formula at the end of the scene (see Ex. 4. 6). What lies in between is a different matter, for although there are brief references to D (especially effective in the culmination of the fifth maid's defiant affront to the others ['Oh, if I could see you all hanged by the neck in a dark shed because of what you have done to Elektra!']) the key is avoided throughout the scene.[12]

Still, within this main body there are some important harmonic points of articulation. The first is not so much a chord, but a complex of two juxtaposed chords: B minor and F minor. Beginning in the tenth bar (reh. 1) this B–F complex acts like a secondary eruption as Elektra enters and sees the women at the well. Strauss uses these violent tritone juxtapositions to highlight her frenzied, mimed reaction to them (Ex. 4. 5).

This tritone complex reappears at the end of the scene when it evokes the violent beating that the fifth serving maid receives after defending Elektra. Its placement is critical, for it thwarts the ultimate resolution to the tonic D in the drawn out, otherwise traditional, I^6_4–V^7–I cadence mentioned above (Ex. 4. 6).

Thus this B–F minor complex acts as an important secondary frame, in close proximity to the tonic at the outset and at the

together by its animating conception—is the secco recitative. By fusing its chordal procedure with the *accompagnato* technique, Strauss introduced the musically exterritorial recitative far deeper into organized composition than even Wagner had done . . . In this respect, the scene of the maid-servants in *Elektra* probably marks a high point which he never again equaled.'

[11] Anthony Newcomb, 'The Birth of Music out of the Spirit of Drama', *19th-Century Music*, 5 (1981), 49–50.

[12] D—in its minor or major guise—recurs over a half-dozen times, but usually these reappearances are extremely brief. See reh. 4, 2 before reh. 8, 4 before reh. 16, 4 before reh. 17, reh. 19, reh. 23, 1 after reh. 28, reh. 31, etc.

Ex. 4.5

(Elektra springt zurück wie ein Tier in seinen Schlupfwinkel, den einen Arm vor dem Gesicht.)

Ex. 4.6 Reduction; compare with reh. 31, etc.

Sagt sie das oder nicht? Ja, ja! Sagt sie das oder nicht? Ja, ja! Sie schlagen mich!

$\mathrm{I}^{6\sharp}_{4}$ $\mathrm{i}^{6\natural}_{4}$ V^{7}

end of the scene, and it plays a significant role in the Klytämnestra scene, which will be discussed later.

After the arresting opening D-minor sonority, followed by brutal alternations of B minor and F minor shortly thereafter, Strauss presents us with yet another potent, non-functional sonority: a polytonal chord combining D flat major and E major, the Elektra chord mentioned above. This unresolved sonority serves as a vital destablizing force in the scene. It appears to be a kind of culmination of tritonal relationship between B and F minor (see Ex. 4. 5).

There is another important key touched upon in scene 1 that is second only to D in its importance: the key of B flat minor/B flat major. Strauss first touches upon B flat minor as the third maid quotes Elektra saying: 'I'm feeding a vulture in my body!' The composer shifts to B flat major as the fifth maid asks: 'Is she not a royal daughter and suffers such disgrace?' B flat minor, the key of Elektra's solitude, and B flat major, the key of Elektra's royal lineage, play a small but significant role in the opening scene. The tension between B flat minor and major is played out more fully in the next scene, Elektra's monologue.

Elektra's Monologue (Scene 2)

Now that the serving maids have left the stage Elektra once again steps out of the darkness, and her monologue is a seminal, expository scene in the work. In it she traces events of a gloomy past and foresees the ultimate retribution. Elements vaguely touched upon in the previous scene now coalesce in sharper focus. More important, however, the monologue anticipates musical events that will affect the entire work.

Unlike the previous scene, the monologue is based on a clear, balanced key scheme:

B flat minor –	C minor	B flat major –	C major
[6 after reh. 36]	[reh. 44]	[3 after reh. 56]	[7 after reh. 61]

Strauss thus establishes a block of two minor keys a major second apart and transforms them into the major mode. But the more critical transformation in this prophetic scene is the one from C minor to C major: the dramatic movement from Agamemnon's death to the victory dance after his death has been avenged. The fact that—as late as the fair-sketch stage—Strauss had originally planned to modulate directly to C major at 3 bars after reh. 56 (thus bypassing B flat major altogether) underscores the overriding importance of the C-minor to C-major transformation.[13]

Strauss articulates the beginning of the monologue with the polytonal Elektra chord, but in a significantly different way than in the previous scene. No longer a static, unstable chord, it now resolves to B flat minor. Those hints of B flat minor from scene 1 are now fully realized (Ex. 4. 7).

Ex. 4.7 Reduction; see 1st and subsequent bars after reh. 36

With the resolution to B flat minor, Elektra invokes the name 'Agamemnon'; the motive that opened the opera is now texted for the first time. She asks for his whereabouts ('Do you not have the strength to lift your face towards me?'), and as his countenance becomes clearer in her mind's eye, the harmony shifts from B flat minor towards C minor, culminating in the moment she visualizes his open wound: '. . . around your forehead a royal wreath of purple . . . feeds upon the wound of your head.' Strauss intends to make this important shift clear to the listener, for at reh. 43 he begins a steady, downward chromatic descent in the bass line from D to G^7, one bar before reh. 44. A preliminary sketchbook

[13] This original plan is discussed in greater detail in Chapter 6.

(Tr. 17) shows that Strauss worked on this chord progression before composing any continuity sketch for the scene (Ex. 4. 8).

Ex. 4.8 Tr. 17, fol. 7

Shortly after this almost exaggerated resolution to C minor, Strauss makes a brief excursion to A flat major, as Elektra asks Agamemnon: 'Show yourself to your child.' This short A-flat passage culminates in a full-blown aria for Elektra towards the beginning of the Recognition Scene ('Es rührt sich niemand') at 3 bars before reh. 149a.

Elektra's sense of isolation, represented by B flat minor, is overcome 3 bars after reh. 56 with a cadence on B flat major as she imagines that all three of Agamemnon's children will dance on their father's grave after mother and stepfather have been killed. Likewise, the C minor of the mortally wounded Agamemnon becomes C major (7 after reh. 61) as she describes this dance as a victory dance. Strauss charges the dominant seventh of the cadence with extra power first by having Elektra sing a sustained G for two and a third bars and, second, by propelling the G^7 chord upward through the ranks of the orchestra in a rapid crescendo only to follow it with a sudden *Generalpause* before the cadence on C. Strauss's overt diatonicism as Elektra ends her monologue has the quality of a cathartic act of purification, purging the chromaticism that preceded it and, at least temporarily, celebrating the envisioned retribution against Klytämnestra and Aegisthus (Ex. 4. 9).

In Example 4.9 Strauss makes an important thematic relationship as well; the bold, ascending Agamemnon theme

Ex. 4.9 2 bars after reh. 61

♩‿♬♬♩‿♬♬ has also been rhythmically transformed, conforming to the rhythm of Elektra's victory dance. Strauss closes the scene with a short instrumental *Nachspiel* that ends with a sudden shift to E major. This swift change to the major mediant provides the sensation of a localized shock effect; it is not prepared for earlier in the monologue. Yet the relationship between E and C major—the bacchic and the victorious—is an important one, and the composer ultimately intertwines and juxtaposes these two keys in the final scene of the opera.

Elektra's opening monologue is, therefore, an exposition in every sense of the word. In it Hofmannsthal calls our attention to important events of the past and future, while Strauss establishes a referential key plan that affects tonal events to follow.[14] Indeed, in certain ways her monologue is a tonal microcosm for the entire work. A brief memorandum by Strauss on the inside front cover of an *Elektra* fair sketchbook sheds further light on this scene: 'Electra alone B flat minor; intensified against the world B minor. | Agamemnon C minor; victory dance C major. [Electra allein B Moll; der Welt gegenüber gesteigert H Moll. | Agamemnon C Moll; Siegestanz C Dur.]'[15] The above was intended as a memorandum for scene 2, but, as we shall see, this relationship between B flat, B, and C (the central tonal elements of the Klytämnestra scene) is important to the entire opera as well.

Chrysothemis–Elektra I (Scene 3)

Scene 3 of the opera stands apart from the others in a number of important ways. Unambiguously centred around E flat major, it is the most diatonic scene in the opera—an effective counterweight against the next scene with Klytämnestra. Early sketches show that Strauss identified E flat with

[14] There are even local references to F and F sharp, the keys of Aegisthus and Klytämnestra, respectively.

[15] This compositional memorandum exemplifies Strauss's original desire not to include B flat major as a tonal area in Elektra's monologue.

Chrysothemis from the start.[16] In doing so Strauss sought to strike contrast between her and Elektra. This contrast is sharpened by the composer's formal approach to the scene, which consists essentially of a recitative (dialogue) and aria (solo).[17] Although more dialogue (i.e. recitative) follows the aria as Klytämnestra approaches, this latter dialogue serves more as an elision to the next scene than as the second of two bookends with an aria in the middle, although that intentional symmetry is undeniable. Strauss's reversion to a more conventional approach—in both harmonic treatment and formal layout—serves as a musical confirmation of the younger sister's 'traditional' view of a woman's destiny.

In the opening dialogue between Elektra and her sister Strauss avoids any sense of tonal centre until the very end. Similar to scene 1, this avoidance is achieved chiefly through recitative; the composer punctuates their animated exchange with a host of referential harmonies:

1. The Elektra chord (followed immediately by polytonal B–Fm complex): Chrysothemis startles her sister out of her vision [4 after reh. 64]
2. E flat major ($V^{6}_{5}/E\flat$): to contrast the above with the Chrysothemis persona [4 after reh. 65 and 2 after reh. 66]
3. C minor: (Elektra:) 'As our father lifted his hands' [4 after reh. 66]
44. F sharp major: 3 Klytämnestra themes in succession (as wife, mother, and queen) [5 after reh. 67]
5. F major: Elektra refers to Aegisthus ('the other woman, the coward') [1 before reh. 69]

Strauss weaves another destabilizing element throughout the dialogue, a series of four hollow, chromatic dyads, a perfect fifth apart, that possibly refer to the tower where Elektra is to

[16] See Gilliam, 'Strauss's Preliminary Opera Sketches', 177–8 and 183–4.

[17] We recall from Chapter 2 that Strauss cut this scene to create the shape of a brief introductory dialogue between Elektra and Chrysothemis followed by an extended solo aria for the latter.

be banished. They appear in three guises (reading from top to bottom): F♯–B, G–C, B♭–E♭, A–D; F–B♭, G♭–C♭, A–D, A♭–D♭; and A♭–D♭, A–D, C–F, B–E. The dialogue finally resolves to B flat minor, which serves as pivot for the ensuing aria, with the final line: '. . . und wünsch den Tod und das Gericht herbei auf sie und ihn.' Indeed, Strauss writes 'B^b minor tonic' in the right-hand margin by that line in his copy of the play.[18]

Chrysothemis' aria is the focus of the scene, and it consists of two basic parts:

I—'Ich hab's wie Feuer in der Brust' [E♭—Cm—$B♭^7$]
II—'Kinder will ich haben' [E♭–Cm (A♭m) Cm—E♭]

Although both are in E flat, part I is considerably more modulatory and less regular in period structure than the more lyrical part II. Part II, furthermore, may be divided into three sections: the lyrical opening (A), a more declamatory middle section (B), and a musical—but not textual—return to A. Music and text do not work together in Strauss's musically symmetrical layout; indeed musical form seems imposed upon the text in part II, where the return to A falls mid-sentence.[19] Moreover, the form evokes a vague vestige of an Italian two-part aria form, with a through-composed first part and a binary second part—however, part II lacks the customary tempo change. Strauss may or may not have had this Italian model in mind, but the musically atavistic quality of her monologue was no doubt deliberate.

Klytämnestra–Elektra (Scene 4)

This scene is, on the one hand, the keystone to Hofmannsthal's and Strauss's arch-like structure, yet, on the other, it is harmonically the most obscure scene in the opera. That is not

[18] Page 15 of Hofmannsthal's text (5th edn.), RSA.

[19] Indeed, sources show that 'Kinder will ich haben' was conceived—at the earliest stages—without specific text in mind. See Gilliam, 'Strauss's Preliminary Opera Sketches', 183 ff.

to say that the deeper tonal underpinnings in this scene are not clear and affective, for Strauss constructs a thick, dissonant, chromatic surface that obscures an orderly arrangement of tonal points of articulation. This dissonant surface is created through various techniques such as polytonality (and other non-functional chord progressions), quartal sonorities, and the avoidance of the tonic through recitative technique (such as was used in scene 1 and the opening of scene 3).[20] Indeed, the flow of harmonic events in this scene is linked more closely with the flow of dramatic events—of human conflict—than with any other.

The scene divides into three sections:

1. Introduction: Klytämnestra expresses her desire to speak with her daughter
2. Dialogue: (a) Klytämnestra complains of nightmares and seeks a cure
   (b) Elektra says that she knows a cure, but does not reveal it
3. Climax: (a) Elektra finally reveals her prescription.
   (b) Elektra's threat is undercut by news of Orestes' death

The steadily increasing dramatic intensity of this scene is without equal in the opera. After a relatively slow paced introduction the conflict begins. Klytämnestra entreats Elektra to tell her what sacrifice will end her nightmares. Elektra answers in riddles ('When the right victim falls beneath the axe, you will no longer dream'), and her replies become increasingly sharp. The turning point of the dialogue occurs when Elektra asks whether Orestes may return; the mention of his name has been forbidden in the palace. Tension reaches its zenith as Klytämnestra threatens to chain her daughter up if she will not reveal the necessary sacrificial blood. It is as if, in the second part, Elektra loads the revolver with carefully-wrought, enigmatic replies to her mother's queries. The

[20] The annotation 'Recitativ' appears no less than eight times in Strauss's copy of the play.

weapon fires at the outset of part III when she reveals the proper sacrifice: 'What must bleed? Your own neck must bleed when the hunter has moved in for the kill!'

Elektra's role has increased steadily in scene 4, and the texted part of this scene ends in her triumph; Klytämnestra cowers in fear. But Klytämnestra ultimately prevails; she receives news that Orestes has been killed moments after Elektra's climactic finale. This powerful end to the scene, when Elektra's moment of victory has dissolved as quickly as it erupted, is all the more compelling by its being conveyed solely in gesture, for Klytämnestra's torch-bearing confidante whispers the news in her ear.

Strauss's harmonic treatment of this scene bolsters these dramatic events. The principal harmonic conflict (a sonic allegory to the human conflict) in this scene concerns relationships between B minor, C minor, and B flat major—these last two keys, we recall, comprise a major part of Elektra's monologue. Tonal events are fairly loosely defined at the outset of scene 4, and as the pace quickens these tonal relationships tighten up significantly—harmonic points of articulation that did not seem as clear at the beginning are clarified by the end of the scene. Strauss's tonal strategy for the Klytämnestra scene may be summarized as shown in Fig. 4. 3.

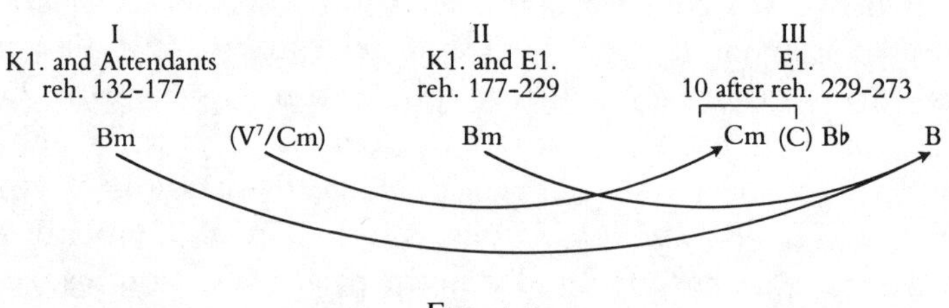

FIG. 4.3

In part I Strauss tries to strike a balance between dissonant, chromatic moments and more stable, consonant stretches. The three most prominent consonant moments are in F sharp major (reh. 144), C minor (reh. 164), and C major (reh. 173)—all part of the semitone tension in scene 4. F sharp major—Klytämnestra's key—suggests her temporary transport into a state of reverie at the sound of Elektra's voice ('Das klingt mir so bekannt. Und nur als hätt' ich's vergessen').[21] The brief appearance of C minor not only refers to the murdered Agamemnon, but anticipates the shift to the realm of C at the outset of part III. The long dominant pedal (with C in 6/4 position, followed by V^7) solidifies that relationship.

Strauss makes B minor a stronger point of reference in part II, despite numerous non-functional referential harmonies that underlie much of the animated exchange between Elektra and Klytämnestra. As with part I (reh. 135), he clearly establishes B minor at the outset (reh. 177) of the section, but in the latter part of the section he iterates it and reiterates it in a way he had not done before. In establishing B minor at reh. 177, Strauss also refers to the B–F minor complex that he had established in the first scene; indeed this complex acts as a substitute for B minor in part II. First alternately (7 after reh. 177), then simultaneously (reh. 178), this complex culminates at reh. 193 and reaches its climax at reh. 204, as Elektra declares: 'When the right victim falls beneath the axe, you will no longer dream.' By the end of part II (reh. 224), when Klytämnestra threatens Elektra in order to get the name of the sacrifice ('And in one way or another I will force the right word from your lips') the tempo picks up with a veritable stretto on B in the bass. After a brief interruption, he once again hammers away on B up until the very end of part II.

Part III begins with the abrupt shift to C minor as Elektra ('springing out of the darkness') turns the tables on her mother, and the pace quickens considerably. At the end of Elektra's succinct and powerful speech Strauss creates a double climax: the penultimate one in C major (reh. 258) and the ultimate one in B flat major (reh. 259). In going from C

[21] Strauss often used F sharp major to evoke dreamlike or fanciful states. We recall Don Quixote's F-sharp dream of dragons to be slain and ladies to be saved 3 after reh. 35 as well as the moment in *Der Rosenkavalier* where time seems to stand still: the presentation of the rose (Act II). In Act I of *Die Frau ohne Schatten*, the Empress awakens from a dream in F sharp major (reh. 49).

to B flat, Strauss reverses the process of B flat to C that he had set up in Elektra's monologue. Her apparent victory over her mother in this scene is short-lived, and he illustrates her fleeting jubilation by supporting her climactic high note (c^3) over a C^6_4 chord—the bass line then moves down-ward by semitone to an F^7 chord before it cadences on B flat (Ex. 4. 10).

Ex. 4.10 Summary of harmonic motion at the end of Elektra's speech, scene 4, reh. 258 to 259

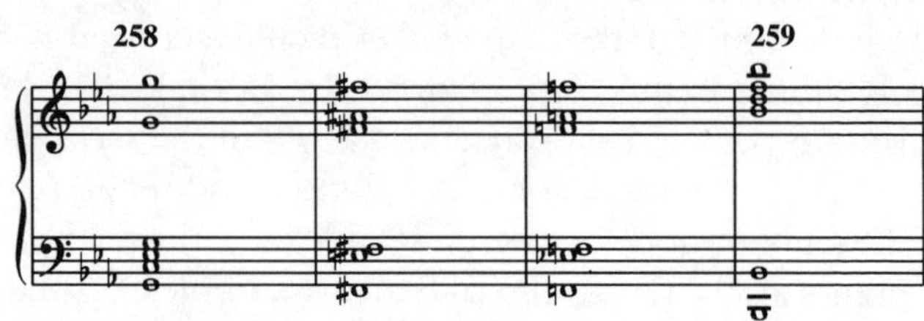

But the tables are turned once again, this time in favour of Klytämnestra, and in a lengthy instrumental passage her confidante, trainbearer, and serving maids rush about the stage with news of Orestes' death. This passage is not a transition to the next scene, but an integral part of section III. It climaxes in B major—the scene has come full circle.

Chrysothemis–Elektra II (Scene 5)

The end of scene 4 marks the turning point of the opera, and Strauss, himself, decided to renumber rehearsal cues (i.e.: reh. 1a, 2a, etc.) with scene 5.[22] This next scene—an animated exchange between sisters—also initiates the first return of a major tonal block (E flat major), yet its treatment is far more complex than in scene 3, which was little more than an aria for Chrysothemis. Elektra pleads with her sister

[22] A copy of an *Elektra* piano-vocal score (dated 18 June 1930) at the Bavarian State Library (Mus. Mss. 12735) contains musical commentary in Strauss's hand indicating how *Elektra* might be divided if it were performed as a two-act opera; the point of demarcation is reh. 1a.

to help in the murders, she tries to flatter her, makes promises and quasi-incestual overtures, although Strauss eliminated many of the sexual overtones that originally pervaded this scene.

The pace of events immediately following Klytämnestra's victory is frantic: Chrysothemis rushes onstage with the news of Orestes' death, a young servant rides off to tell the news to Aegisthus, and Elektra resolves that she and her sister will have to undertake the deed themselves.[23] The so-called Cook–Servants Scene (just under 60 bars in length), which was a separate scene in the play (and significantly longer), is now no more than a brief interruption at the outset of scene 5. Although Hofmannsthal suggested cutting the scene entirely, Strauss chose to preserve the bare essence of it.

Scene 5 consists of two parts:

1. Introduction
2. Main section (Elektra entreats Chrysothemis)

Strauss articulates three discrete subsections in this introduction: Chrysothemis' entrance ('Orest ist tot!'—reh. 1a), the servants' interruption ('Platz da!'—reh. 26a), and Elektra's decision ('Nun muss es von uns geschehn.'—reh. 34a). The key plan for the introduction is as follows:

Introduction

1. E♭ minor (D minor/major)	'Orest ist tot!' (reh. 1a to 26a)
2. F	'Platz da!' (reh. 26a–33a)
3. Mod. (V^7/E♭)	'Nun muss es von uns . . .' (reh. 34a to 52a)

Strauss introduces E flat minor for the first time in the opera at reh. 1a, and the key not only has important ramifications in scene 5, but, as we shall see, later on in the Aegisthus Scene and in the final bars of the opera as well. Within the frame of E flat minor in section 1 of the introduction, Strauss also emphasizes D minor/major (see

[23] All of this takes place within the first 240 bars of scene 5—before the main section of the scene gets underway.

reh. 4a, 5a, 4 before reh. 10a, and 17a).[24] The second section, an abrupt shift to F major, is charged with the spirit of Aegisthus. The rhythm of his motive is articulated from the outset, culminating in its full-fledged form at reh. 30a. The young servant's exit ushers in section 3, an unstable section that works its way to a climactic drawn-out V^7/E♭ as Elektra sings: 'Du! Du! Denn du bist stark.'[25] The climax is reached in the first bar of the main section of the scene.

The second part of scene 5 is less a dialogue between the sisters than a series of speeches, or entreaties, by Elektra that are consistently rebuffed by Chrysothemis (see the summary in Table 4.1).

TABLE 4.1 Main section (scene 5)

Reh. no.	Key	
52a	E♭	'Wie stark du bist!' (Elektra's 1st speech)
69a	unstable	'Lass mich!' (Chrysothemis)
82a	G	'Von jetzt an will ich deine Schwester sein' (Elektra's 2nd speech)
88a	unstable	'Nicht, Schwester, nicht' (Chrysothemis)
89a	Dm/D	'O ja! Weit mehr als Schwester bin ich dir' (Elektra's 3rd speech)
3 after 97a	unstable	'O bring mich fort!' (Chrysothemis; more animated repartee ensues)
101a	Cm	'Denn eh' du diesem Haus und mir entkommst' (Elektra)
109a	E♭/Gm	'Sei verflucht!' (Elektra; double cadence)

In her first speech Elektra praises her sister's sensual strength ('You are strong, you are beautiful, you are like a fruit on its day of ripening'). The stability of E flat major and regular periodicity recalls the style of Chrysothemis' 'aria' in

[24] One wonders whether this emphasis is related to the D minor/major of the opening scene, especially since the composer articulates this important turning point at the beginning of scene 5 with those new rehearsal numbers.

[25] Strauss had already hinted at that V^7 three bars after reh. 43a.

scene 3. In a shift to G major (Elektra's second speech) she vows that she will be the sister to Chrysothemis that she had never been before. By the third speech she promises to serve as a slave-midwife. D minor refers to Elektra as slave (a reference to the introductory scene) and Strauss shifts to D major as she speaks of the child that Chrysothemis will bear. As Chrysothemis becomes more horrified, Strauss's harmonic language becomes more complex and turbulent. The ultimate cadence is curious, for although the composer distinctly returns towards the tonic E flat by the end, he creates a startling, deceptive cadence on G minor as Elektra curses her sister. The use of G minor could very well signify that negation of sisterhood that Elektra earlier promised Chrysothemis in G major. Within that resolution on G minor Strauss artfully articulates a resolution on the tonic as well, by integrating the expected E flat into that cadence as Ex. 4.11 shows.

Ex. 4.11 Rch. 109a

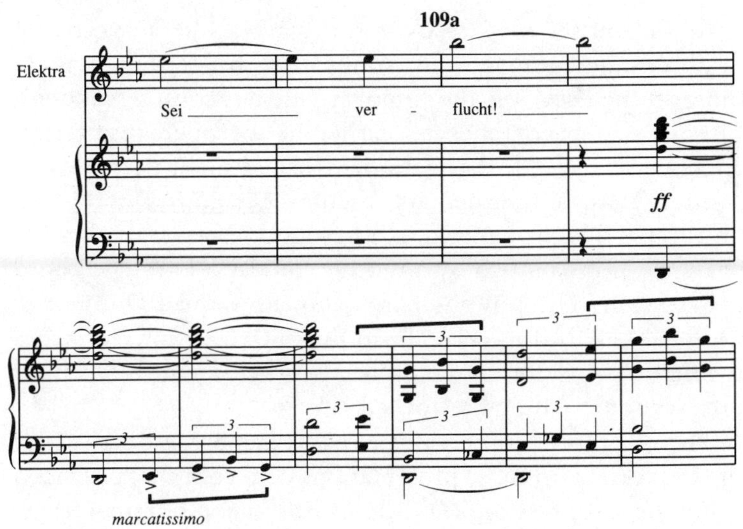

Fig. 4.4 gives a summary of the key plan for scene 5:

Pt. I Pt. II

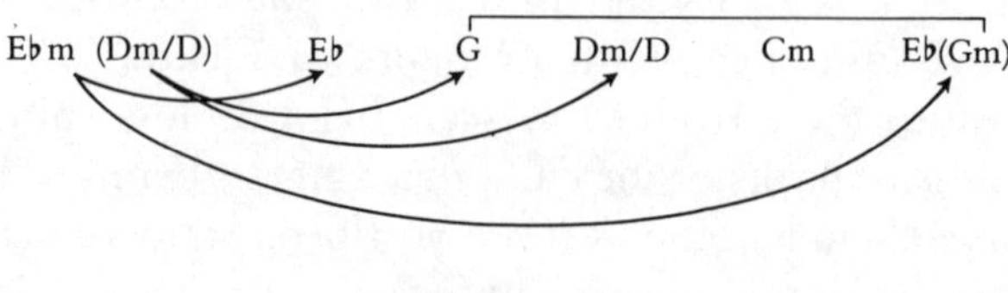

FIG. 4.4

Recognition Scene (Scene 6)

The sixth scene is the dénouement of the drama—the Aristotelian anagnorisis; here the plot begins to unravel. Strauss divides the scene into three parts:

I: The recognition
II: Elektra's aria
III: Elektra's self-reflection, which culminates in her reinforcing Orestes' decision to execute the murders.

At the outset of part I Orestes arrives like a spectre of death. Strauss revives this atmosphere by setting it in D minor—the key of the gloomy introduction. Although Orestes had been rendered earlier in the opera (especially effective in scene 4: 'Lässt du den Bruder nicht nach Hause, Mutter?') by a fragmentary theme his physical arrival is depicted in a new way. Strauss evokes the character not so much by a motive, but by a D minor chord progression. The composer probably envisioned D minor as Orestes' key for this scene from the outset. In early sketches for the Recognition Scene Strauss worked on such D minor progressions, which he labelled 'Orest'.

There are three subsections in part I and Strauss articulates the first one with three presentations of Orestes' open-ended D-minor progression (D minor–B♭ major–G♭ major, D minor–B♭ major–G♭ major–B′, D minor–B major–G minor–A♭^{7}). Elektra's reaction to the messenger, the second subsection, is also strongly framed in D minor (1 before reh. 128a and reh. 130a). In the third subsection, however, Strauss creates instability; the familiar D minor progression is now omitted. Orestes' speech begins in F minor (reh. 130a), but does not remain there. Indeed, by the time Elektra asks 'Wer bist denn du?' the composer shifts to a fleeting dominant pedal on E flat, with an even more short-lived resolution on A flat—the tonic of part II.

Elektra's aria (part II) 'Es rührt sich niemand' is the most conventional portion of the entire opera and dramaturgically gratuitous. Strauss desired a lyrical moment of repose after Elektra's outburst 'Orest!', and he asked Hofmannsthal for extra text to help fill out his preconceived musical plan.[26] The aria rarely ventures beyond its firm A flat major footing and is organized in a simple binary form (AA′) with a coda. The aria is generated (in both key and thematic content) from material that originated in Elektra's monologue (scene 2), more specifically the brief orchestral passage that follows her line: '. . . zeig dich deinem Kind!' (9 after reh. 45), and Strauss clarifies that connection in the coda of her aria (reh. 153a, see Ex. 4.12).

Strauss also subdivides part III of the Recognition Scene:

1. A monologue in which Elektra explains her metamorphosis from princess to 'no more than a corpse of [Orestes'] sister'
2. A duo in which Elektra convinces Orestes to go ahead with the deed.

By now the rapid pace of events has abated and, for the first time, Elektra delves into the past not to recount the deed, but to probe realms of her psyche that had hitherto not been explored. Although Strauss centres part III—the most harmonically unstable of the three parts—around C, the gravitational pull towards that key is not really felt until the duo at the end; before this moment Strauss touches upon a

[26] See letter to Hofmannsthal (22 June 1908) in *Correspondence*, 16.

Ex. 4.12 (*a*) 9 bars after reh. 45

(*b*) reh. 153a

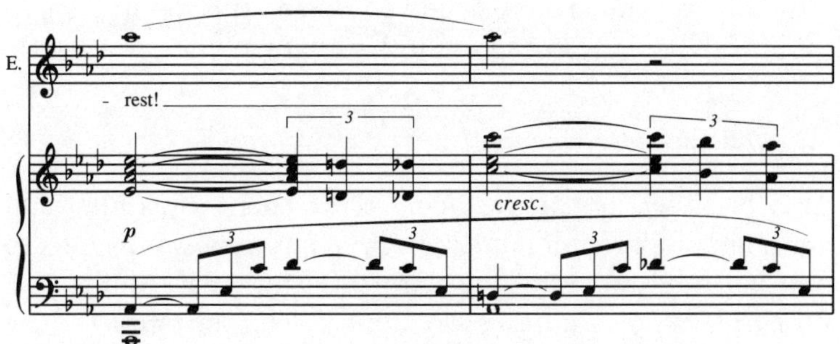

number of referential keys—especially E (most notably at reh. 158a and 163a–166a), which plays such a vital role in the final scene.

Strauss's emphasis on C for the duo between Elektra and Orestes is, thus, far from unwavering, and it is usually presented in the 6/4 position. Furthermore, he leaves C by the end of the scene and shifts to a final cadence on D minor, as a kind of frame for the whole scene, although D minor played a negligible role in parts II and III. This reference to C foreshadows the victory to be celebrated in the final scene, where D minor plays no part at all. Part III also serves as an elision connecting the Recognition Scene and the murders. Strauss's key plan for scene 6 may be summarized as follows:

Pt. I	Pt. II	Pt. III
D m	A♭	C (Dm)

Klytämnestra's Murder

Just after the brief cadence on D minor Orestes' servant hastily enters and beckons his master to enter the palace; the time has arrived. The most important harmonic aspect of this short section is the clash between B and C minor. Thus, the B/C tension that was established in the Klytämnestra scene finally comes to a head at the moment of her murder. Strauss further explores this semitone relationship with a cluster of semitones (c–c♯–d) right after the death blow has been struck. It is immediately followed by an eruption in F sharp minor—Klytämnestra's key in the minor mode.

Aegisthus' Murder

This brief section of the opera represents Aegisthus' only appearance, although there have been numerous references to him harmonized each time with the familiar F^6 sonority. F major plays no significant structural role in the opera—typically a localized tonal reference within the context of another key—and its lengthiest appearance before the murder is the brief servant section. That 'scene' serves as an intrusion on Chrysothemis' E-flat-minor outburst 'Orest ist tot!'; E flat minor is interrupted by F major. For Aegisthus' murder, Strauss reverses the order: the scene begins in F major as Aegisthus enters the scene ('He! Lichter!') and moves quickly toward E flat major as Elektra feigns servility ('Darf ich nicht leuchten?'). Strauss clarifies the connection between E flat minor and E flat major with the use of a motive associated with Orestes' presumed death now transformed into a saccharine motive of obsequiousness as Elektra lights the way to his violent end (see Ex. 4. 13).

Ex. 4.13 Reh. 1a and 204a

Just as Klytämnestra's key had changed to the tonic minor as she was attacked, so does Aegisthus'. But more important than his shift to F minor is the eruption of C minor as Elektra answers Aegisthus' question whether or not anyone hears him ('Agamemnon hört dich!' she replies). Strauss assigns specific stage instructions to that chord: 'Aegisthus' face appears again at the window.' With the dramatic turn to C minor, the final scene is ready to begin.

The Final Scene (Scene 7)

The last scene of *Elektra* is one of unprecedented culminating power. With remarkable thoroughness Strauss constructs a stretto of returning motives as Elektra celebrates her father's avengement. But beneath that surface of motivic energy lies a more powerful harmonic movement to C major. Strauss's keen sense of harmonic pacing (with subtle, yet effective cumulative references to C leading up to scene 7) creates this potency. In Elektra's opening monologue Strauss moves from C minor to C major, but undercuts it with a sudden shift to E major. Elektra's emphatic reply to her mother in the Klytämnestra Scene began in C minor and moved towards C major (albeit in the 6/4 position), but was thwarted by a sudden cadence to B flat. Likewise the movement to C major at the end of the Recognition Scene remained in the 6/4 position. And while there is never any doubt that scene 7 is in C major, the ultimate release of this powerful, built-up tension does not occur until the final bars (7 after reh. 262a). Here Strauss reminds us that Elektra's vision, with its temporary setbacks, has finally been fulfilled by recalling the very cadence from the Klytämnestra Scene where V/C had earlier slipped to B flat (see Ex. 4. 14; compare with Ex. 4. 10).

Although the finale is set in C major, E major serves as a secondary tonic. The entire scene is nothing short of an extended conflict between C and E major. Protracted juxtapositions between these two keys occur in an emphatic—almost relentless—consonant, diatonic, harmonic context. Perhaps Strauss felt such overt clarity a necessary counterweight to previous chromatic moments in the opera; it is as if this unremitting tonal affirmation was designed to purge the spirit of decay that had hitherto permeated the work. The duality between C and E, of course, has its origins

Ex. 4.14 3 bars after reh. 262a

in Elektra's opening monologue, and the symbolic significance and interaction of these two keys at the end of the opera are intimately bound together in Elektra's dance.

For present purposes, we may simply state that C and E major symbolize two different impulses: (1) victory and the restoration of order and (2) bacchic impulse of cathartic celebration, respectively. Table 4.2 summarizes the relationship between these two keys.

To summarize, let us recall the essential harmonic events of *Elektra*'s seven scenes. In scene 1 Strauss constructs an unstable recitative-like setting in D. The next scene presents two clear harmonic blocks (B flat and C), capped off by E, and scene 3, the most diatonic one in the opera, is set in E flat. Although Strauss erects a fairly dissonant and chromatic foreground in scene 4, an unmistakable movement of B–C–B♭–B is in operation. E flat is less affirmative in scene 5 than

TABLE 4.2

E	1.	Chrysothemis (plus chorus): 'Es ist der Bruder . . .' (6 after reh. 220a)
E	2.	Elektra's speech: 'Ob ich nicht höre . . .' (4 after reh. 228a)
C	3.	Elektra/Chrysothemis duet: 'Wir sind bei den Göttern' (reh. 236a)
E	4*a*.	Elektra's dance (reh. 247a)
C	4*b*.	Elektra: 'Schweig und tanze' (5 after reh. 255a)
C	5.	Elektra's death (reh. 261a)

scene 3, but it is none the less solidly weighted in that key. Although Strauss frames scene 6 in D, the brief recurrence of that key at the end of the scene seems gratuitous, since by then the scene has distinctly shifted towards C. Scene 7 consists mainly of the clash between E and C, and the latter key prevails.

We may summarize this tonal organization as shown in Ex. 4. 15.

Ex. 4.15

At the outset of this chapter I pointed out the expository quality of Elektra's monologue (scene 2), and the above reduction puts that observation into sharper focus. It serves as a kind of tonal microcosm for the entire work, exemplifying a broader harmonic phenomenon operating in *Elektra*: movement either by step (D–C from scene 1 to 2, B♭–C in scene 2, E–E♭ from scene 2 to 3, the stepwise movement in scene 4, E♭–D from scene 5 to 6, as well as the stepwise motion in sc. 6), or movement by third (D–B♭ from scene 1 to 2, C–E in scene 2, E♭ [D♯]–B from scene 3 to 4, B–E♭ from scene 4 to 5, E♭–C from scene 5 to 6, and E–C in scene 7). Both relationships (represented by B♭–C and C–E in scene 2) comprise an integral part of that second scene. In Ex. 4. 15*a* we also see how the B♭–C relationship of scene 2 is pitted against the framework of B (the semitone in between that relationship) in scene 4, and likewise how the C–E relationship of that second scene is finally worked out in scene 7.

A reduction to a more fundamental level reinforces the pivotal importance of the fourth scene. As Example 4. 15*b* shows, the most essential harmonic movement in the opera is that of a semitone: the descent to B in scene 4 returning to C at the end. At this primary level we also see the underlying synthesis of Hofmannsthal's dramaturgy and the composer's music; scene 4 contains the greatest psychological conflict, which translates musically into harmonic motion essentially by semitone.[27] Strauss articulates C at the outset with Elektra's dream of Orestes' return, and it is temporarily submerged by B in the Klytämnestra scene with the news of his alleged death; C then resurfaces triumphant after the return of Orestes and the execution of the murders.

Yet even in the final scene this semitone tension between B and C is exploited, but now, of course, within the context of the juxtaposition of E and C.[28] A comparison of a passage beginning two bars before reh. 242a and a passage starting two bars before reh. 245a is but one example of this important semitone duality (Ex. 4. 16).

A summary of tonal structure in *Elektra* illuminates two comments that, years later, Strauss made about the opera, comments touched upon earlier in this study. He observed that his musical setting both intensified the dramaturgy, especially through 'the force of its climaxes', and structural

[27] Interestingly, the harmonic motion of scene 4 is an inversion of the overall tonal movement for the opera: B–C–B vs. C–B–C, respectively.

[28] Here the B–C duality no longer symbolizes the tension between mother and daughter, but the dichotomy of the maenadic vs. round dance, which will be discussed in Chapter 7.

Ex. 4.16a

Chrysothemis
Elektra
weiß glüh'n - de Ge - sicht des
242a Allmählich immer fließender.
poco a poco sempre scioltamente di più
C.
Wer hat uns je ge -
E.
Monds.
pp espr.
C.
- liebt?
E.
Wenn ei - ner auf mich sieht, muß er den
3
cresc.

Ex. 4.16b

unity.[29] As for the latter, we see how Hofmannsthal's architecture and Strauss's tonal structure represent a compelling, unified whole. Strauss himself remarked that *Elektra* surpassed *Salome* in structural unity, adding that it is to *Salome* what 'the more flawless, and stylistically uniform *Lohengrin* is to the inspired [earlier] venture of *Tannhäuser*'.[30] Whatever the case, one thing is for sure: *Elektra*'s rigorous tonal symmetry—catalysed by Hofmannsthal's drama—remains unique in Strauss's operatic output.

[29] Richard Strauss, *Recollections and Reflections*, ed. Willi Schuh, trans. L. J. Lawrence (London, 1953), 154.

[30] *Recollections*, 155.

5 *The Annotated* Elektra *Libretto: Strauss's Preliminary Musical Thought*

Two surviving textual sources for *Elektra* contain musical commentary by Strauss; they document some of his earliest musical ideas about the opera. The first source is Strauss's copy (RSA) of the fifth edition (1904) of Hofmannsthal's play. Furthermore, there also exist two separate folios, originally part of the Anna Bahr-Mildenburg Nachlass, owned, since 1947, by the Theatre Collection of the Österreichische Nationalbibliothek (ÖNB). These two folios, written entirely in the composer's hand, contain only part of the play: the Recognition Scene to the end of the scene with Aegisthus. But before delving into these manuscripts and the significance of the musical material contained in them, we should first establish a general framework outlining Strauss's compositional methods.

Strauss never gave a specific account of his working procedure, a fact that is further obscured by a lack of good documentation for those instances when he did address the subject. Perhaps the most often-quoted passage concerning Strauss's method of composing—referring in this case to opera—originated from a chapter ('The Composer Speaks') in a book on contemporary composers by David Ewen. It is taken from an undated, unnamed American newspaper:

I compose everywhere, walking or driving, eating or drinking, at home or abroad, in noisy hotels, in my garden, in railway carriages. My sketchbook never leaves me, and as soon as a motif strikes me I jot it down. One of the most important melodies from my opera, *Der Rosenkavalier*, struck me while I was playing a Bavarian card game. But before I improvise even the smallest sketch for an opera, I allow the texts to permeate my thoughts for at least six months or so, that the situation and characters may be thoroughly assimilated. Then only do I let musical thought enter my mind. The sub-sketches then become sketches. They are copied out, worked out, arranged for the piano and rearranged as often as four times. This is the difficult part of the work. The score I write in my study, straightway, without troubling, working at it twelve hours a day.[1]

What can we learn from this admittedly unsubstantiated account? Certain statements made in the above passage are corroborated by musical sources: namely, the recording of motives and melodies in preliminary sketchbooks followed by more elaborate sketches (fair sketches?), which are then 'arranged for the piano' (probably the Particell or *Klavierskizze* as Strauss would label it).

But some contradictions are apparent in the composer's summary as well. Strauss did not always wait 'at least six months' to allow the text to ripen in his mind, although this statement is probably accurate with regard to *Elektra*. By his own admission Strauss began composing a portion of *Der Rosenkavalier* upon receipt of Hofmannsthal's Act I text,[2] and it has frequently been noted that he began making some musical annotations in the margins of Hedwig Lachmann's translation of Wilde's *Salome* during the first reading.[3] But, more importantly, Garmisch sources also point to various chronological layers of work that the composer neglects to mention, notably compositional thought *before* the preliminary sketches and *after* the fair sketches.

[1] 'The Composer Speaks: Richard Strauss', in *The Book of Modern Composers*, ed. David Ewen (New York, 1942), 54, 55.

[2] See letter of 4 May 1909 in *Correspondence*, 30.

[3] But one should add that Strauss had been preoccupied with the idea of composing *Salome* for some time.

STAGES OF COMPOSITION IN *ELEKTRA*

The composition of *Elektra* entailed four fundamental compositional stages; these stages typify Strauss's creative procedure with other operas as well:

1. Musically annotated libretto
2. Sketchbooks
3. Particell
4. Orchestral score[4]

During the first stage Strauss establishes much of the tonal framework.[5] Several scholars have commented on the composer's practice of annotating a libretto with musical marginalia.[6] Most agree on two counts: (1) many of these pre-sketch annotations represent the earliest layer of Strauss's compositional technique, and (2) these musical glossings consist mainly of harmonic annotations—with some motivic commentary as well—that designate both local and broader regions for the opera at hand. We shall see how the *Elektra* text, with its numerous motivic jottings, differs in part from this latter generalization.

The second step—the sketchbook stage—can be subdivided into two basic layers: preliminary and fair sketches, or *Roh-* and *Reinschriftskizzen*, as Strauss would often describe them. Most preliminary sketchbooks are smaller in size than fair

[4] These generalizations stem from the examination of sources relating to *Elektra*, *Der Rosenkavalier*, *Ariadne auf Naxos*, *Arabella*, and *Daphne*. My doctoral work, 'Richard Strauss's Daphne: Opera and Symphonic Continuity,' Ph.D. Diss., (Harvard University, 1984) was in part a study of *Daphne* sources.

[5] Indeed, one-time Strauss librettist Stefan Zweig described the composer's libretto as a kind of scaffold for his musical ideas. See *The World of Yesterday* (Lincoln, Nebraska, 1964), 369.

[6] See, for example, Willi Schuh, 'Hugo von Hofmannsthal und Richard Strauss: Legende und Wirklichkeit', in *Umgang mit Musik* (Zurich, 1970), 173–202; Charlotte Erwin, 'Richard Strauss's Presketch Planning for *Ariadne auf Naxos*', *The Musical Quarterly*, 67 (1981), 348–65; Bryan Gilliam, 'Strauss's Preliminary Opera Sketches: Thematic Fragments and Symphonic Continuity', *19th-Century Music*, 9 (1986), 176–88. In a personal communication with this author (15 Oct. 1978), Karl Böhm described his first-hand observation of Strauss making marginal annotations in the *Daphne* text.

sketchbooks (this generalization becomes more consistent later on in Strauss's career). The former type of sketchbook fitted easily into an inside coat pocket, allowing Strauss (who did not compose at the piano) to compose almost anywhere.[7] The third stage—the Particell—comprises the entire opera in a quasi-piano-vocal score format. The Particell consists of bound bifolios, one act per volume, and is typically in ink; stages one and two are more often in pencil.

The final stage, the orchestral score, is a *tour de force* of calligraphic neatness and precision, in which the composer took great pride. 'You may say what you like about his [Strauss's] music; but if you don't praise his handwriting he will be cross with you,' declared the composer's wife, Pauline, to Alfred Kalisch on one occasion.[8] The orchestral score also consists of bound bifolios (one volume per act) and is ready for the publisher. The *Elektra* score is handsomely half-bound in leather with maroon linen boards; the title 'Elektra' is stamped on the leather in gold *Jugendstil* lettering.

Compositional layers in *Elektra*, however, should not necessarily be confused with strict compositional chronology. In Chapter 3 we recall that when Strauss had reached a creative impasse (beginning 7 October 1907) at the moment of Orestes' return, he stopped sketching and began scoring the work from the opening scene to the beginning of the Recognition Scene. He did not resume sketching that scene until 21 June 1908.

These musical annotations in the libretto form a vital part of Strauss's working method.[9] Schuh explains that, generally, certain '"tonal images" . . . [would] present themselves to Strauss after the first reading of a poem or libretto,' and that

[7] The average size of the smaller format sketchbook is *c.*8 × 13 cm., and the larger format averages *c.*13 × 18 cm.

[8] Ernest Newman, *Richard Strauss*, preface by Alfred Kalisch (London, 1908), xiv.

[9] By libretto—as it pertains to *Elektra*—I mean Strauss's edited copy of Hofmannsthal's play.

he would often jot them down in the margin.[10] When examining Strauss's annotated libretti, one does not easily comprehend the composer's tonal plan at first glance. One senses the distance between 'tonal images' that surfaced in the composer's mind and what appears on paper, for these marginal jottings are often little more than mnemonic devices that might refer to a local or broader tonal region. Furthermore, these annotations are not solely harmonic glossings, for Strauss often jots thematic fragments in the margins or, less often, the vocal setting for a particular phrase of text—sometimes just above the text, other times in the margin beside it. Such annotations, likewise, carry multi-level implications. A thematic fragment beside a phrase of text might be intended for that particular line or could be a recurring motive for a larger portion.

A point that scholars have neglected to stress is that these musical marginalia do not necessarily represent a closed, pre-sketchbook stage musical layer. While many of these musical remarks are, no doubt, the result of early glossing, it is fair to assume that as he was sketching, Strauss would also refer to the text and might add further musical comments. The arrangement of his annotations in the *Elektra* text point to such multiple layers.

In her article on Strauss's musical annotations in the libretto to *Ariadne auf Naxos*, Charlotte Erwin establishes four basic categories of musical commentary:

1. Simple harmonic designations [*Tonangaben*]
2. Short thematic ideas
3. Metric and tempo markings
4. Other verbal notations.[11]

Erwin asserts that the first category represents the predominant type of annotation.

[10] Schuh, 'Hofmannsthal und Strauss', 184.
[11] Erwin, 'Strauss's Presketch Planning', 349.

A primary point here is that the predominance of harmonic over other kinds of designations in the *Ariadne* libretto is typical. In the *Vorspiel* manuscript, out of a total of thirty-one different annotations by Strauss, twenty-one are harmonic designations. The *Rosenkavalier* libretto shows a total of thirteen harmonic annotations within the first four pages alone. The final text of *Arabella*, though less heavily annotated overall, still shows harmonic designations to be the primary type of marginalia totaling twenty-four, with a proportionately higher number of musical sketches [thematic sketches?] totaling twenty-two.[12]

Her cogent remarks about the importance of harmonic annotations are central to understanding Strauss's musical commentary and its relation to the genesis of a particular opera. None the less, the importance of marginal thematic jottings must not be neglected; they, too, form an essential part of Strauss's early musical plan, as the *Elektra* annotations clearly indicate.

Elektra: The Musically Annotated Text

Let us turn to the two textual sources containing musical commentary by Strauss: the published play at the RSA and the handwritten fragment at the Theatre Collection of the ÖNB. The *Elektra* text—including the ÖNB fragment—contradicts Erwin's hypothesis, for there we find forty thematic fragments, versus thirty-one harmonic indications; in a few rare instances these thematic fragments represent vocal settings of a phrase of text. This relation of harmonic jottings to thematic annotations underscores the importance of the latter.

Moreover, the *Elektra* text exhibits three sub-categories that fall under the general rubric 'other verbal notations': (1) style of singing (such as 'recitative' or 'quite free in the declamation'), (2) suggestions for instrumentation, and

[12] Ibid., 351.

(3) more general compositional memoranda (such as 'begin again with the *Steigerung*' or '*sinfonisch!*' and the like). Such instructions are to be found, with just one exception, only in Strauss's printed copy of the play.

A number of Strauss experts, including two of his librettists, have expressed their amazement at the composer's ability to size up the musical possibilities of a play or libretto after only two readings. The composer's cuts and marginal annotations in *Elektra* attest to his sound dramatic instincts. But these annotations, as mnemonic devices, frequently appear fragmentary, arbitrary, and inconsistent at first glance. With the major source—Strauss's creative mind—missing (as well as some possible written sources), it is impossible to reconnect, to fill in, to order logically many of Strauss's initial reactions to the text as they appear in their written form.

Accepting this important limitation, what are we to make of such large gaps in the *Elektra* text? How typical is this source? Only the first four pages of Strauss's copy of the adjacent *Rosenkavalier* text are extant,[13] so we must look to the composer's copy of *Salome* to find the chronologically closest autograph libretto for comparison.[14] Here one finds musical jottings for the first dozen pages or so (through Jochanaan's entrance from the cistern), and they drop off until Salome's final monologue, where we find a plethora of annotations. Thus this text, too, generates more questions than answers.

How should we interpret this lack of musical commentary for whole scenes (or large portions of scenes) in his copy of *Salome* or *Elektra*? And what do the musical annotations in these particular documents represent: a composer writing down the first ideas that came to his mind after one or two readings, or do they represent only a fraction of his musical

[13] These four pages were a gift from Strauss to Willi Schuh, and they are reproduced in his *Umgang mit Musik*.

[14] For the *Salome* 'libretto', Strauss edited and annotated the 1st edn. (1903) of Lachmann's German translation of Wilde's play.

thought at that time? After a cursory examination of the *Elektra* libretto the reader might be tempted to make one of two assumptions: (1) that these lacunae evince undocumented thought, or (2) that they show a composer who had not yet come up with any ideas for those particular sections at such an early stage.

In the case of the Recognition Scene, which—in the printed text—is practically devoid of compositional annotations by Strauss, we know that he glossed this scene in the ÖNB fragment and at a later date. Yet can we conclude that he had no significant musical ideas when he read through the scene prior to Hofmannsthal's textual addendum? Elektra's monologue (scene 2) is likewise short on the composer's commentary, but does contain two isolated, metrical specifications in the margin: '4/4' at 'Wo bist du Vater?' and 'allmählich/6/8 breit' beside the lines, '. . . und sie ahnen den Tod und wiehern in die Todesluft und sterben, und wir schlachten dir die Hunde mit dir gejagt. . . .' Although the composer apparently did not follow through with the latter annotation, these metrical annotations indicate that he probably apprehended some basic musical shape.

Another problem requires further exploration before we examine the annotated *Elektra* texts: the relationship between the first two compositional stages in Strauss's opera. Both Schuh and Erwin separate the 'pre-sketchbook' and the 'sketchbook' stages of composition, and it is indeed important to differentiate these two stages. But it seems artificial—perhaps even unhelpful—to segregate them as chronologically discrete layers of creativity; Strauss surely consulted his textbook while sketching the opera. Most of his textual cuts were in pencil, and although many of his musical annotations match that pencil point, there are other annotations (in a different pencil point) that suggest a further layer, and there are a few thematic jottings in ink. In short, one apprehends a certain fluidity between stages one and two.

There is clearly no dearth of questions or qualifications surrounding Strauss's marginal annotations in the *Elektra* text, and examining them may not produce an abundance of conclusions. Yet Strauss's comments—cryptic as they may be at times—require our evaluation, for they point to some of his earliest musical thoughts about the opera.

The 1904 Text

The fifth edition (1904) was not Strauss's only copy of the play; he also owned the seventh edition of 1906. But this later edition—with its neatly-wrought cuts and tipped-in additions—was intended for the printing of the libretto published by Fürstner. It contains no musical commentary, is identical to the published opera text and therefore is of little interest to this study. Strauss's earlier copy of *Elektra*, however, contains musical commentary (in some form or another) in every scene. The amount of marginal jotting varies significantly from scene to scene; most of Strauss's annotations are centred around the Klytämnestra Scene—especially the dialogue portion—and Elektra's second scene with Chrysothemis. What follows is a survey of Strauss's musical thought at this early stage of composition as evinced by his commentary in this fifth edition.

Scene 1

From the standpoint of marginal glossing in the text, the opening scene of *Elektra* differs from *Salome*. On the first page alone of the earlier play, he maps out the opening twenty-nine bars in significant detail, while scene 1 of *Elektra* is practically devoid of musical commentary; we find no indications of keys, tempi, or thematic ideas. Strauss indicates only the vocal dispositions for the serving maids—written above each voice ('Alt', 'Mezzosopran', 'hoch Sopran', etc.)—and makes two suggestions concerning instrumentation:

1. 'Woodwinds and muted trumpet' ['Holz u. sord. Tromp.'] beside the line: 'Immer wenn die Sonne tief steht, liegt sie und stöhnt.'
2. 'Timpani' beside the line: '"Fort, Fliegen!" schrie sie, "fort!"'

Strauss's assignment of vocal parts corresponds with the final version: the first serving maid is an alto, serving maids two and three are mezzo-sopranos, the remaining two maids are sopranos, and the overseer is also a soprano.[15] The composer's brief ideas concerning instrumental assignments are not as far-reaching, although he ultimately uses woodwinds (with various permutations of the Agamemnon motive [2 after reh. 3]) to accompany the first serving maid ('Immer wenn die Sonne tief steht . . .'). Such glosses evince how soon the composer's imagination for timbre was stimulated—even at this early stage of glossing the play. Similarly in the *Salome* text we find dramatic situations or lines of text that generate specific timbral responses by the composer.

Scene 3

There are more marginal annotations in scene 3 than in either of the two previous scenes. Most of Strauss's commentary is concentrated around the opening of Chrysothemis' lyrical, aria-like outburst: 'Ich hab's wie Feuer in der Brust' (Ex. 5.1). This page of the autograph libretto reveals both thematic and harmonic jottings, although we see more of the latter in this instance. And within this cluster of designated keys (E♭ major, C minor, D♭ major) there are different levels of tonal reference not clearly indicated by the composer. The E flat in the upper right-hand corner probably refers to the tonal setting for this monologue, which, as the composer indicates, is

[15] Strauss refers to the sopranos as 'hoch Sopran' or sometimes just 'hoch' to distinguish them from their alto and mezzo-soprano counterparts.

Ex. 5.1 Diplomatic copy of Strauss's text (RSA); Strauss's annotations in italics

Chrysothemis:

Ich kann nicht sitzen und ins Dunkel starren *3/4*
wie du. Ich hab's wie Feuer in der Brust, *Es dur* *Hörner*
es treibt mich immerfort herum im Haus,
in keiner Kammer leidet's mich, ich muß
von einer Schwelle auf die andre, ach!
treppauf, treppab, mir ist, als rief' es mich,
und komm'ich hin, so stiert ein leeres Zimmer *C moll*
mich an. Ich habe solche Angst, mir zittern
die Knie bei Tag und Nacht, mir ist die Kehle
wie zugeschnürt, ich kann nicht einmal weinen,
wie Stein ist alles! Schwester, hab Erbarmen! *Des dur dominant sept.*

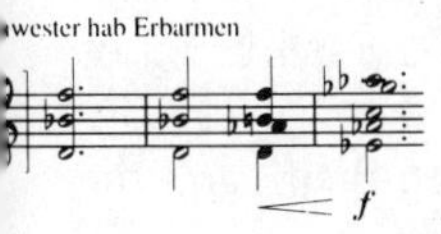

set in 3/4 metre. The motivic fragment in the upper left-hand margin serves not only as a harmonic bridge leading to this passage, but also as an important recurring figure throughout a good portion of her monologue. Strauss's references to C minor and V^7 of D flat on this page are thus local excursions from his broader plan. Annotations on either side of Chrysothemis' last line of her first speech ('wie Stein ist alles! Schwester, *hab Erbarmen*!') make it clear that he wished to articulate the final few words of that line with a sudden and fleeting shift to the dominant of D flat, although in the final version that shift is to D flat minor.

In another portion of this scene there are important compositional memoranda by Strauss—just after Chrysothemis' climactic 'Kinder will ich haben'. Here she reaches her emotional nadir in this scene midway through her speech. Beyond their ability to bear children what do they have, Chrysothemis asks Elektra: no father, an estranged mother, no brother ('no messenger from our brother, not even the messenger of a messenger, nothing!'). She compares Elektra and herself to two caged birds, which 'turn their heads left to right' as they wait for their brother. Beside those lines Strauss writes 'ganz dumpf | piano', which marks the most quiet and austere moment in scene 3.

Chrysothemis' low point is short-lived, for Hofmannsthal creates a compelling chain of images as she ponders the passing of time:

> With knives each passing day carves its mark on your face and mine, and outside, the sun rises and sets, and women whom I have known slender are heavy with blessing, and toil on their way to the well and scarcely lift the pail, and all at once they are delivered of their weight and come to the well again and they themselves flow with sweet drink, and, suckling, a new life clings to them, and the children grow.

It is tempting to marvel at an inherent musicality in Hofmannsthal's text: a highly profiled lyrical affirmation of a 'woman's destiny', followed by a gloomy realization of the present, which then leads to a sequence of metaphors concerning time and mutability that act as a transition to Chrysothemis' recapitulatory reaffirmation of her desire to bear children ('No, I am a woman and want a woman's destiny!'). But Strauss provided much of that shape himself with his own editing of the text. Chrysothemis' reference to the fettered birds originally followed the last line in the transitional passage quoted above, but Strauss, who saw the importance of the above passage as a musico-dramatic retransition, eliminated any obstacle to that sequential forward thrust. He inserted the caged-bird passage, instead, right after the lines, 'Der Vater, der ist tot. Der Bruder kommt nicht heim.'

Strauss's text shows that, early on, he evidently perceived the sequential nature of Hofmannsthal's language at that moment of retransition (see Ex. 5.2).

Ex. 5.2 Diplomatic copy of Strauss's text (RSA); Strauss's annotations in italics

Chrysothemis:

Hab Mitleid mit dir selber und mit mir
Wem frommt denn diese Qual? ~~Dem Vater etwa?~~
Der Vater, der ist tot. Der Bruder kommt nicht heim.
~~Du siehst ja doch, dass er nicht kommt.~~† Mit Messern 
gräbt Tag um Tag in dein und mein Gesicht
sein Mal und draussen geht die Sonne auf
und ab, und Frauen, die ich schlank gekannt hab',
sind schwer von Segen, mühen sich zum Brunnen
und heben kaum den Eimer, und auf einmal
sind sie entbunden ihrer Last und kommen
zum Brunnen wieder und aus ihnen selber
rinnt süsser Trank und säugend hängt ein Leben
an ihnen, und die Kinder werden gross—

bis

wieder mit der Steigerung beginnen

In the right-hand margin he writes: 'again begin with the build-up' ('Wieder mit der Steigerung beginnen'). In the margin directly opposite, the composer sketches out a sequential figure that he plans to use in this build-up: essentially the head motive of 'Kinder will ich haben'. But Strauss ultimately chose to present that head motive in augmentation, making the connection between sequential material and the recapitulation less apparent and ultimately more powerful.

Scene 4

The fourth scene displays the widest variety of annotations thus far (metrical, tonal, thematic, style of singing, and orchestrational); they centre mostly on the rapid exchange between Elektra and her mother, and they evince Strauss's concern for textual clarity and intelligibility. We shall see in the next chapter that he continued to wrestle with the problem even in the fair sketches for scene 4. Does the dearth of commentary outside this portion of the dialogue mean that Strauss had not yet come up with any ideas concerning more important parts of this scene, such as Klytämnestra's introductory monologue or Elektra's final confrontation with her mother? Or were these sections so clear in the composer's mind that he did not feel it necessary to put them down at the time?

There is no clear answer, but one thing is for certain: Strauss not only realized the dramaturgical importance of this dialogue, he also recognized how important it was for the audience to understand the text. This is the only scene where Strauss annotates vocal style; he writes, for example, 'Recitativ' next to Klytämnestra's part no less than eight times. At this point in the play Hofmannsthal employs a Socratic method of getting to the root of Klytämnestra's problem, yet her queries are met with puzzling responses by Elektra. All eight instances of Strauss specifying 'Recitativ' are for interrogatives by the mother:

1. 'You know then with which consecrated beast?' *Recitativ*
2. 'Is it tied up inside?' *Recitativ*
3. 'And what sort of rites?' *Recit*[ativ]
4. 'Say the name of the sacrificial victim!' *Recitativ*
5. 'And how sacrificed? What hour? And where?' *Recitativ*
6. 'Reveal the rites! How would I perform them?' *Recitativ*
7. 'Who else then? Who does it?' *Recitativ*
8. 'Who? Answer me. Someone from this house? *Recitativ/(stringend)* Or must a stranger come?'

Klytämnestra's constant probing gives this dialogue shape and momentum; clarity is essential.

Perhaps the best example of his desire for utter clarity of text for the singers is the moment when Elektra refers to Orestes for the first time in their conversation; it is the turning point in this scene (Ex. 5.3).

Elektra's question about Orestes is her first since part I of scene 4 ('Do you dream, Mother?'), marking the end of the

Ex. 5.3 Diplomatic copy of Strauss's text (RSA); Strauss's annotations in italics

Elektra:
zu Boden stierend, wie abwesend

Ja, ja, ein Fremder. Aber freilich
ist er vom Haus.

Klytämnestra:

Gib mir nicht Rätsel auf.
Elektra, hör mich an. Ich freue mich,
daß ich dich heut' einmal nicht störrisch finde. *Pause*

Elektra:
leise

ganz frei in der Deklamation Läßt du den Bruder nicht nach Hause, Mutter? *zuerst Tuben*

Klytämnestra:
Von ihm zu reden hab' ich dir verboten.

Elektra:
So hast du Furcht vor ihm?

dialogue between mother and daughter. Elektra's explosive reply ('What must bleed? Your own neck . . .'), which articulates the onset of part III, will soon begin. Strauss's original idea was to dramatize this pivotal moment (see Ex. 5.3) in the text first by preceding it with a sudden pause, followed by Elektra's singing in a style 'quite free in the declamation' ['ganz frei in der Deklamation']; Klytämnestra's reply was intended to be in that declamatory style as well. As Elektra utters the word 'brother' Strauss envisioned an entrance of the tubas (probably two or more tenor tubas).

But the composer's ultimate solution, which differs significantly from what is described above, is simply: silence —Elektra asks about Orestes (in a recitative, articulated by tubas) and Klytämnestra replies (in recitative as well). Strauss preserves the essence of the above, but handles it in a more subtle and compelling way (see Ex. 5.4).

There is, for example, no stark *Generalpause* preceding Elektra's forbidden question, but there is a significant cessation of musical activity in the orchestra that essentially dwindles down to a sustained D (Orestes' key). The horns adumbrate the Orestes theme by repeating the head motive in a decoration of this D pedal. With the shift to E flat in the bass, we hear that theme in full, then the cadence on A flat (the key of their childhood) along with the childhood theme in the oboe. Elektra asks the forbidden question not 'in the declamation', but using the childhood theme. The only known sketch for this moment is a fair sketch, but even at this late stage Strauss has her sing in recitative (Ex. 5.5).

None of the composer's tonal annotations are at the structural level in scene 4. Still, most of his marginal comments relating to the assignment of specific keys shed further light on tonal symbolism in Strauss's music.[16] Two examples illustrate Strauss's method of jotting down certain keys associated with particular characters or events. The first example is from part I of this scene, before Klytämnestra descends and talks with her daughter: the moment of Klytämnestra's temporary reverie as the sound of Elektra's voice transports her back to times past ('Das klingt mir so bekannt. Und nur als hätt' ich's vergessen'). It is also one of the longest consonant stretches of any one key in the scene—in this instance F sharp major, the key that, as sketches show, Strauss associates with Klytämnestra. In the margin to the left of this short speech, which Strauss had originally deleted, the composer writes 'Fis moll'.[17]

[16] See pp. 90–2.

[17] In the previous chapter we have already discussed the near lack of structural distinction between major and minor modes in Strauss's chromatic harmony around the time of *Elektra*.

Ex. 5.4 8 bars after reh. 215

Ex. 5.4 cont.

216 sehr schnell 𝅗𝅥 = 72 molto allegro
217
2 ob.
2 B♭ cl.
1 F cl.
b. cl.
3 bns.
1 2 hns. in F 3
tr. 3
1 3 tbns. 2,3
Elektra
(leise)
Läßt du den Bru - der nicht nach Hause, Mutter?
So hast du Furcht vor ihm?
Klytämn.
Von ihm zu re - den hab' ich dich verboten.
Wer
1,2 vn. 3
1 va. 2,3
vc.
a 2
a 3
I.
dim.
p espr.

Ex. 5.5 Tokyo sketchbook, p. 95

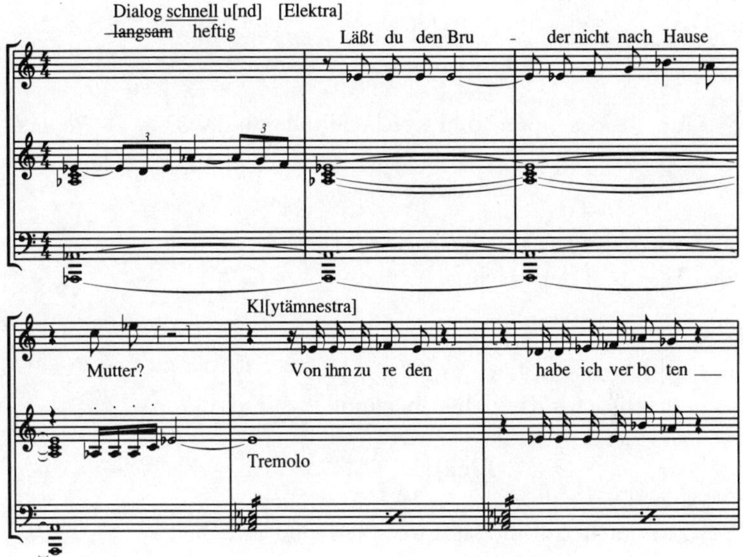

We see even more specific character delineation through tonalities in the dialogue portion of scene 4. Midway through this section, as Klytämnestra demands to know what rites will rid her of her dreams, Strauss subliminally suggests (with symbolic keys) unnamed characters who lie just beneath the surface of this puzzling conversation.

In the short exchange shown in Ex. 5.6, the composer articulates C major, D minor, and F major—the keys of Agamemnon, Orestes, and Aegisthus, respectively, thereby conjuring up the spirit of Elektra's father as she caustically replies: 'No. This time you do not hunt with net and axe.' D minor gives us the answer to Elektra's evasive reply ('A man') to her mother's query as to who will carry out the rite. 'Aegisthus?' The F major chord refers to Klytämnestra's question.

There are only a few examples of thematic marginalia in this scene, and they are of two types: either a theme or thematic fragment intended to rule a particular stretch of

Ex. 5.6 Diplomatic copy of Strauss's text (RSA); Strauss's annotations in italics

Klytämnestra:
dringend
Und wie das Opfer? und welche Stunde? und wo? *Recitativ*

Elektra:
ruhig
An jedem Ort, zu jeder Stunde
des Tags und der Nacht.

Klytämnestra:
Die Bräuche sag! *Recitativ*
Wie brächt ich's dar? ich selber muß—

C dur **Elektra:**
Nein. Diesmal
gehst du nicht auf die Jagd mit Netz und mit Beil. *cis*
a
e
d

Klytämnestra:
Wer denn? wer brächt' es dar? *Recitativ*

Elektra:
Ein Mann. *D moll*

Klytämnestra:
Aegisth? *F dur*

Elektra:
lacht
Ich sagte doch: ein Mann!

Klytämnestra:
Wer? gib mir Antwort.
Vom Hause jemand? oder muß ein Fremder herbei? *Recitativ (stringend)*

text, or a theme intended for a single referential purpose. We see the former in the scene where Klytämnestra calls to end the riddles, just before Elektra asks about Orestes (see Ex. 5.3). Here Strauss refers to the recurring, saccharine parallel thirds that suggest Elektra's feigned benevolence toward her mother [5 after reh. 148 *passim*]; these thirds—now outlining a vii^7 of D—constitute the essential motivic material of the mother's plea. But they continue against the D drone in the bass that leads into Elektra's forbidden question (see reh. 215–16).

The second type is illustrated just four lines later, when Klytämnestra asks. 'Who says that [I fear Orestes]?' ('Wer sagt das?') (Ex. 5.7). In the margin to the right of that line the composer writes: 'Hier erst das Thema lauernde Unsicherheit.' Strauss provides neither staff nor clef, but it is clearly the sinuous Klytämnestra theme first introduced in Elektra's monologue (1 after reh. 39); with it he intends to suggest her uneasiness with the subject of Orestes. The composer ultimately did not use the theme at that spot, but placed it five bars later—in juxtaposition with the Orestes theme—in order to undercut Klytämnestra's false claim that her son is feeble and stammers (see 7 after reh. 217).

Ex. 5.7 Diplomatic copy of Strauss's text (RSA); Strauss's annotations in italics

Elektra
So hast du Furcht vor ihm?

Klytämnestra
Wer sagt das? *Hier erstes Thema*

lauernde Unsicherheit

Scene 5

Here we find the greatest concentration of musical annotations by Strauss in his 1904 edition of the play. Moreover, the type of remarks made by the composer indicate that early on he viewed the scene in a two-part format:

(1) Introduction (with three subsections):
(*a*) Chrysothemis enters with the news of Orestes' death
(*b*) the brief interruption of the servants
(*c*) Elektra's decision that she and her sister must undertake the murders.

(2) Main Section (the dialogue between Elektra and Chrysothemis, with four principal subsections):
(*a*) 'Du! Du! denn du bist stark!'
(*b*) 'Von jetzt an will ich deine Schwester sein.'
(*c*) 'O ja! weit mehr als Schwester . . .'
(*d*) 'Dir führt kein Weg hinaus als der.'

Most of the marginal jottings in this scene show how Strauss highlighted these sections and subgroupings within each section.

In the introduction, he articulates, for example, the end of the first subsection [see reh. 22a] with the following striking theme (he had already articulated the beginning of this subsection with the head motive of this theme):

Although no head motive is indicated, we find the prototype for the above theme (hastily jotted down in pencil)—at the same spot in the textbook (i.e. the end of the first subsection). It is one of the longest thematic sketches in Strauss's edition of the play and differs in certain details from the final version of that theme:

Did Strauss already have this promising head motive in mind before he jotted down the theme? No such motive is to be found at the beginning of this subsection. At first glance it seems that Strauss intended to articulate only the end of the first subsection with this theme. However, the theme was written down later than the other annotations; it is squeezed into the bottom of the page beneath some added text (in ink) that postdates Strauss's initial editorial pencil. The composer could have already been sketching this scene, and what we see at the bottom of that page is motivic expansion, for Strauss fuses the childhood motive at the end of the theme.

In the ensuing rapid, parlando subsection (the interruption of the two servants) Strauss appears to be preoccupied with the rhythm and declamation of the text. Much of the thematic sketching here suggests that the composer desired to stress the connection between these servants and Aegisthus. Indeed, the trochaic and anapaestic aspects of the Aegisthus motive pervade this short section, and a clear statement of the motive occurs by reh. 30a.

The third subsection is nearly devoid of any musical comments save at the outset, where Strauss sets the harmony and rhythm for Elektra's opening, 'Nun muss es von uns geschehen.' More important, he jots down a significant chord progression to the right of Chrysothemis's reply 'Elektra?' 

It recalls . Chrysothemis' opening line of the opera, although in a different transposition, is one of many repetitions that occur at important structural moments in the opera—indeed up until the very end (see 5 after reh. 254a). Significantly, the above represents its only appearance as an annotation in Strauss's text.

There are no further marginal comments until the opening of the main section, which Strauss articulates (in his text) with a shift to 3/4 metre at Chrysothemis' repeated cry: 'Elektra!' The composer's change to triple metre in the final score does not take place until three lines later as Elektra exclaims 'Wie stark du bist!' At that moment in the margin of the text Strauss writes 'sinfonisch!', a not inappropriate remark since much of this main section is a symphonic recapitulation of material from the first scene with Chrysothemis.

The principal function of Strauss's musical annotations in the main section is to articulate the important subdivisions outlined above and discussed in the previous chapter (see p. 94, Chapter 4). They comprise Elektra's four entreaties that are rejected by Chrysothemis:

(1) Wie stark du bist! dich haben *sinfonisch!*
die jungfräulichen Nächte stark gemacht.

[. . .]

(2) *zwischen Übergang*

Von jetzt an will ich deine Schwester sein, ¢

[. . .]

(3) ¢ O ja! weit mehr als Schwester bin ich dir
von diesem Tage an: ich diene dir

[. . .]

(4) *C moll* Denn eh' du diesem Haus
quartsept und mir entkommst, musst du es tun! [. . .]

2/4 Dir führt
nach der kein Weg hinaus als der. Ich lass dich nicht
Deklamation phrasieren

Scene 6

We recall how problematic this scene was for Strauss; despite preliminary cuts and textual rearranging he was unable to set the Recognition Scene as it stood. After struggling with the scene as late as October, he decided to postpone sketching and began scoring the work starting with scene 1, working his way through to scene 5 by the latter part of June 1908. By then he was able to find a solution to his creative impasse. What he needed was additional text at the moment Elektra recognizes Orestes.

Garmisch, 22 June 1908

Dear Herr von Hofmannsthal,

In *Elektra*, page 77, I need a great moment of repose after Elektra's first shout: 'Orest!'

I shall fit in a delicately vibrant orchestral interlude while Electra gazes upon Orestes, now safely restored to her. I can make her repeat the stammered words: 'Orest, Orest, Orest!' several times; of the remainder only the words: 'Es rührt sich niemand!' and 'O lass Deine Augen mich sehen!' fit into this mood. Couldn't you insert here a few beautiful verses until (as Orestes is about to embrace her gently) I switch over to the sombre mood, starting with the words: 'Nein, Du sollst mich nicht berühren . . ., etc?[18]

Hofmannsthal sent Strauss the requested lines three days later; these additional eleven lines make up Elektra's A flat major aria. Rather than trying to squeeze them into the published play, the composer wrote out the Recognition Scene afresh, incorporating the additions as well as some cuts and textual rearranging.

Thus, there are two textual layers for scene 6: the 1904 edition and the handwritten document at the ÖNB. The printed text—the earlier, problematic layer—contains fewer musical ideas. None the less, there are two annotations in the printed text worthy of comment; they concern the moment

[18] Letter of 22 June 1908 in *Correspondence*, 16.

that Elektra recognizes her brother. The original text is as follows:

Orest
(sanft):
Die Hunde auf dem Hof erkennen mich,
und meine Schwester nicht?

Elektra
(schreit auf):
Orest! *langes*
Orest *Orchesterzwischenspiel*
(fieberhaft):
~~Wenn einer dich im Hause hat, der~~ *u. Übergang*
~~hat jetzt mein Leben in der Hand.~~

Elektra *langes zärtliches Orchester-*
(ganz leise, bebend): *zwischenspiel*

Orest! Orest! Orest! *Orest!*
Es rührt sich niemand. O lass deine Augen
mich sehen! Nein, du sollst mich nicht berühren!
Tritt weg, ich schäme mich vor dir. [etc.][19]

Whether Strauss refers to two orchestral interludes, or whether the second annotation is merely a more refined description of the first one, is not clear. Yet one thing is certain: the interlude that the composer ultimately devised is the boldest, most dissonant and chromatic instrumental passage in the opera. Strauss's descriptions 'tender' or 'delicately vibrant' are inapplicable, although the passage dramatically subsides as it makes a transition to Elektra's quieter aria ('Es rührt sich niemand').

The second annotation (just below Orestes' deleted text in the above example) is impossible to date precisely, although it probably stems from the time of the June 1908 letter to Hofmannsthal. Then Strauss was of a different mind con-

[19] Of course in between 'O lass deine Augen mich sehen!' and 'Nein, du sollst mich . . .' Strauss inserted the text he had requested from Hofmannsthal.

cerning the nature of that orchestral passage, and the delicate and tender impulse ultimately found its way into Elektra's A-flat-major aria that immediately follows. More interesting, however, is the theme ('zart') that he jots down along with that description (see above). Although he intended it for the earlier conceived interlude, this theme—cast in an entirely different mood—instead plays a prominent role at the outset and throughout the jubilant C major duet between Elektra and Chrysothemis at the end of the opera (see Ex. 5.8).

Klytämnestra's Murder

Strauss's handwritten text [ÖNB] includes Klytämnestra's murder and continues through Aegisthus' exit as he goes into the palace. There is, thus, a double layer of text from the Recognition Scene to the moment preceding Aegisthus' murder. The existence of a second layer explains the spareseness of annotations for Klytämnestra's murder as well as the Aegisthus scene in Strauss's 1904 edition. The composer's sole musical comment at the moment Orestes disappears into the palace illustrates, once again, the precision of his musical imagination at this early stage. The annotation relates to the following stage direction (underlining by Strauss):

Elektra
(allein in entsetzlicher Spannung.
Sie läuft auf einem Strich vor der Tür hin und her, mit gesenktem Kopf, wie das gefangene Tier im Käfig. Plötzlich steht sie still und sagt): *dazu Läufe im Quartett u.*

Ich habe ihm das Beil nicht geben können!
Sie sind gegangen und ich habe ihm
das Beil nicht geben können. Es sind keine
Götter im Himmel!

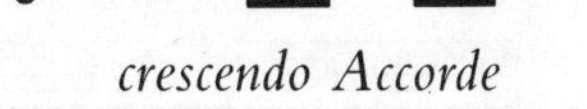

crescendo Accorde
volles Orchester

Ex. 5.8 Rch. 237a

(Abermals ein furchtbares Warten. Da tönt von drinnen, gellend, der Schrei der Klytämnestra.)

Elektra
(schreit auf wie ein Dämon):
Triff noch einmal!

These annotations are among the few in ink and, thus, probably postdate the earlier pencilled ones. Here we see Strauss translating Elektra's aimless rushing about into musical gesture; her running becomes runs in the cellos and double-basses, which are divided into four parts (hence, 'Quartett'). He establishes these runs on the head motive which originated from the outset of Elektra's confrontational 'Was bluten muss?'—the final section of the Klytämnestra scene. In the above passage Strauss sketches that head motive in G minor, although it appears in C minor in both scene 4 and this murder scene.

The musical figure just under 'Triff noch einmal' is noteworthy, for it illustrates that, at this early stage, not only did Strauss choose to use the Agamemnon motive—which previously had always spanned octaves—but that he would mutate it by having the figure arch upward in minor ninths. The close proximity of these two musical annotations also reinforces a connection that we already perceived: the rhythmic relationship between this latter Agamemnon theme and Elektra's confrontational motive (Ex. 5.9).

Ex. 5.9

Aegisthus' Murder

This short section is practically devoid of any annotations, save a two-bar theme to the left of Aegisthus' questions: 'What is that in your voice? . . . Why do you stagger back and forth with your light? . . . What are you dancing for?' (See Ex. 5.10.)

Ex. 5.10 Diplomatic copy of Strauss's text (RSA)

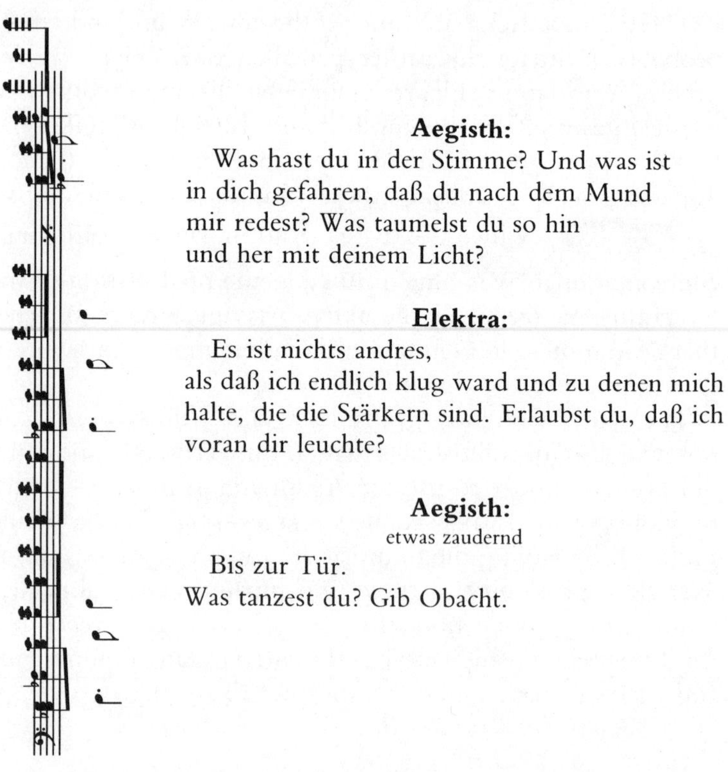

Aegisth:

Was hast du in der Stimme? Und was ist
in dich gefahren, daß du nach dem Mund
mir redest? Was taumelst du so hin
und her mit deinem Licht?

Elektra:

Es ist nichts andres,
als daß ich endlich klug ward und zu denen mich
halte, die die Stärkern sind. Erlaubst du, daß ich
voran dir leuchte?

Aegisth:

etwas zaudernd

Bis zur Tür.
Was tanzest du? Gib Obacht.

The dotted rhythmic gesture below the triplets refers to Elektra's victory dance; it occurs as early as Elektra's opening monologue. But Strauss ultimately chose not to use the above, but rather a different style of dance, a dance (including upward glissandi in cello and bass) that looks back to the seductive style of *Salome* as Elektra lures her stepfather to his death.[20] The pervasive Orestes figure is blended into this alluring atmosphere (Ex. 5.11).

Final Scene

Strauss probably did not use his copy of the play as the primary textual source for sketching this scene. We see no sign of cuts on these pages, yet Strauss indeed cut or rearranged most of Chrysothemis' last speech, 'Hörst du den nicht', as well as some stage directions. More important, this scene, like the Recognition Scene, contains some significant textual additions by Hofmannsthal, in this case an extended duet for Elektra and Chrysothemis ('Wir sind bei den Göttern').

Garmisch, 6.7.08

Dear Herr von Hofmannsthal,

Your kind letter of the 4th received with thanks. Enclosed herewith your final verses which I am asking you to extend as much as possible as a *simultaneous duet* between Elektra and Chrysothemis. [. . .][21]

Curiously, the 1904 edition of the play bears no evidence of this thought on the part of the composer. There is surely a missing textual source that contained the remainder of the drama: from Aegisthus' murder ('Hört mich niemand?') to the end of the work. This and other issues will be dealt with in the final part of this chapter, which is a discussion of Strauss's handwritten copy of part of the text at the ÖNB.

The ÖNB *Elektra* Text

This document consists of two separate folios of different sizes.[22] Strauss writes *Elektra* text on both sides of each folio:

[20] Indeed, in both instances a young woman tries to seduce her stepfather.

[21] Letter of 6 July 1908 in *Correspondence*, 18.

[22] Fol. 1 measures 29 × 23 cm. and fol. 2 measures 33.8 × 21 cm. (Fol. 2 was severed at the middle, has been repaired, and is now protected by onion-skin contact

Ex. 5.11 Reh. 206a

fol. 1^v includes the additional text that he had requested from Hofmannsthal. Thus we can date this document fairly precisely, for it postdates Hofmannsthal's submission of the extra lines on 25 June 1908. But it cannot date beyond the first week of July of that year, because he finished sketching the Recognition Scene and began sketching the rest of the opera around 6 July. On the verso side of fol. 2 (see Illustration II), indeed, we find nearly three-quarters of the page concerned with pencilled calculations of the disposition of orchestral parts for two (or perhaps three) pages of the full score. Two of the three series of calculations are headed by the numbers 214 and 215, respectively. These numbers refer to pages 214 and 215 of the autograph score; page 216 begins the Recognition Scene.

Strauss frequently calculated the layout of orchestral parts on scrap paper, which he usually threw away.[23] Thus, having scored the final page of the previous scene, Strauss evidently began writing down the text to the now expanded Recognition Scene on the clean reverse side of that scrap. The

paper.) The provenance is the estate of Anna Bahr-Mildenburg, who made a fine career as Klytämnestra early in the 20th century, especially in Vienna. Although there is no inscription on either folio, Strauss probably gave them to her. He had given her an *Elektra* sketchbook, which bears the inscription: 'To the brilliant interpreter of Klytämnestra in Vienna | Fräulein von Mildenburg | with friendly memories | from your greatest admirer. | The thankful composer of *Elektra* | Dr Richard Strauss | Garmisch, 7 May 1909.' ['Der genialen Darstellerin | der Klytämnestra in Wien | Frl. von Mildenburg | zu freundlicher Erinnerung | an ihren grössten Bewunderer. | Der dankbare Componist der Elektra. | Dr Richard Strauss. | Garmisch, 7. Mai 1909.'] Bahr-Mildenburg, who was married to the Viennese playwright and critic Hermann Bahr, died in January 1947; both of these documents went to the *Theatersammlung* of the ÖNB that year.

These folios were catalogued in *Richard Strauss: Autographen in München und Wien*, although neither is dated by Brosche (Günter Brosche and Karl Dachs, eds., *Richard Strauss: Autographen in München und Wien*, Veröffentlichungen der Richard-Strauss-Gesellschaft, München, vol. iii (Tutzing, 1979).) Moreover, the folios curiously are numbered in reverse order since fol. 2 begins with the opening of the Recognition Scene and fol. 1 is a continuation of it. I have preserved Brosche's published numbering for the sake of consistency.

[23] Franz Trenner, who helped the Strauss family sort through the estate shortly after the composer's death, described this practice to the author a number of years ago. In that discussion he explained that he had found a number of such scraps that were wadded up and thrown away in a box that had not yet been disposed of.

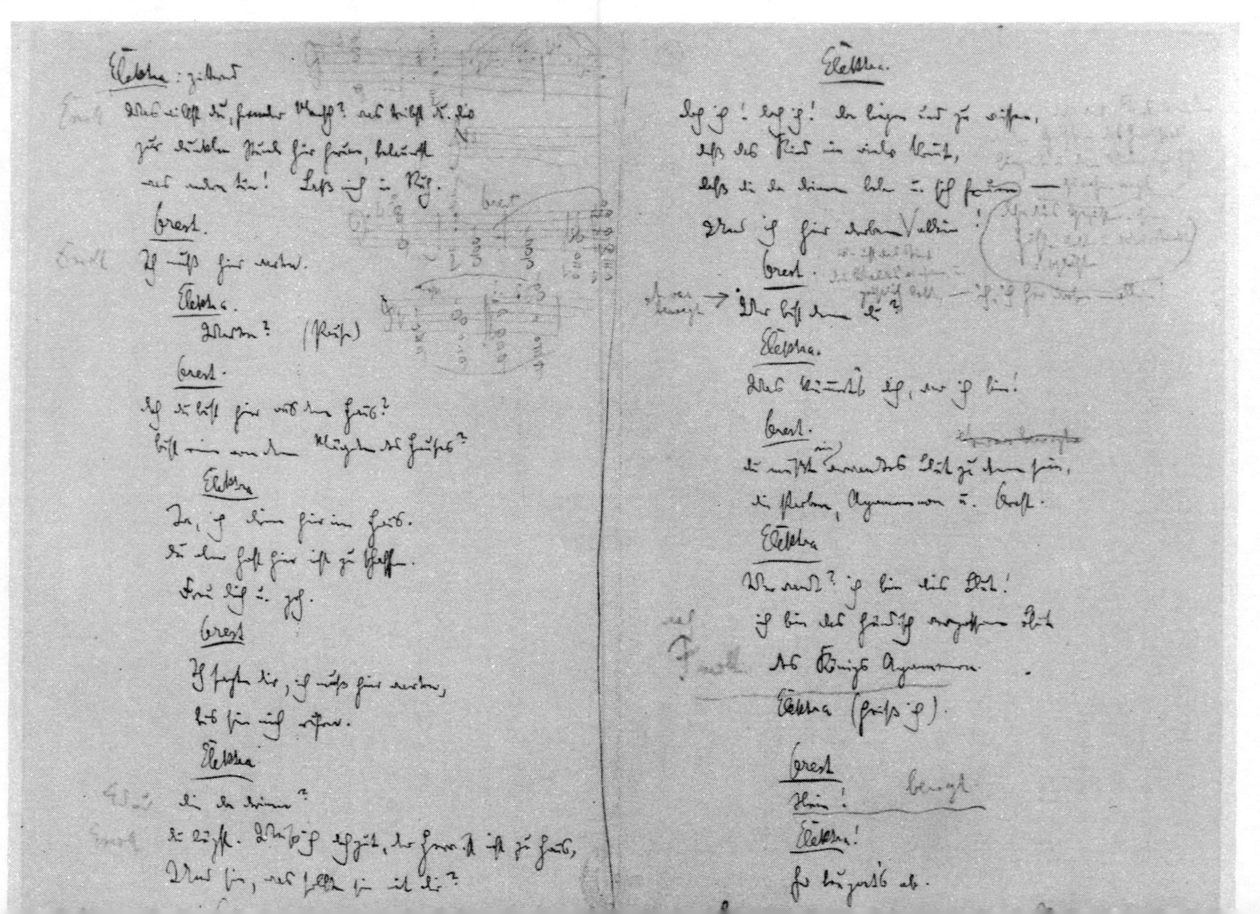

ILLUSTRATION I *Elektra*, text fragment, ÖNB, fol. 2

[illegible],
wir haben einen Auftrag hier an die Frau.

Elektra (schreit)

C moll

Orest

Wir sind zu ihr geschickt,
weil wir bezeugen können, daß ihr Sohn
Orest gestorben ist vor unsern Augen.
Denn ihn erschlugen seine eigenen Pferde.
Ich war so alt wie er, und sein Geselle
bei Tag und Nacht.

Elektra.

Muß ich dich noch sehn?
Schleppst du dich hieher in meinen traurigen Winkel,
Herold des Unglücks!
Kannst du nicht die Botschaft austrompeten,
dort, wo sie sich freun!
Du lebst — und er, der besser war als du
und edler tausendmal und tausendmal
so wichtig, daß er lebte — er ist hin!

Thema 3

Thema 1.

Orest:

Laß den Orest.
Ihn freute sich zu sehr
an seinem Leben, und die Götter droben
vertragen nicht den allzuhellen Laut der Lust.
So mußte er denn sterben.

Elektra: [illegible] ich nicht Vater u. nicht Bruder hab,
bin ich der Spott der Buben.

Orest

Elektra! Elektra!
Du bist es? Du bist es wirklich? Du!
(schnell)
Sie haben dich hungern lassen oder —
sie haben dich geschlagen?

Elektra

Laß mein Kleid, wühle nicht mit deinem Blick darein.

Orest

Elektra! Was haben sie gemacht
mit deinen Nächten!
Furchtbar sind deine Augen.

Elektra:

Laß mich!

Orest:

Hohl sind deine Wangen.

Elektra

Geh ins Haus, drin hab ich eine Schwester,
die bewahrt sich für Freudenfeste auf!

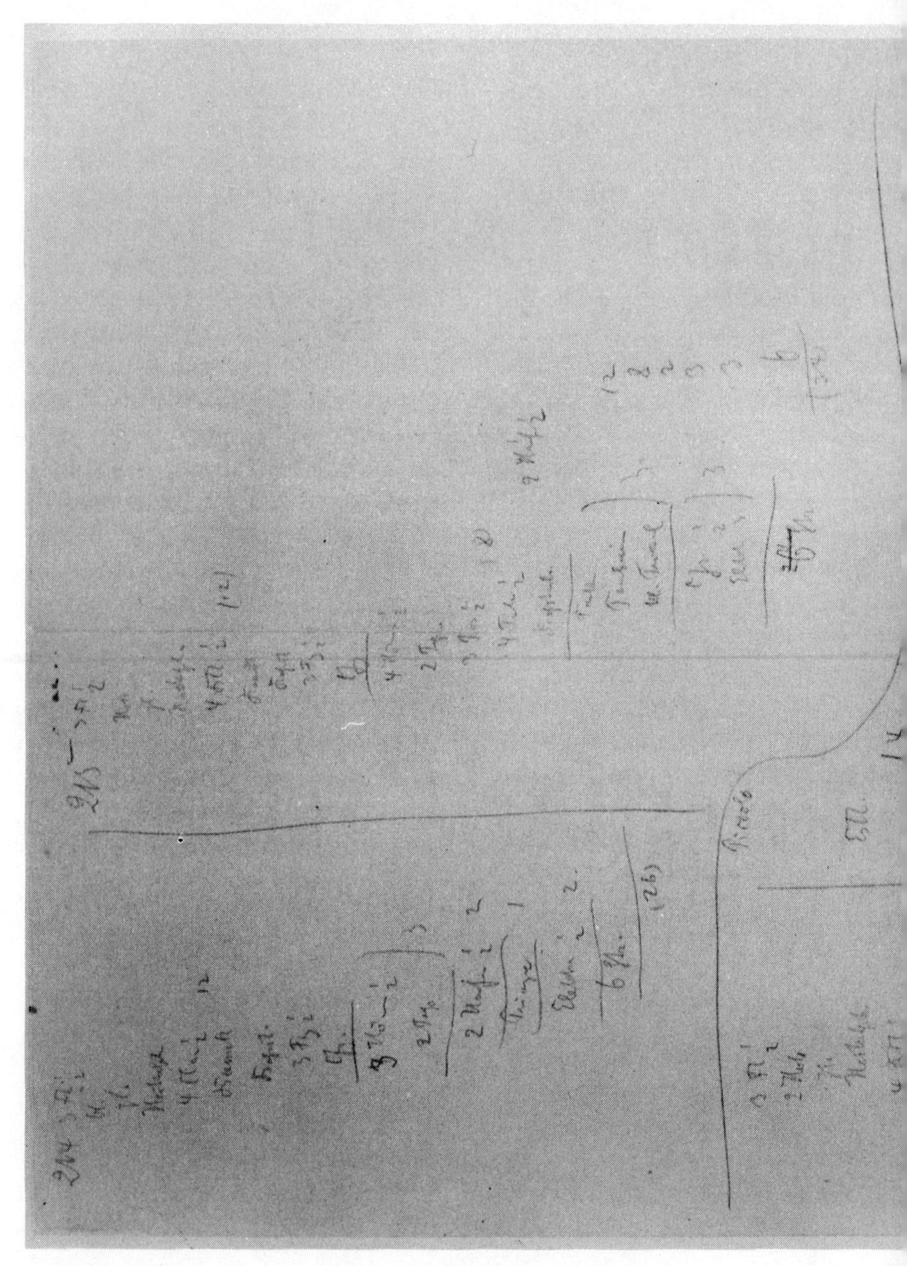

ILLUSTRATION II *Elektra*, text fragment, ÖNB, fol. 2v

30. 2000

12	4 Hörner 1/2	2 Trp. 6
5	4 Tuben 1/2 5	
3	[illegible]	Pauken 1
7	Orgel 1, 2, [illegible] 3	(3 1)
	[illegible] Str.	7 Str.
24		31

Die alten [illegible] deiner [illegible],
küsst sich an [illegible], küsst seine Füsse,
richtet sich auf, umschaut um sich spähend
und schleicht lautlos wieder ab.

Elektra (kaum ihrer mächtig)
Wer bist du denn? Ich fürchte mich.

Orest (sanft)
Die Hunde auf dem Hof erkennen mich,
und meine Schwester nicht?

Elektra (schreit auf) Orest !!

[illegible], hör ich.

Elektra
Ich will nicht wissen, wer du bist.
Ich will niemand sehn.

Orest
Hör zu: ich hab nicht Zeit. Hör zu:
~~Ich darf nicht laut reden.~~
Hör zu mir: Orestes lebt.

Elektra (wirft sich herum)

Orest
~~Gib keinen Laut von dir.~~
Wenn du dich regst, verrätst du ihn.

Elektra
So ist er frei? wo ist er?

Orest
Er ist unversehrt wie ich.

Elektra
So rette dich, bevor sie dich erwürgen.

Orest
Bei meines Vaters Leichnam! dazu kam ich her!

Elektra (getroffen) Wer bist du?

Allegro Thema 2

676

44
14.20
65.35
100
223.60

2.15

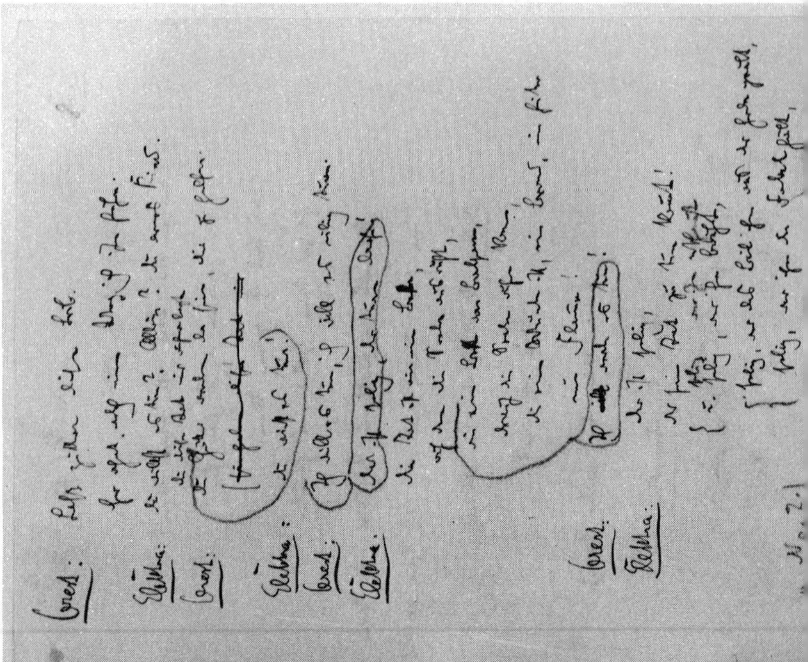

ILLUSTRATION III *Elektra*. text fragment, ÖNB, fol. 1

war solches Haar, vor dem die Männer zittern,
dies Haar, versträhnt, beschmutzt, erniedrigt, dies!
Verstehst du's, Bruder! Diese süßen Schauder
hab ich dem Vater opfern müssen.
Meinst du, wenn ich an meinem Leib mich freute,
drangen nicht seine Seufzer, drang sein Stöhnen
nicht bis an mein Bette? Eifersüchtig sind
die Toten: und er schickte mir den Haß,
den hohläugigen Haß als Bräutigam.
Ich habe alles, was ich war, hingeben müssen.
Meine Scham hab ich geopfert, die mir süßer
Räubern bin ich gefallen, die mir auch das
letzte Gewand vom Leibe rissen —
Und eine Prophetin bin ich immerfort gewesen
und habe nichts hervorgeholt aus mir
und meinem Leib
als Flüche u. Verzweiflung. —
Was schaust du ängstlich um dich? Sprich zu mir!
Sprich doch! Du zitterst ja am ganzen Leib!

Der Pfleger:
Seid ihr von Sinnen, daß ihr euren Mund
nicht bändigt, wo ein Hauch, ein Laut
uns und das Werk verderben kann.
Sie wartet drinnen.
Ihre Mägde suchen nach dir.
Es ist kein Mann im Haus. Orest!

Orest reckt sich auf, seinen Schauder bezwingend.
Die Tür des Hauses erhellt sich und es erscheint eine Dienerin
mit einer Fackel, hinter ihr die Vertraute.
Elektra ist zurückgesprungen, steht im Dunkel.
Die Vertraute verneigt sich gegen die beiden Fremden,
winkt, ihr hinein zu folgen. Die Dienerin befestigt
die Fackel an der Tür.
Orest u. der Pfleger gehen hinein. Orest schließt einen
Augenblick schwindelnd die Augen, der Pfleger ist
dicht hinter ihm, sie tauschen einen schnellen Blick.
Die Tür schließt sich hinter ihnen.

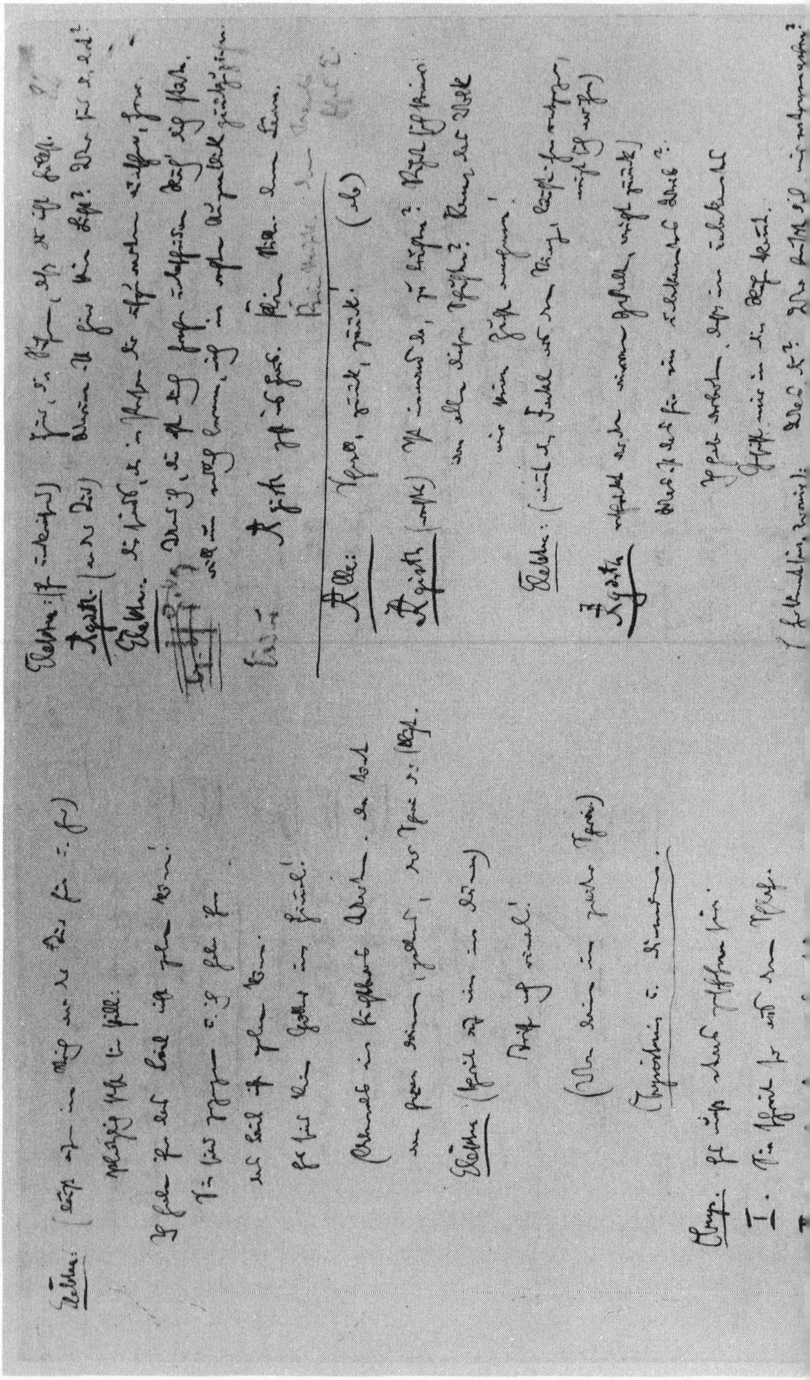

ILLUSTRATION IV *Elektra*, text fragment, ÖNB, fol. 1[v]

III. Alle Türen sind verriegelt.

IV. Es sind Mörder! Es sind Mörder im Haus!

I. (schreit auf) Oh!

Alle: Was ist?

I. Seht ihr denn nicht: dort in der Tür steht einer!

Chrys. Das ist Elektra! das ist ja Elektra!

II. Warum spricht sie denn nicht?

Chrys. Elektra, warum sprichst du denn nicht?

I. Ich will hinaus, die Männer holen. (läuft rechts hinaus)

Chrys. Mach auf doch die Tür, Elektra!

Mehrere: Elektra, laß uns in das Haus!

I. (durch die Hoftür zurückkommend) schreit: Zurück!

(Alle erschrecken)

I. Aegisth! zurück in unsre Kammern! schnell!

Aegisth kommt durch den Hof! Wenn er uns findet und wenn im Hause was geschehen ist, läßt er uns töten.

Äg. ..., ich ... ?
zu leuchten allen an. Wo sind sie denn die fremden Männer, die das von Orest uns melden?

Elektra: Drinnen. Sie fanden eine liebe Wirtin, und sie ergetzen sich mit ihr.

Äg. Und melden also wirklich, daß er gestorben ist, und melden so, daß nicht zu zweifeln ist?

Elektra: O Herr, sie melden es nicht mit Worten bloß, nein, mit leibhaftigen Zeichen, an denen auch kein Zweifel möglich ist.

Äg. Was hast du in der Stimme? Und was ist in dich gefahren, daß du nach dem Mund mir redest? Was taumelst du so hin und her mit deinem Licht?

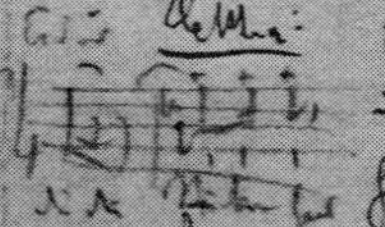

Elektra: Es ist nichts anders, als daß ich endlich klug ward und zu denen mich halte, die die Stärkern sind.

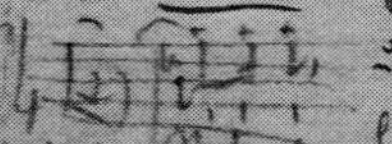

Erlaubst du, daß ich voran dir leuchte?

Äg. Bis zur Tür. Was tanzest du? Gib Obacht.

V Ba M M
V 323 Th

text is organized into two columns on each page. The contents are as follows:

Fol. 2: [Elektra]'Was willst du, fremder Mensch?' through [Elektra] 'Geh' ins Haus, drin hab' ich eine Schwester, die bewahrt sich für Freudenfeste auf!' (Illustration I)

Fol. 2^{v}: [Orestes] 'Elektra, hör mich' (column 2) to [Elektra] 'Orest!!' (column 1). (Illustration II)

Fol. 1: [Elektra] 'Es rührt sich niemand' to [Pfleger] 'Es ist kein Mann im Haus, Orest.' (Illustration III)

Fol. 1^{v}: [Elektra] 'Ich habe ihm das Beil nicht geben können!' to [Elektra] '. . . [ich] will nun endlich lernen, mich im rechten Augenblick zurückzuziehen'.[24] (Illustration IV)

One wonders whether Strauss stopped writing out the text at the end of fol. 1^{v}, or perhaps continued to the end of the play. The continuation—which would have included Hofmannsthal's textual additions for the sisters' duet—could not have comprised more than another folio. Those additions that the playwright sent him are in Garmisch and contain no music annotations by the composer; this final part of the composer's edition of the play is devoid of any textual editing or musical commentary.

Strauss's musical annotations on these two folios differ in three ways from those of the printed edition. In the first place, a much higher percentage of his musical ideas in the two folios find their way to the final score, although Hofmannsthal's additional lines are devoid of any comments. This closer correspondence between musical marginalia and final score is hardly surprising when we recall Strauss's compositional schedule surrounding the scene; he had been pondering the Recognition Scene for some time. In the second place, these folios are more heavily annotated than any scene in the printed text. They surely evince a second

[24] The *Elektra* text is entirely in ink, while his musical annotations are in pencil. There is also a curious '82' pencilled in the upper right-hand corner of fol. 1^{v}. This number, in a foreign hand, was perhaps a catalogue or inventory number used by Bahr-Mildenburg; the number '81' (in the same hand) appears on a blank page of the Bahr-Mildenburg *Elektra* sketchbook.

glossing, and this time he was able to give this scene his full attention. Finally, although there are some important motivic jottings, most of Strauss's musical ideas consist of the assignment of keys that are intended to mirror or even evoke various states of mind. What follows is an overview of the most important musical annotations.

Folio 2–2ᵛ (Illustrations I and II)

As the list of contents shows, these two folios logically divide up the Recognition Scene: the second folio begins with Orestes' entrance and ends with the moment Elektra recognizes him; the first begins with her lyrical 'Es rührt sich niemand' and continues until Orestes' exit up to the end of the scene with Aegisthus. In other words fol. 2 comprises the D minor part I of the Recognition Scene, and fol. 1 covers parts II and III as well as most of the Aegisthus scene. It is clear that Strauss wanted to get all of part I on fol. 2, for—as Illustration II shows—Elektra's last line 'Orest!' is squeezed on to the bottom of the page. Indeed, we cannot rule out the fact that Strauss did not write out the text for parts II and III, etc. before the opening; these two folios are not the same size.

With few exceptions the marginal annotations in fol. 2 consist of various keys jotted into the margins. This folio offers a fine example of Strauss's practice of tonal symbolism, for most of these keys seems to have extra-musical significance directly related to the text beside. On the recto side of the folio (Illustration I) we see the keys E minor, D minor, E major, C sharp minor, A major, and F minor sketched into the margins. On the verso side (Illustration II) we find only E flat major as well as two chords that are spelt out on ledger lines:

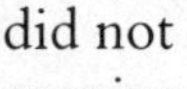

and

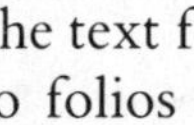

But one should evaluate these keys with caution, for they are, after all, mnemonic devices, not meant to distinguish consistently between referential and structural keys.

In the upper left-hand corner of Illustration I (as Elektra trembles at the sight of the disguised Orestes) Strauss writes 'E minor' and pencils in a theme that undoubtedly is meant to suggest her sense of agitation:

Ex. 5.12 *Elektra* text fragment (ÖNB)

Strauss does not indicate D minor until Orestes' line 'Ich muss hier warten.' He ultimately discarded the notion of opening the scene in E minor and chose to suggest her trembling with a D/C♯ tremolo pedal along with a different, agitated theme. (See Ex. 5.13)

The overwhelming sense of D, suggested by the pedal, prepares us for Orestes' first progression, already seen in the form of a marginal jotting:

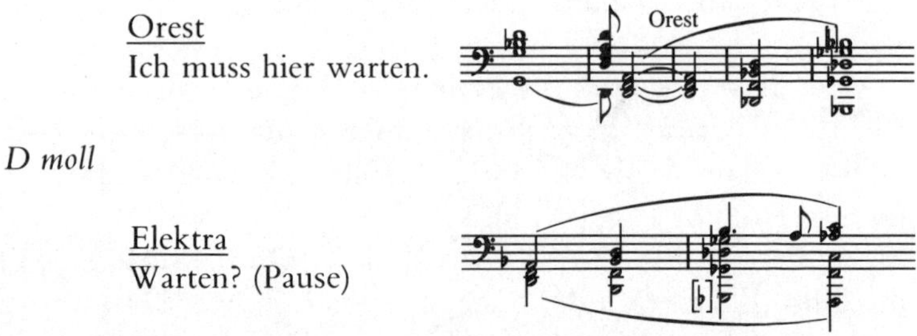
Orest
Ich muss hier warten.
Orest
D moll
Elektra
Warten? (Pause)

Sometimes Strauss's suggestions for key are at a most minute level, such as when Elektra asks, 'Die da drinnen? Du lügst' (see approximately midway down column 1 of Illustration I). In this case the composer indicates 'E major' for 'Die da drinnen?' and 'E minor' for 'Du lügst,' and these ideas find their way into the final score (see Ex. 5.14).

Ex. 5.13 4 bars after reh. 120a

Ex. 5.14 Reh. 125a

It is puzzling that these two chords receive such specific treatment when so many other chordal progressions go unmentioned, but the appearance of arbitrariness is inevitable when examining a composer's *aides mémoires*.

For the disguised Orestes' explanation that he has come to give witness to Orestes' death by his own horses, Strauss suggests a shift to C sharp minor, which remains the key of that narration. Dotted quavers and semiquavers in semitone motion pervade his speech; Elektra's response parallels Orestes' music, although a semitone higher. Strauss's annotations show how he prepares for this shift by moving down a third from C sharp minor to A major.[25] This dominant pivot back to the D-minor tonic coincides with her line 'Herold des Unglücks!', and Strauss not only writes the pitches above each syllable of that line, but writes out the same theme beside it:

	Elektra
A dur	Muss ich dich noch sehen?
	Schleppst du dich hierher in meinen traurigen Winkel?

a h cis e d
Herold des Unglücks

[25] These four marginal annotations evince a certain movement by thirds (outlining V of D) leading to the dominant and then the resolution to the tonic.

D moll Kannst du deine Botschaft nicht austrompeten
dort, wo sie sich freuen!

Illustration I shows how the composer inserts what was originally the last part of her reply as the continuation of her speech.

Compare the play and 'libretto' versions:

Play

Hab' ich dich
noch sehen müssen! hast du dich hierher
in meinen traurigen Winkel schleppen müssen,
Herold des Unglücks! Kannst du deine Botschaft
nicht austrompeten dort, wo sie sich freuen!
Du lebst—und er, der besser war als du
und edler tausendmal und tausendmal
so wichtig, dass er lebte—er ist hin!
Dein Aug' da starrt mich an und seins ist Gallert.
Dein Mund geht auf und zu und seiner ist
mit Erde vollgestopft. Könnt' ich den deinen
mit Flüchen stopfen! geh mir den Augen.

'Libretto'

Muss ich dich
noch sehn? schleppst du dich hierher
in meinen traurigen Winkel,
Herold des Unglücks! Kannst du nicht die Botschaft
austrompeten dort, wo sie sich freu'n!
Dein Aug' da starrt mich an und seins ist Gallert.
Dein Mund geht auf und zu und seiner ist
mit Erde vollgestopft.
Du lebst und er, der besser war als du
und edler, tausendmal und tausendmal so wichtig,
dass er lebte, er ist hin.

He also writes 'Thema 3' as a musical rubric for that insertion. Strauss refers to either themes 1, 2, or 3 in four instances in fols. 1 and 2; these themes appear nowhere in these ÖNB MSS nor do they appear in Strauss's annotated edition of the text. Clearly, then, the composer refers to a missing sketchbook, giving us further evidence of the fluidity between the libretto layer and the sketchbook layer, especially at this point in *Elektra*'s composition.

Indeed, these three themes to which Strauss refers might very well be the ones written on the last page of a bifolio that was torn out of a sketchbook; this bifolio is now at the Bayerische Staatsbibliothek and will be discussed further in the next chapter.[26] The bifolio consists of four pages of preliminary sketches that generally relate to the Recognition Scene. Folio 1 contains four attempts at an Orestes motive (all in D minor); fol 1^{v} contains a twelve-bar Orestes passage in C major; fol. 2 not only has a thematic fragment representing the title role, but a four-bar *Casanova* theme. Fol. 2^{v} presents the three themes that relate mostly to the first part of the Recognition Scene.

The themes on all four pages are in the same ink and pen point, which would date them around the time Strauss was thinking about *Casanova*, thus between early March and late May 1906.[27] The three themes on fol. 2^{v} are shown in Ex. 5.15.

These three themes were originally unlabelled and not numbered; the numbers '1' and '2', as well as the words 'Lass den Orest', 'anders', 'Allegro Hör mich an! Orestes lebt' are all in pencil.[28] Moreover, theme 3—the only one not labelled—is entirely in pencil and probably stems from a later date, perhaps from the time of the ÖNB folios. With its dotted quavers descending by semitone, it is clearly a

[26] The sketchbook from which this fragment was torn is evidently in private hands; the owner seems to tear out a bifolio every now and then and put it up for sale. Bifolios that directly correspond to this one have been sold by Stargardt in Marburg and Kronenberg in Basle.

[27] Strauss had toyed with the idea of composing an opera (*Christines Heimreise*) based on the adventures of Casanova before settling on the *Elektra* project in June 1906.

[28] Throughout Strauss's career, the composer seems to have written down promising themes (or fragments) in ink, while writing preliminary and continuity sketches in pencil. These pencilled labels clearly postdate the themes.

Ex. 5.15 Munich fragment, fol. 2v

prototype to the final version mentioned above with regard to Orestes' narration. Strauss refers to 'Thema 1' (see Illustration I) as Orestes sings 'Lass den Orest' and 'Allegro Thema 2' (see Illustration II) as Orestes declares to his sister that Orestes indeed lives.

At the bottom of fol. 2v (Illustration II, column 2) we see Strauss's musical answer to Elektra's question, 'Wer bist du?':

the short thematic fragment representing Orestes.[29] The composer had used this fragment in a similarly subliminal way in the Klytämnestra scene, just before Elektra asks, 'Lässt du den Bruder nicht nach Hause, Mutter?' Perhaps for that reason he ultimately decided not to repeat that process in the Recognition Scene.

Folio 1–1ᵛ (Illustrations III and IV)

Although fewer in number, the cogent musical ideas in the margins of fol. 1 (Illustration III) exemplify the composer's firm grasp of the text. The long, sinuous marginal theme that winds its way downward (midway down col. 1), suggesting how her hair has gone from the height of beauty to the nadir of ugliness, is practially identical to the theme we hear in the basset horn at reh. 162a, when Elektra says, 'Dies Haar versträhnt, beschmutzt, erniedrigt.'

Just below Strauss writes: 'E dur, die | süssen Schauder.' At first glance, it seems as if he refers directly to that line in the text (see 7 after reh. 166a): 'Diese süssen Schauder hab' ich dem Vater opfern müssen.' But the fact that he uses a definite article ('the') rather than the demonstrative pronoun ('these') of the text suggests that E major has broader purpose, namely to establish the erotic atmosphere suggested by 'sweet shivers'. Illustration III shows how Strauss circumscribes a latter portion ('Ich habe alles, was ich war . . .') of Elektra's long monologue and moves it up a number of lines earlier in order that it may precede the lines, 'Diese süssen Schauder [etc.].'[30]

E major—the key of Eros in *Elektra* and most of Strauss's later works—evokes the erotic imagery implicit in Hofmannsthal's text. The composer transfers that musical mood

[29] The text for Elektra's question is identical with the play. For the printed libretto the line was changed to 'Wer bist denn du?'

[30] Strauss actually cut part of the text circled in pencil. More specifically the lines: '. . . so wie unter Räuber bin ich gefallen, die mir auch das letzte Gewand vom Leibe rissen—'.

to the lines preceding her actual lines 'Diese süssen Schauder', etc. In the final score those lines are (see reh. 163a ff):

All that I was, I have had to surrender. I sacrificed my shame, the shame which is sweeter than all, which like the silvery haze around the moon envelops every woman and which turns infamy away from her and her soul.

There is another theme at the bottom of this folio, a theme articulated by two basic components: the rising triplet figure associated with Elektra's royal lineage and dotted semitone gestures. Strauss did not use this theme, therefore it is difficult to understand how he wanted to use it, although it seems probable that the triplet figure relates to Elektra as she calls herself a prophet ('So bin ich eine Prophetin immerfort gewesen'); indeed Strauss underlines the word *Prophetin* (six lines from the bottom of Illustration III). Instead of using the triplet figure, he continues with the motive of Elektra's hatred that appeared four bars before (see after reh. 169a): '[He sent me . . .] hollow-eyed hatred as a bridegroom.' The two motives are, in fact, not so different, for intervallically they are nearly identical.

Ex. 5.16

Strauss, however, did use the semitone idea—with some changes—to suggest Elektra's despair (see reh. 171a): 'I have been a prophetess and have called forth nothing from me and my body except curses and despair.'

Midway down column two of fol. 1, as Orestes' Tutor enters, Strauss recalls the second theme 'No. 2 | D moll Thema. . . .' from the sketchbook fragment (see Ex. 5.15). The important gesture here is that of the two semiquavers and a quaver in descending and ascending fourths, which has suggested the atonement for Agamemnon's murder throughout the opera, indeed it plays the most prominent role in the final bars (Ex. 5.17).

Ex. 5.17 3 bars after reh. 262a

Although there are no more annotations for the Recognition Scene, there are a couple of glosses that pertain to Elektra's brief dialogue with Aegisthus. The first one, at the bottom of fol. 1[v] (col. 2) [see Illustration IV] offers us the tonal underpinnings of this scene in a nutshell:

Es dur Elektra: Es ist nichts anderes, als dass ich endlich klug ward
und zu denen mich halte, die die Stärkern sind.
Erlaubst du, dass ich voran dir leuchte?

Ägisth: Bis zur Tür. Was tanzest du? Gib Obacht.

We recall that Strauss uses E flat major—the key of the weaker, compliant Chrysothemis—to characterize Elektra's mock ingratiation to her stepfather. But Strauss also uses F major—the jocular key of *Till Eulenspiegel*—to characterize the weak, effeminate Aegisthus. He seeks to strengthen that sense of weakness by ironically connecting the F-major motive with Elektra's lines: 'die die Stärkern sind'. At the top of column 2 we see Strauss's clear-cut musico-dramatic ideas about the ending of this scene. He not only intends to end it with the obsequious key of E flat, but wishes to draw our attention to its relationship with E flat minor—the key of Orestes' supposed death, and he does it by recalling the four-note theme [musical notation] now transposed to the major.

Moreover, Strauss's musical details concerning Aegisthus' exit are quite specific:

Es dur Ägisth geht ins Haus. *Kleine Stille, dann Lärm.*
Keine Musik, dann Tremolo
sofort E [dur]

He envisions two important, and almost simultaneous, musical juxtapositions as Aegisthus goes into the house to meet his death: that of silence and sound, and that of E flat and E major (Ex. 5.18).

In the former, a short, nervous pause is interrupted by a quiet, sustained E, first in the bass line, which moves upward by glissando in the harp to a tense, high-pitched tremolo on E hovering over the scene in the first violins. The use of glissando, as well as a hovering tremolo, to create an atmosphere of tension before a murder foreshadows the upward glissando ending on a sustained tremolo B in Act III, scene 2 of *Wozzeck* shortly before Franz kills Marie.[31]

But the juxtaposition of E flat major and E major as Elektra utters her final line, '. . . now I will finally learn to withdraw at the right moment,' is equally important to Strauss's dramatic aim. Elektra's act of obsequiousness fades

[31] See reh. 85 (Act III) of *Wozzeck*.

Ex. 5.18

d.bn.
hp.1
glissando
vn. 1
d.b.
Schnell. (Allegro assai)
b.cl.
1
3 bn.
2,3
d.bn.
1,3
4 hn. in F
2,4
1,2
3 tbn.
3
Schnell. (Allegro assai)
vn. 1,2
desks 1,2
desks vc. 3,4
desks 5,6
d.b.
cresc.

Ex. 518 cont.

213a
M. ♩=152
b.cl.
1
3 bn.
2,3
d.bn.
a 2
1,2
3 tpt.
in C
3
b.tpt.
in C
1,2
3 tbn.
3
d.b.tbn.
timp.
213a
(schreiend)
(Aegisth erscheint an einem kleinen Fenster, reißt den Vorhang weg.)
Aegisth
Helft! Mör - - - - - der!
M. ♩=152
1,2
vn.
3
va.tutti
desks
1,2
desks
vc.
3,4
desks
5,6
d.b.

as quickly as its representative E flat, and Strauss creates a sudden but quiet shift up a semitone. The choice of E (the key of bacchic jubilation) foreshadows Chrysothemis' E-major entrance: 'Es ist der Bruder drin im Haus!' (see 5 after reh. 220a).

The musical annotations in the ÖNB fragment differ significantly in type from those in the RSA printed text. In the former we find a predominance of tonal glossings and these annotations more accurately relate to the final score. When examining this document, it is important to keep in mind Strauss's compositional chronology. Most of Strauss's musical jottings in the 1904 edition date from the time of his early reading of the play—more or less simultaneous with most of his cuts and rearrangements of text—and perhaps later on, while he was sketching the opera up to the Recognition Scene. This involvement can be summarized as follows:

1. Autumn 1905? until late spring 1906: Strauss's pre-sketch planning and the first layer of musical glossings of the text.
2. June 1906 to early October 1907: an additional layer of annotations that may have resulted from preliminary sketching of the opera.

We can pinpoint Strauss's activity with the ÖNB document more narrowly:

1. *c.* 21 June 1908: Strauss writes out the Recognition Scene up to Aegisthus' exit by hand and begins glossing the text. The Recognition Scene is fully sketched by *c.*6 July 1908.
2. Strauss either added the brief annotations pertaining to Aegisthus' scene within the above time frame or shortly thereafter.

As the above timetable suggests, Strauss sketched out the Recognition Scene in a remarkably short period of time: roughly two weeks. Thus, marginal jottings and work in the sketchbooks could not have been that far apart; they might even have been simultaneous. But it is hardly surprising that the composer could have worked so rapidly when we remember that he had probably been thinking about that scene, off and on, for some ten months.

Taken as a whole, the annotations in both sources reveal much about Strauss's early thought with regard to *Elektra*. Judging by his cuts and rearrangements of text, as well as early layers of musical annotations in the margins, we see a composer who has a remarkably quick and solid grasp of the musico-dramatic possibilities inherent in Hofmannsthal's play. Strauss's practical, theatrical instincts as opposed to Hofmannsthal's, at times, less practical aims complemented each other quite well. These two contrasting views, one of a pragmatic man of the theatre and the other of a refined poet, are apparent in the earliest *Elektra* letters, and they defined a relationship that would continue for another two decades.

We also find solid evidence of Strauss's tonal symbolism: the use of various representational keys. His marginal comments show how broad or specific these references could be. Furthermore, there are annotations that illustrate how early Strauss envisioned various orchestral timbres: specific sound qualities that were stimulated by certain situations or moments in the drama. Finally, although the evolution of a network of themes is not obvious, we none the less see the origin of certain important motives to be expanded, along with others, in the next layer: the preliminary sketchbooks, which are a major focus of the remainder of this study.

6 *The* Elektra *Sketches*

The Richard-Strauss-Archiv in Garmisch houses the largest single collection of Strauss's sketches, some 144 sketchbooks in all. These sketches span approximately from the time of *Till Eulenspiegel* up until the last year of his life, and they offer the scholar a fascinating cross-section of Strauss's compositional methods. Moreover, they provide an important frame of reference for the *Elektra* sketches. Regrettably, it is impossible to determine what part of the entire corpus of Strauss sketches the Garmisch collection represents. There might well be just as many, if not more, sketchbooks in private hands, for once a work was completed the sketchbooks were usually of little value to the composer, and he gave them to friends and acquaintances throughout his life. Fortunately some of the sketchbooks that had been in private hands are now in various libraries and archives throughout the world.

Over a decade ago the Garmisch sketchbooks were catalogued, in a rough chronological order, by Franz Trenner.[1] Since Strauss dated few of his sketches, Trenner occasionally had to make some arbitrary decisions concerning dating, for many sketchbooks contain material relating to more than one work. Space permitting, Strauss would sometimes fill empty pages of an older sketchbook. One such sketchbook (Tr. 19), for example, contains material as early as *Elektra* and as late as *Die ägyptische Helena*. Thus Trenner determined the catalogue order by the date of the earliest musical material. Besides giving a physical description of each sketchbook, he also attempted to compile an inventory

[1] Franz Trenner, ed., *Die Skizzenbücher von Richard Strauss aus dem Richard-Strauss-Archiv in Garmisch*, Veröffentlichungen der Richard-Strauss-Gesellschaft, München, vol. i (Tutzing, 1977).

of each one, but the lists of contents are often incomplete: some pages are listed in detail, while others go unmentioned. But this criticism is certainly small compared to the immense contribution that his catalogue has made for Strauss research; it has opened up a body of manuscripts that had been only partially known.

Strauss mentions three types of sketchbooks in his writings and other sources: *Rohskizzen*, *Reinschriftskizzen*, and *Klavierskizzen* (preliminary sketches, fair sketches, and Particell). Although not consistent early on, the preliminary sketchbooks are typically small, commercially-bound manuscript books measuring approximately 12.5 × 16.5 cm. before 1912 and 8 × 13 cm. thereafter. These little books fitted easily in his coat pocket and allowed him to sketch out ideas almost anywhere. We find two distinct layers in these preliminary sketches: first, motivic fragments jotted down as they occurred to the composer, sometimes briefly worked out (these fragments may be found in a sketchbook consisting solely of these or interspersed among continuity drafts); second, early attempts at continuity sketching, which might consist of various layers in a given preliminary sketchbook.

The size of a fair sketchbook is usually slightly larger, measuring approximately 13 × 18 cm. These sketches are well-developed continuity drafts, devoid of numerous scratch-outs and erasures, and typically comprise a single compositional layer per book. Both preliminary and fair sketchbooks are written mostly in pencil. Strauss uses pen more to annotate than to compose, although sometimes a single theme or motive is written in ink. Furthermore, in both types of sketchbooks, Strauss often writes the appropriate text, in ink, on the inside front and back covers. The typical Particell consists of an oblong single volume, for each act, consisting of bound single folios, measuring approximately 27 × 35 cm. and averaging three to four systems per page.

Strauss often refers to the Particell as a *Klavierskizze*, but it should not be confused with a piano-vocal score. Although it is often in that format, Strauss sometimes opts for a short-score arrangement with as many as four staves for the orchestral part, especially when the orchestral texture becomes thicker. The term *Klavierskizze* is also misleading for the fact that one finds little evidence of real sketching in such a source; there is rarely any significant departure from the final product. Strauss writes out the Particell in ink, using pencil for annotations: usually orchestrational suggestions or calculations of how many bars per system will be allotted in the orchestral score. The sparsity of the instrumentational mnemonic devices surely indicates how early Strauss envisioned orchestral timbre: in some instances simultaneous with the earliest musical ideas. We recall from the previous chapter such suggestions as 'winds and muted trumpet', 'horns', 'at first tubas', and 'timpani' in the margins of Strauss's *Elektra* text.

The fair sketches and Particell need little further general description. Generally speaking, the only significant changes in a fair sketchbook relate to a change in the vocal part, or perhaps a block of music transposed to a different key. In this sense the one surviving *Elektra* fair sketchbook is exemplary. The Particell, as mentioned before, contains few anomalies at all. Preliminary sketchbooks, on the other hand, are more complicated and the most interesting and require further commentary.

Preliminary Sketchbooks: Thematic Fragments and Continuity Sketches

The first layer of composition in preliminary sketchbooks (i.e., the search for a promising theme or motive) was fundamentally important to Strauss. The preceding chapter has already illustrated the close relationship between this layer and the marginal annotations in Strauss's *Elektra* text, where Strauss, too, jots down themes as well as establishes certain keys. Manipulating themes posed few problems for the composer, whose technique could sometimes be his own worst enemy. He had little difficulty in weaving the thematic fabric for an opera; the problem lay in choosing the proper threads. Strauss explained the problem in his essay, 'On Inspiration in Music', where he drew a distinction between inspiration and industry. Inspiration, he wrote, is the 'invention of a motive', whereas industry consists of motivic expansion.[2] The composer could expand upon a theme on almost any occasion, but the invention of a promising theme, according to Strauss, required a special frame of mind. '[Themes originate] spontaneously out of situations and words,' he once explained to Stefan Zweig.[3]

Thus, in preliminary sketchbooks, Strauss's first compositional task was to compose themes or motives largely in response to dramatic situations. Such themes appear almost anywhere in the sketchbooks: isolated on a single page, grouped among related themes, or even on a page of unrelated material. Example 6.1 illustrates a preliminary sketchbook page of related motives for *Elektra* taken from Tr. 17 (?1906–18), one of three *Elektra* sketchbooks in Garmisch. Many pages of Tr. 17 contain nothing but motivic labels with corresponding music; fol. 1 of this sketchbook is exemplary.

At the top of fol. 1, Strauss jots down 'das Schicksal der Atriden' ('the fate of the house of Atreus') with a corresponding theme. On the right-hand side of the next system appears the 'Agamemnon' motive, which assumes many guises throughout the work.[4] In the third system Strauss precedes 'Elektras Hass!' with a variant of 'das Schicksal der Atriden'.[5] Significantly, these early sketches for *Elektra* are not unlike many early sketches for Strauss's symphonic

[2] Richard Strauss, 'On Inspiration in Music', in *Recollections and Reflections*, ed. Willi Schuh, trans. L. J. Lawrence (London, 1953), 114, 115.

[3] Stefan Zweig, *The World of Yesterday* (Lincoln, Nebraska, 1964), 369.

[4] In this sense Agamemnon is much like Keikobad in *Die Frau ohne Schatten*. Neither character makes an appearance on stage; both remain omnipresent figures who dwell in the orchestra.

[5] In the third system Strauss uses the synonym 'Geschick' rather than 'Schicksal'.

Ex. 6.1 Tr. 17, fol. 1

poems, which also contain motivic labels with corresponding music.

One finds such 'captions' for musical fragments in other *Elektra* sketchbooks as well. A number of pages of Tr. 18, another preliminary sketchbook, contain only dramatic images or stage directions with underlying music, such as 'Klytämnestra appears', 'Grieving over the death of Orestes', 'Elektra entreats Chrysothemis'. Similarly, a sketchbook

(Tr. 3 [?1894–7]) containing material relating to *Don Quixote*, *Till Eulenspiegel*, and *Also Sprach Zarathustra* contains narrative images with corresponding music, such as 'Don Quixote's informed answer', 'Sighs at Dulcinea'. Similarities between symphonic and operatic sketches at this preliminary stage are not surprising, for at this level of composition—even in opera—Strauss's orientation is primarily orchestral. In *Elektra*, the earliest continuity sketches evince Strauss's reliance on the orchestra as the fundamental expressive vehicle.[6]

On fol. 14 of Tr. 18, Strauss composes a five-bar theme headed 'Chrysot[hemis]' (see Ex. 6.2). Although Strauss does not use it specifically as a Chrysothemis motive, it none the less provides essential motivic and harmonic material for a significant portion of a monologue, more precisely, 'Kinder will ich haben' (4 after reh. 84). Indeed, immediately thereafter (on fol. 14^v) Strauss proceeds to work out a twenty-two-bar sketch for that passage (Ex. 6.3).

Ex. 6.2 Tr. 18, fol. 14

The theme ('Lebhaft') is textless, although the composer admittedly could have memorized that part of the libretto. But the evidence that Strauss was not setting text at this stage lies in the close relationship between Examples 6.2 and 6.3—between thematic fragment and the twenty-two-bar draft that expands upon it. That relationship suggests that 'Kinder will ich haben' is more an outgrowth of a thematic rendering of the character Chrysothemis than a lyrical response to specific lines of text.

[6] See Bryan Gilliam, 'Strauss's Preliminary Opera Sketches: Thematic Fragments and Symphonic Continuity', *19th-Century Music*, 9 (1986), 176–88.

Ex. 6.3 Tr. 18, fol. 14^{v}

The most fundamental relationship between Examples 6.2 and 6.3 is that both are set in E flat major, the key representing Chrysothemis. We know from earlier chapters that Strauss's choice of E flat stems, in part, from its functional and programmatic relationship to A flat major, the key of the so-called childhood motive, first appearing in Elektra's monologue just after she sings, 'zeig dich deinem Kind!' (see 9 after reh. 45). The predominant ♩‿♫♩ figure in this motive is related to that persistent rhythmic gesture in Example 6.2; in Example 6.3 the same figure is transformed into a triple-metre 𝅗𝅥 ♫. Finally, and most important, Strauss borrows the harmonic pattern underlying 'Chryso-t[hemis]', using it, with little variation, at bars 9 ff of Example 6.3, repeating the pattern at bars 15 ff.

A substantial continuity sketch for Chrysothemis' opening monologue ('Ich hab's wie Feuer in der Brust') begins on the next folio of Tr. 18. On the third folio of this continuity draft (see Ex. 6.4) we see the passage corresponding to 'Lebhaft',

Ex. 6.4 Tr. 18, fol. 17v

where Strauss makes considerable alterations in the continuity sketch. In this later layer the composer adds a vocal part differing slightly from the final version (see bars 4 ff. and bar 16). There are other significant modifications as well. Strauss extends the 𝅗𝅥 | ♩ 𝅗𝅥 | ♩ sequential chain in Example 6.4 and expands the end of that phrase at bar 15. Another difference between Examples 6.3 and 6.4 is the change in melody and harmony in the last four bars. In the former sketch, the four bars represent a point of termination; the fragment simply stops at that point. In the latter sketch, these bars have a new context; they are part of a continuum.

In sum, if we recall Ex. 5.2 from the preceding chapter—where Strauss establishes E flat major as Chrysothemis' key in the margin of the text—we see a good example of the composer conceiving a harmonic image that anticipates a short theme as seen in Ex. 6.2, which in turn provides essential material for a more extended, textless passage. Ex. 6.4 not only shows that, in this instance, the vocal part was inserted at a later stage, but moreover that it is secondary to the orchestral line, where a clear sense of periodicity is established. The soprano, on the other hand, begins with an awkward setting of the word 'Kinder', giving undue stress to an unaccented syllable. By the fourth bar of the final version, the voice does little more than elaborate a sustained B♭ for five bars. Thereafter it doubles the orchestra.

Overview of *Elektra* Sketches

There are five sketchbooks with material relating to *Elektra*, as well as some loose folios.[7]

1. Preliminary sketchbook, Tr. 17 (RSA)
2. Preliminary sketchbook, Tr. 18 (RSA)
3. Preliminary sketchbook, Tr. 19 (RSA)
4. Preliminary sketchbook (Theatersammlung, ÖNB: henceforth, Vienna sketchbook)
5. Preliminary sketches: 3 separate bifolios (BSt: henceforth, Munich fragment; the other two now in private hands)
6. Fair sketch ['*Elektra* Reinschrift'] (Musashino College of Music, Tokyo: henceforth, Tokyo sketchbook)

Taken together these sketches represent only a fraction of the whole. Indeed, to say that there are five *Elektra* sketchbooks

[7] See Appendix II for a full inventory and description of the *Elektra* sketchbooks.

is a bit misleading, for Tr. 19 contains only a handful of folios pertaining to *Elektra* and more than half of the pages of the Vienna sketchbook are blank. If we compare these *Elektra* sources to those relating to Strauss's later *Daphne* we can better appreciate the situation.

The source situation with respect to *Daphne* is in itself far from ideal; there are important gaps in these sketches as well. Yet, as incomplete as they may be, they still comprise some thirteen sketchbooks: eight *Rohskizzen* and five *Reinschrift-skizzen*.[8] Extant sketchbooks for the earlier operas are significantly sparser than the later ones: *Salome* is no better than *Elektra*, and the situation with *Guntram* and *Feuersnot* is even worse. Obviously Strauss had the opportunity to give away earlier ones over a longer span of time.

Figure 6.1 offers us a bird's-eye view of *Elektra* material contained in most of the sketchbooks. It does not include Tr. 19, which contains only a handful of *Elektra* thematic fragments that mostly relate to scene 6.

As Fig. 6.1 indicates, a remarkable amount of *Elektra* (most of scene 5 and all of scene 6) is not represented by the surviving sketchbooks, preliminary or fair. The lack of material relating to scene 6 (the Recognition Scene) is especially regrettable. We recall Strauss's creative impasse with the Recognition Scene, in late September or early October 1907. A significant portion of sketches relating to that scene, especially preliminary ones, would help us better understand Strauss's problems as he tried to grapple with Orestes' entrance and recognition. The *Elektra* fragments suggest that such a sketchbook survives, but is in private hands.

Most of the preliminary sketches pertain to the first half of the opera, but even there we find important gaps: most of Elektra's monologue, the opening of her first scene with Chrysothemis, and about a third of the Klytämnestra scene. Beyond that scene, only preliminary sketches relating to the

[8] See Gilliam, 'Richard Strauss's Daphne: Opera and Symphonic Continuity', Ph.D. Diss. (Harvard University, 1984).

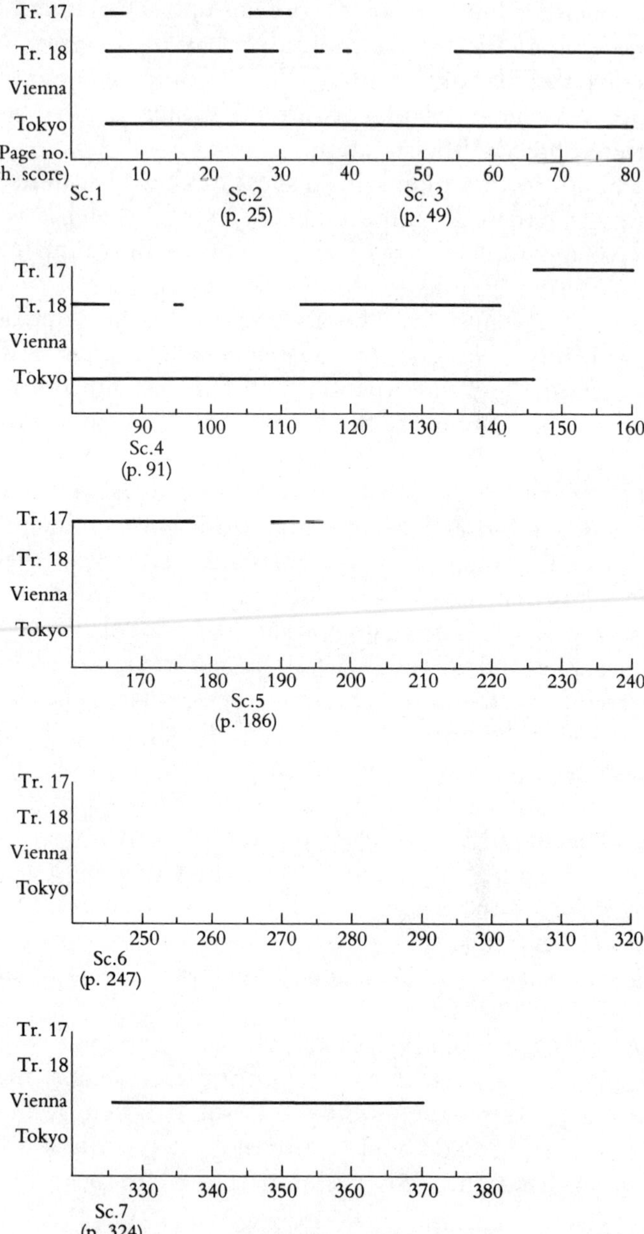

FIG. 6.1 Summary of the *Elektra* sketches

final scene can be found in any significant amount. The sole surviving fair sketchbook begins with the opening bars, continues through scenes 2 and 3, and drops off approximately midway through the Klytämnestra scene. Judging from the *Daphne* fair sketches, which all basically comprise a single, continuous layer, there are probably no more than three or four missing *Elektra* fair sketchbooks; it is impossible to determine the number of missing preliminary sketchbooks.

Dating the *Elektra* Sketches

Only in rare instances, such as in *Salome*, did Strauss date his sketches. The composer typically dated the last page of a Particell and the first and last pages of an orchestral score, although, with *Elektra*, Strauss does not even date the Particell. Without dates how does one properly order these few surviving *Elektra* sketches? All the available evidence, as sparse as it may be, indicates that Strauss sketched *Elektra* scene by scene, in correct dramaturgical order. The only deviation from that methodical approach was when he stopped sketching the Recognition Scene and began orchestrating the opening of the opera in early October 1907 (see Table 3.2). But even then he never sketched a scene out of sequence, but rather interrupted his sketching in order to orchestrate. This scene-by-scene approach is not unusual for Strauss; he reveals his preference for this method in a letter (4 May 1909) to Hofmannsthal during the early stages of *Der Rosenkavalier*:

> The final scene [of *Der Rosenkavalier* Act I] is magnificent: I've already done a bit of experimenting with it today. I wish I'd got there already. But since, for the sake of symphonic unity, I must compose the music from the beginning to the end I'll just have to be patient.[9]

[9] Letter of 4 May 1909 in *Correspondence*, 30.

The *Salome* sketches and those of other operas reinforce Strauss's admission as well.

The picture of *Elektra*'s compositional chronology is far from detailed; Strauss makes no mention of the Particell (*Klavierskizze*) until he is working on the penultimate scene in summer 1908. Thus the last two scenes of the opera offer the most detail concerning Strauss's composing *Elektra*. Table 3.2 shows that Strauss began sketching the Recognition Scene on 21 June 1908, finished sketching that scene around 6 July, finished it in Particell a week later, and began orchestrating it on the next day. Likewise, Strauss finished sketching the opera around 20 August 1908, finished the Particell on 11 September, and finished the score eleven days later. Therefore, work in the Vienna sketchbook probably spans the first few weeks of August 1908, and possibly even the end of July.

The other preliminary sketches are more problematic, for all that we know of Strauss's sketching the first four scenes of the opera is that he began work on scene 1 in June 1906 and finished scene 2 by 16 July. Thus, although most of Tr. 18 should date from the summer of 1906, we cannot precisely date the sketches for scene 4 (the second third of that scene) contained in the sketchbook. Likewise only part of Tr. 17 can be accounted for in an accurate chronology. The small portion of fragmentary sketches relating to the opening of scene 2 and the slightly larger ones pertaining to the beginning of scene 5 stem from June 1906 and September 1907, respectively. There are also many pages of individual sketches where Strauss has jotted down—and occasionally has worked out—various thematic fragments that, for the most part, predate Tr. 18. Some of these Tr. 17 sketches may represent Strauss's earliest ideas for the opera. But the largest block of sketches in Tr. 17 concerns the final third of that undated scene 4, which goes beyond the latest sketch of Tr. 18. In short, given the significant amount of overlap between Tr. 17 and 18, it is difficult to prise these two sketchbooks apart when trying to establish a chronological order.

The sketchbook fragments (BSt, Tr. 19, etc.) present fewer problems, for—with one small exception—they all relate either to the Recognition Scene of the entrance of Aegisthus, which was composed between 21 June and early July 1908. But dating becomes more complex when we consider the fair sketches and Particell. Beyond the level of preliminary sketches specific dates become more difficult to pin down. For example, when Strauss reported (16 July 1906) to his friend Willi Levin that he had finished the first two scenes, did he mean that he had just completed the preliminary sketches, fair sketches, or had he even got as far as the Particell? We know that, for the last two scenes, Strauss went from sketch to Particell to orchestral score with each scene. But can we assume that Strauss would exhaust each layer of composition before moving on to the next scene? It hardly seems likely; we already know that he sketched scenes 1 to 5 before orchestrating.

The Tokyo fair sketchbook puts the problem into sharper focus. In the preliminary sketchbooks Strauss establishes the fundamental motivic material, which is in turn expanded into blocks or stretches of continuity sketches—often in multiple layers. In the fair sketchbook he connects these various blocks in one continuous layer. But when did Strauss compose the fair sketches contained in the Tokyo sketchbook? Did he compose them scene by scene, or did he wait until he had finished a number of them as preliminary sketches? The paucity of sources makes definitively answering these questions a difficult, perhaps impossible, task.

The following arrangement of the *Elektra* sketches is admittedly hypothetical. Yet, despite these difficulties, the ordering of sources below makes the most sense, and the brief discussion of each source which follows will help explain why.

1. Tr. 17: Spring 1906 and possibly until early September 1907
2. Tr. 18: Summer 1906 (part of this sketchbook probably later [spring 1907?])

3. Tokyo sketchbook: Second half of July 1906 to no later than September 1907
4. Sketchbook fragments (BSt, Tr. 19, and private MSS): 21 June to *c.*6 July 1908
5. Vienna sketchbook: approx. late July to approx. 20 August 1908

Sketchbook Tr. 17

Tr. 17 contains a wide-ranging number of works dating from 1906 to 1918. In his chronological catalogue Trenner decided to order such sketchbooks according to the earliest sketches contained therein, and, to a certain extent, the above table follows Trenner's logic. In Tr. 17 there are sketches to Op. 56 No. 6 ('Die heiligen drei Könige aus Morgenland'), Op. 69 No. 3 ('Einerlei'), *Der Rosenkavalier*, *Deutsche Motette*, *Eine Alpensinfonie*, and some unidentified works. The preliminary sketches to *Elektra* contain both blocks of continuity sketches as well as non-continuous thematic fragments. Tr. 17 stands apart from the others in that it contains so much of the latter: numerous pages of sketches for individual themes and motives.

Indeed, on the inside cover Strauss writes, in pencil and in large script, 'Elektrathemen'. Curiously, he makes no mention of the lengthy continuity sketch for scene 4: perhaps the label predates it, or perhaps—as we shall see—it was because he was dissatisfied with it. (In smaller script and in ink—and probably later—the composer lists more recent works contained in the book.[10]) Much of Tr. 17 illustrates Strauss's search for motivic ideas relating to characters, important moments in the drama, or specific actions. More than any other *Elektra* sketchbook, Tr. 17 shows the remarkable

[10] 'Die heiligen drei Könige', 'Reinheit' [*Deutsche Motette*?], 'Heroisches Thema' [*Eine Alpensinfonie*], and 'O du liebes Einerlei'. Below this list we find house and garden plans for the new villa in Garmisch, which was begun in April 1907 and completed in early June 1908. On the back inside cover of Tr. 17 the composer's wife has written out the text for the *Deutsche Motette*. The text contains many musical annotations by Strauss.

similarities between opera and tone poem at this early stage of creativity. Stimulated by actions and situations, Strauss creates motives and themes destined for further expansion.

On folio 5[v], for example, we see three different depictions of Elektra (see Ex. 6.5):

Ex. 6.5 Tr. 17, fol. 5[v]

Thus Elektra appears as: a proud princess, crouched in grief, and an aggressive avenger. We first see the Elektra-as-princess theme (in the same B-flat-major setting) in scene 1, when the fifth servant reminds the others who Elektra once was. The other two Elektra themes are both early manifestations of Elektra's hatred, but have not yet been fused with the familiar Elektra chord . As they now stand, these latter two themes are essentially diminutions of the first Elektra theme, as if 'Elektra's hatred' is a distortion of the once proud Elektra.

In two try-outs (fols. 1[v] and 2) for the opening bars of the opera, the importance that Strauss placed on the 'schmerz gebeugt' fragment becomes readily apparent (see Ex. 6.6). Both examples share the idea of opening the work with the powerful Agamemnon motive; they differ in the placement of Elektra's 'schmerz gebeugt' theme. At first Strauss

Ex. 6.6 Tr. 17, fols. 1v and 2

combines it with the Agamemnon motive; in layer two these two themes are separated a bit. A comparison of these two themes to the next surviving layer (Tr. 18) shows that Strauss decided to delay any Elektra theme until the moment in which she rushes in and out near the outset of scene 1 (Ex. 6.7). The only significant difference between the ideas shown in Ex. 6.7 and the final version is the guise of the Elektra theme, which is now combined with the so-called Elektra chord.

The sketchbook contains many other thematic fragments relating to various characters and situations. Towards the beginning of the sketchbook, some are intended as material for Elektra's opening monologue, which is, of course, an important exposition for many motives. There, Strauss composes themes for Klytämnestra, Aegisthus, Orestes, and Agamemnon; he depicts Elektra cowering before Klytäm-

Ex. 6.7 Tr. 18, fols. 2^v and 3

nestra, or filled with pain and grief.[11] He also jots down particular tonalities he might use to symbolize certain characters: D minor for Agamemnon (fol. 3^v), A minor and C minor to depict Elektra (fol. 3^v), and E major to evoke Elektra's victory dance (fol. 1^v). The fact that Strauss wrote 'Elektrathemen' so prominently at the top of the inside cover, not mentioning the continuity sketch, surely illustrates the importance that Strauss put on these themes.

[11] See, e.g., fols. 3–7 in Tr. 17.

The only major continuity sketch in Tr. 17 involves roughly the final third of the Klytämnestra scene. The sketch is fairly long (35 pages in all) and begins shortly after Elektra dares mention her brother to Klytämnestra ([Elektra:] 'Wie?' [Klytämnestra:] 'Es heisst er stammelt.') The opening of this passage is only some forty-five bars beyond the point where the Tr. 18 sketch for scene 4 leaves off—[Elektra:] 'An jedem Ort zu jeder Stunde des Tags und der Nacht.' The scene 4 sketches in both Tr. 17 and 18 support Strauss's admission that the Klytämnestra scene was the most difficult for him to compose; the anecdote that Strauss had to compose the scene two or three times appears in various works.[12] Even in the Tokyo *Reinschrift* this scene is far from finalized. Here, as well as in Tr. 18, the composer seems to have problems establishing a definitive harmonic and motivic shape for the scene, not to mention problems with the vocal line. In Tr. 17 things become especially thorny after the opening of the third part of scene 4, which is, as we recall, Elektra's powerful and culminating response to her mother's various queries about how she might end her dreams ('Was bluten muss? Dein eigenes Genick, wenn dich der Jäger abgefangen hat!').

By the next line ('Ich hör ihn durch die Zimmern gehn . . .') Strauss no longer sets text melodically, but opts for a purely rhythmic setting of the text below the empty vocal staff and, thus, concentrates more on the orchestral material (Ex. 6.8).

Ex. 6.8 Tr. 17, fol. 29v

[12] See William Mann, *Richard Strauss: A Critical Study of the Operas* (London, 1964), 71; and Max Steinitzer, *Richard Strauss* (Stuttgart, 1927), 198.

Occasionally we find no rhythmic setting for the text at all.

As Strauss reaches the high point of Elektra's confrontation ('Da steh ich vor dir, und nun liest du mit starrem Aug' das ungeheure Wort . . .') he interrupts his sketching and goes back to 'Was bluten muss' for a second pass, continuing all the way to the end of the scene. In this second layer he sets much of the text left unset in layer one, although often the rhythm bears no resemblance to his rhythmic mnemonic devices in the first layer. In layer two Strauss firms up the orchestral part; the motivic threads are more tightly woven, yet much of it differs from layer one as well. There are some brief blocks of sketches for the interlude between scenes 4 and 5, and the composer tries his hand at composing some of the opening of that next scene (as Chrysothemis rushes in with the news of Orestes' supposed death), but Strauss does not get beyond that moment in the drama. Tr. 17 basically ends with the opening of scene 5 in a state of flux.

Sketchbook Tr. 18

This sketchbook is inscribed to the opera's dedicatee, Willi Levin,[13] and although most of the sketches in Tr. 18 pertain to *Elektra*, there are sketches to two other pieces as well: the *Parademarsch für Cavallerie*, a work for the Kaiser that Strauss composed during his stay at Bad Nauheim in June 1907, and

[13] On the cover page of this sketchbook Strauss writes: 'Property of Herr Willi Levin | in memory of the Eibsee | July–August 1906 | Richard Strauss.' ['Eigentum des Herrn Willi Levin zum Andenken an den Eibsee Juli–August 1906. Richard Strauss.'] Strauss had intended to give this sketchbook to his friend and Skat partner Willi Levin, a prominent Berlin banker, to whom—along with his wife—*Elektra* was dedicated. Strauss, Levin, and their families had vacationed on the Eibsee in late July and early August. We do not know when Strauss wrote the inscription, which is in itself unusual in that he records only the date of their vacation rather than the time in which he allegedly gave the book to Levin. (This is the only dedication known to this author where Strauss does not record the date in which he gave the sketchbook to the recipient. The phrase, 'Eigentum des Herrn Willi Levin', is also unusual for Strauss; the dedication in the Vienna sketchbook is more typical.) Strauss very well may not have given the sketchbook to Levin at all, since it remained a part of the Strauss estate. Therefore the composer's inscription offers no real assistance in dating this important source.

Vier Frauengestalten der National Gallery, a project that never materialized.[14]

Often Strauss wrote down the portion of text (on the inside front and/or back covers) he intended to set. On the inside back cover page (verso) of Tr. 18 we find the text for a portion of the Klytämnestra scene (roughly the second half of part II, which is the dialogue portion of their scene) although he sets more text than that in this sketchbook.[15] (We recall that the dialogue section of the scene was the only annotated portion of scene 4 in Strauss's 1904 textbook.)

Tr. 18 contains both blocks of continuity sketches as well as sketch fragments. Scene 1 is a fairly lengthy stretch of continuity sketching, which comprises a single compositional layer. This sketch, which spans ten folios, is far enough evolved so that the next layer is very likely the fair-sketch stage. The dramaturgical significance of this scene is the establishment of an atmosphere of death and decay; it is achieved by the use of important referential keys and motives. Strauss solidifies both elements in Tr. 18, although he seems a bit unsure about the construction of the final cadence on D. In these sketches the orchestral continuum is established, but the mostly declamatory vocal lines are less well defined. In a number of instances one finds only text above an empty vocal staff.

Strauss's ideas for Elektra's monologue (as seen in Tr. 18) are not nearly as definitive as those for scene 1. One finds only some sixty bars of continuous sketches for scene 2, and they pertain to the opening B-flat-minor section of her speech:

[14] For this project Strauss intended to create four musical portraits based upon paintings in London's National Gallery: Paul Veronese's *Sleeping Girl*, William Hogarth's *The Shrimp Girl*, Joshua Reynolds' *Heads of Angels*, and George Romney's portrait of Lady Hamilton. The only surviving sketches are for 'Lady Hamilton' ('Thema con variazioni') and the 'Crevette Girl' ('Schnell'), and they comprise nine or ten pages. There is a one-page sketch labelled 'Lady Hamilton' in Tr. 17.

[15] There are also a number of non-musical details on these pages as well. On the recto side of the back cover page, for example, we again find building details for his Garmisch villa. That Strauss wrote the text to scene 4 on the back side of these preliminary building instructions indicates that he might have sketched at least part of that scene in the late spring or early summer 1907.

roughly the first fifty bars.[16] These scene 2 sketches further suggest the close relationship between Tr. 17 and 18; we recall those fragmentary ideas for Elektra's monologue in Tr. 17. There is surely another source between the sketches for this scene—in both sketchbooks—and the fair sketch of it in the Tokyo source.

Strauss jots down two ideas on the page preceding the scene 2 sketch: Elektra alone, conjuring up the spirit of Agamemnon, as well as a brief passage labelled 'Klytämnestra' (see Ex. 6.9).

Ex. 6.9 Tr. 18, fol. 10v

Strauss described this Agamemnon motive as '[the father] as shadow' in Tr. 17; the motive in the fourth bar was labelled simply 'the father'. Just below the Agamemnon passage, Strauss creates a contrasting theme for Klytämnestra, making us aware of both the similarities and differences between these themes for 'the father' and 'Klytämnestra'. Both begin with the prominent two shorts and a long, but the Klytämnestra theme—with its triplet configuration and sinuous shape—is intentionally more obscure.

[16] These additional words go against the grain of Hofmannsthal's original intent, for in her monologue and throughout most the play Elektra does not mention her father by name. Elektra's cry ('Agamemnon hears you!') to Aegisthus towards the end of the play is therefore made much more powerful.

The continuity sketch for scene 3, spanning some eleven folios, is only slightly longer than the one for the first scene and is also essentially in one layer. It begins not with the introductory dialogue between the sisters, but with Chrysothemis' lyrical outpouring ('Ich hab's wie Feuer in der Brust') and continues to the very end of the scene as they hear Klytämnestra approaching. Like the scene 1 sketches, Strauss realized the basic overall shape for this third scene; the step from this preliminary sketch to the fair sketch is a very short one. And it is perhaps hardly surprising that in this lyrical passage the vocal line should be more clearly defined at times than the orchestral part.

The sketches for scene 4 further illustrate the problems that Strauss experienced with this central moment in the opera. His work centres around their dialogue: basically from Klytämnestra: 'Ich habe keine gute Nächte' to Elektra: 'An jedem Ort [zu] jeder Stunde des Tags und der Nacht.' Once again we find Strauss primarily establishing the basic motivic continuity and harmonic underpinnings, although much of this material—especially towards the end—diverges significantly from the final version. Fol. 38^{v} ff. is exemplary (Ex. 6.10).

In the excerpt shown in Ex. 6.10 Elektra explains that when the right victim falls beneath the axe her mother will no longer dream. Strauss works with three basic motives associated with Orestes, Klytämnestra, and the victory dance. Just after 'Also wüsstest du [mit welchem geweihten Tier?'] the composer plans motivic continuation ('gut als Fortführung') with the Orestes theme, although he did not follow through on that motivic plan.

Besides the continuity drafts in Tr. 18, there are a number of pages of individual sketches as well: brief themes or longer passages. Many of these are found towards the end of the sketchbook (after the scene 4 sketch breaks off) and consist of ideas to be expanded upon in the continuation of the Klytämnestra scene, especially the last section of the scene where Elektra temporarily has the upper hand. Almost all of

Ex. 6.10 Tr. 18, fols. 38v and 39

these thematic fragments bear labels, such as: 'Elektra's solemn triumph', 'triumphant/E major', and 'Elektra on the heels of Kl[ytämnestra]'. The last one is taken from Elektra's line in this final section of the scene, 'I am like a dog on your heels' (see Ex. 6.11). The theme that Strauss sketches

Ex. 6.11 Tr. 18, fol. 48; vocal score, 5 bars before reh. 187a, and 192a

articulates the opening of that final section of the Klytämnestra scene. Not only does it pervade the last part of scene 4, but it makes a prominent return as Orestes goes in to the palace to murder his mother.

The Tokyo Sketchbook

The Tokyo sketchbook is a fair sketchbook, and the provenance of this source is not altogether clear.[17] While one of the most important aims of the *Elektra* preliminary sketches is to establish the basic motivic continuity and harmonic shape, a major goal of the fair sketches is to solidify, or even refine, the vocal line (often undeveloped in the *Elektra* preliminary sketches) and also to add more detail to the orchestral part. This sketchbook contains music for scenes 1, 2, 3, and roughly two-thirds of scene 4; at this stage of composition Strauss tries to forge together in a coherent whole various units or blocks of preliminary sketches. And while one can easily imagine the composer going directly from the sketches to scenes 1 and 3 in Tr. 18, it is just as difficult to imagine that there is not some further source separating the Tokyo sketchbook and Trs. 17/18, when it comes to scenes 2 and 4. Thus, we shall briefly focus on these two scenes; scenes 1 and 3 vary little from the final version.

[17] The source bears no inscription, although Mueller von Asow listed it as belonging to the collection of Dr Kurt Levin in Cambridge, England; von Asow does not indicate whether or not Dr Levin was an heir to Willi Levin. (See E. H. Mueller von Asow, *Richard Strauss: Thematisches Verzeichnis* (Vienna, 1955–74), pp. 408–9.) Von Asow was also apparently unaware that the sketchbook was auctioned off by Christie, Manson, and Woods on 16 November 1955. The catalogue description reads: 'Strauss (Richard): Autograph Musical Manuscript of the Opera *Elektra*, text by Hugo von Hofmannsthal, about the first two-fifths of the whole work, written in pencil, unsigned, 96 pages (pp. 89 and 90 struck together by the composer), sm. oblong 8vo., exercise book (1908).' (*Catalogue of Valuable Printed Books and Some Manuscripts* [London: Christie, Manson, and Woods, Ltd., 1955], item 400, p. 48.) It now belongs to the Musashino College of Music in Tokyo, whose catalogue (published in German) has the following listing: 'Strausz [*sic*], Richard. 1864–1949 | *Elektra* | Erste Skizze, kleine Taschenformat | 96 Seiten mit Bleistift in des Komponisten zierlicher Handschrift | geschrieben | Umfasst ungefähr die erste zwei Fünftel des Werks . . .' See *Litterae Rarae Liber Primus* (Tokyo: Biblioteca Musashino Academica Musicae, 1962).

It is admittedly difficult, perhaps impossible, to determine exactly how Strauss went about composing this sketchbook; until scene 4 we see what appears to be one continuous sketch with only occasional scratch-outs or corrections. Scenes 1 and 2 appear as if they were written without much interruption.[18] Scene 3, however, is definitely in a lighter shade of pencil, and, although there is no evidence of a break between scenes 3 and 4, Strauss at least paused enough to play through (on the piano or in his head) the sketchbook to the end of the third scene.[19]

On the cover page Strauss writes: 'Elektra Reinschrift'. The passage on the verso side was briefly mentioned—in a different context—in Chapter 4:

> Electra alone B flat minor, intensified against the world B minor | Agamemnon C minor, victory dance C major.
>
> [Electra allein B moll, der Welt gegenüber gesteigert H moll. | Agamemnon C moll, Siegestanz C dur.]

The above type of text is unusual for a fair sketchbook, because by then Strauss had usually already worked out his tonal plan. Although it is not labelled as such, the above harmonic description specifically applies to scene 2, Elektra's monologue. However, the harmonic motion suggested in the above differs from Elektra's ultimate monologue, which spans B flat minor (6 after reh. 36)—C minor (reh. 44)—B flat major (3 after reh. 56)—C major (7 after reh. 61). B flat major goes unmentioned in Strauss's memorandum, and indeed there is no B flat major in the Reinschrift version of scene 2: at the equivalent of 3 bars after reh. 56 in the fair sketch, the climax is in C major, not B flat (see Ex. 6.12).

On page 22 of the Tokyo fair sketch, Strauss changes this harmonic direction towards C by simply transposing a seventy-five-bar stretch of the monologue down a whole

[18] We recall Strauss's letter (16 July 1906) to Levin that 'the first two scenes are already finished.' He probably meant that they were finished at the fair-sketch stage.

[19] At the bottom of the last page of scene 3 he writes: 'up until this point 20 minutes' ['bis hierher 20 Minuten'].

Ex. 6.12 Tokyo sketchbook, p. 25; vocal score, reh. 56 ff.

tone. Below the *Elektra* chord at the equivalent of 3 bars after reh. 48 in the printed score, the composer writes: 'alles von hier ab ein Ton tiefer' (Ex. 6.13).

Why did Strauss transpose that block of seventy-five bars, thereby adding a new key area to scene 2? Certainly his earlier decision to go directly from C minor to C major underscores the importance that the composer put on the transformation from C minor to C major which symbolizes Agamemnon's murder and avengement. But Strauss's ultimate decision to add B flat was made for two reasons. First of all there is the obvious sense of symmetry that is created by going from B flat minor to C minor then B flat major to C major. And a strong musico-dramatic parallel is created as well: in B flat minor Elektra is alone, in B flat major she imagines her siblings around her dancing on their father's grave. Second of all, there is the more pragmatic consideration of pacing and variety. Had that portion remained in C it would have undercut the culminating power of the ultimate cadence on C. Elektra would have sung a high C for *both* climaxes which are, after all, only thirty-two bars apart.

Besides the crucial whole-tone transposition, Strauss did not alter very much of scene 2; it closely resembles the final version, as do scenes 1 and 3. Scene 4 is a different matter, where we find a number of corrections made by Strauss, who seems to have gone back over this section of the sketchbook with a thick pencil.[20] Furthermore, only a part of scene 4 is contained in the Tokyo sketchbook. These sketches end—right before Elektra asks 'Lässt du den Bruder nicht nach Hause, Mutter?'—on page 94 of this ninety-six-page sketchbook. Judging from the fair sketches to *Daphne*, Strauss most likely continued scene 4—right where it left off—in another fair sketchbook.[21]

Strauss's comments concerning this segment of the Klytämnestra scene are especially revealing. Scene 4 is the

[20] The author has examined only the microfilm of this document.

[21] Sketches on pp. 95 and 96, which correspond to earlier material, predate the scene 4 continuity sketch.

Ex. 6.13 Tokyo sketchbook, p. 22; vocal score, reh. 48 ff.

centrepiece of the opera; the words exchanged between daughter and mother—words that are simultaneously powerful yet enigmatic—are especially important. Annotations show that Strauss emended this scene in order to ensure that the text would be better highlighted and understood. His careful focus on the text and the way it is declaimed is manifested in two basic ways. First, he believed that as it stood there simply was not enough space between certain phrases of text; in a number of places the dialogue was moving along too fast. Page 61 of the Tokyo sketchbook well illustrates Strauss's concern (Ex. 6.14).

Ex. 6.14 Tokyo sketchbook, p. 61

Der ganze Dialog mit mehr Pausen (dehnen!)

Beneath the system Strauss has written: 'The entire dialogue with more pauses (expand!).' ['Der ganze Dialog mit mehr Pausen (dehnen!)'] He wanted to give the words a chance to resonate, to breathe. But we see another concern in Ex. 6.14 as well: his interest that the text (i.e. the vocal line) not be obscured by the orchestra. The arrow indicates that the instrumental figure (ultimately scored for flute) under the line '. . . Kraft zu jäten', should be played *after* Klytämnestra finishes the line, not simultaneous with it. Time and time again we see Strauss drawing such arrows, allowing the orchestra to react to what is being said rather than obscure it. He articulates the problem eight pages later in the Tokyo sketchbook. On this page (p. 69) Strauss either inserts material between phrases of text or makes what was once simultaneous between voice and orchestra now successive. At the bottom of that page, for example, he suggests: 'The words always on the chord [i.e., the downbeat], a bar later the [instrumental] answer.' Ultimately the instrumental answer comes half a bar later. Strauss's focus on the vocal line in the Tokyo sketchbook exemplifies the composer's overall concern for the voice at this stage of sketching.

Tr. 19

Except for sketches to *Parergon zur Symphonia Domestica* and *Fanfare für die Wiener Philharmoniker*, there are few continuity sketches of any significant length in Tr. 19, and *Elektra* is no exception: only six and a half folios of sketches in all (six of these folios are grouped together in one block).[22] Although most of these *Elektra* sketches are thematic fragments—some labelled and some not—they all seem to correspond to the Recognition Scene and shortly thereafter. Here Strauss's principal concern is finding a way to depict Orestes upon his entrance in scene 6 as well as establishing some musical ideas for Aegisthus' entrance following that scene.

Sketches from both Tr. 19 and the Munich fragment document Strauss's search for a new Orestes theme in scene 6; in Tr. 19 there are three themes labelled 'Orest', and in the Munich fragment there are five. Strauss, of course, had already devised an Orestes motive, which played an especially important role towards the end of scene 4. We might think of this theme as the Orestes of the past. But, for the opening of the Recognition Scene, the composer also desired a musical depiction of the Orestes of the present, who—as Paul Bekker observes—arrives at the palace as a spectre of death. And of the eight total thematic sketches for Orestes, all but one are in D minor: the key of death that pervaded the opening scene.[23]

[22] Tr. 19 is unusual for a number of reasons. It was not manufactured by Max Lieber of Freiburg, but by Hans Licht of Leipzig and is smaller in format, measuring 10.5 × 16 cm., although it comprises more pages. This sketchbook is also a fascinating collection of sketches for many different projects spanning the years 1906–26: *Elektra, Die Frau ohne Schatten*, Lied Op. 69 No. 5 ('Schlechtes Wetter'), *Eine Alpensinfonie, Der Rosenkavalier, Parergon zur Symphonia Domestica, Fanfare für die Wiener Philharmoniker, Die ägyptische Helena*, and the *Militärmarsch* o.Op. 112. It also contains sketches for a number of unrealized projects: *Sonatine für Klavier an Bubi, Semiramis, Christines Heimreise*, and an unidentified *Volkslied*.

[23] The C major sketch—a broad, majestic theme—was not used for Orestes, but it would resurface, untransposed, in two different guises: representing Peneios and Jupiter in *Daphne* (8 bars before reh. 86) and *Die Liebe der Danae* (Act III, 10 bars before reh. 83), respectively.

Ex. 6.15 Tr. 19, fols. 11^{v}, 14, 14^{v}; Munich fragment, fols. 1 and 1^{v}

Strauss ultimately dispensed with the idea of composing a theme and opted for three open-ended chord progressions in D minor instead. We see a kernel of that idea in Ex. 6.15, Tr. 19, fol. 14^{v}. We recall that the earliest sketches of those chord progressions are in the margins of the handwritten text for the Recognition Scene at the ÖNB (Theatersammlung).[24]

[24] See Chapter 5, p. 150.

The Munich Fragment and Other Fragments

As many as seven *Elektra* preliminary sketchbook fragments have been accounted for, but only one (BSt Mu. Mss. 11845) is available to the public. All of these fragmentary sources—including the one from Munich—were sold either by J. A. Stargardt of Marburg or Kronenberg of Basle between the years 1977 and 1988. Six of the seven concern scene 6 of the opera; the remaining one relates to the preceding scene. Evidence points to the possibility that most of these folios come from the same sketchbook, which is now presumably in private hands. This sketchbook could very well help fill the gaping holes for scenes 5 and 6 as illustrated in Figure 6.1.

The Munich fragment was purchased by the Bayerische Staatsbibliothek in 1977. It is the only bifolio of the group and was probably pulled out from the middle of the sketchbook, for all of the *Elektra* sketches on this document are closely related and focus on scene 6. On folios 1 and 1^v Strauss sketches various Orestes themes as discussed above. On folio 2 we find two sketches: a four-bar theme labelled 'Casanova' and another short theme labelled 'Elektra innig'. The first sketch refers to the Casanova comedy *Christines Heimreise* that Strauss and Hofmannsthal had considered for a possible collaboration in 1908.[25] The latter sketch—intended to portray Elektra in a heartfelt, tender way—centres around a semitone dotted gesture, which pervades much of the Recognition Scene: especially at the opening and as Elektra reflects upon her childhood, after her A-flat-major aria (see Ex. 6.16).[26]

On the verso side of this folio the dotted figure appears in a more expanded sketch, as well as two thematic fragments

[25] *Correspondence*, 14, 18, 25. The first letter (p. 14) is erroneously dated as 4 June (rather than 4 July) 1908 in the English translation.

[26] We first see this figure at reh. 116a, as Elektra digs for the axe. At reh. 124a it appears in diminution and pervades much of the scene through Orestes' 'Lass den Orest' at reh. 130a. It is highlighted in the solo oboe (reh. 158a) as Elektra reminds herself and Orestes that she was once the beautiful daughter of Agamemnon.

Ex. 6.16 Munich fragment, fol. 2

in ink, with brief excerpts from the text pencilled above (Ex. 5.15).

The two examples are short motivic explorations intended for further expansion. In the first system, Strauss works with the triplet childhood-motive and in the second the familiar gesture of two shorts and a long, which in this guise will ultimately represent the deed. Thus, these textual jottings above the staff are not meant to be set, but serve as cues for particular sections of the scene, sections where he will expand the motivic ideas that he has outlined in the sketchbook. The emphasis is on the orchestral line, on the development of motivic material, and we find a similar concentration on the motivic material in the orchestra and the expansion of that material into continuity sketches in most of the other fragments as well.

In the Stargardt fragment, auctioned in 1986 [henceforth, Stargardt 86], we see the opening of a preliminary continuity sketch for Elektra's A-flat-major aria 'Es rührt sich niemand' (see Ex. 6.17). The aria is a developmental outgrowth of the triplet childhood-motive. Only the verso side of the folio has been published in facsimile, and the reproduction shows a pencil sketch where Strauss later tries to establish a vocal part by squeezing it—now in ink—into the pre-existing orchestral system.[27]

[27] The catalogue gives no information about the recto side of this folio.

Ex. 6.17 Stargardt fragment 86 (verso side)

Another fragment of a preliminary continuity sketch for scene 6 (see Ex. 6.18) is reproduced in a facsimile of the recto side of Stargardt 88. It pertains to a moment towards the beginning of the scene [reh. 128a], as Elektra asks the yet unrevealed Orestes: 'Kannst du nicht die Botschaft austrompeten dort, wo sie sich freu'n?' Here, too, the text is unset and added only after Strauss has established his orchestral line, which consists mainly of an expansion of the dotted semitone idea discussed above. The composer fits the text wherever space permits: above the treble staff or below it.

Ex. 6.18 Stargardt fragment 88 (recto side)

The auction house Kronenberg sold some *Elektra* sketch-book fragments in 1987 and 1988, but the author has been unable to see catalogue facsimiles for the 1987 auction if, indeed, any exist. The Richard-Strauss-Institut (Munich) reports that three folios relating to the Recognition Scene were sold in May of that year.[28] Another *Elektra* sketchbook folio was auctioned on 8 March 1988, and both sides of that manuscript were reproduced in that March catalogue.

Possibly this folio was torn out of a different book. It relates to a different scene (no. 5) and is entirely in ink. Furthermore, Strauss paginates the recto and verso sides as 'No. 1' and 'No. 2'. On the first page we see a number of brief try-outs that relate to reh. 92a in the score ('. . . dir ein Lebendiges liegt, erschreckend fast, so heb ich's empor . . .'), which is from scene 5. Again, the text is unset and written above the treble staff, although the text drops off after a couple of bars in the second system. The second page contains themes under three headings: 'Elektra beschwört Chrysot[hemis]', 'Klytämnestra', and 'Elektra zart'.

One rarely encounters the use of a pen in preliminary sketchbooks. When Strauss wrote in ink, it was usually for the act of recording rather than composing. Thus, the themes on page two were probably taken from earlier sketchbooks. 'Elektra beschwört Chrysot[hemis]' most likely comes from Tr. 18, fol 2; 'Klytämnestra' is probably taken from fol. 48^v of the same sketchbook; and 'Elektra zart' possibly originates from Tr. 19, fol. 16^v ['Elektra | innig | zärtlich']. Although one torn folio is admittedly slim evidence, it very well might have belonged to a sketchbook that served more as a catalogue of musical ideas that were consolidated from various other sketchbooks. Tr. 10 is one such sketchbook. It is paginated in a similar manner and even has themes inventoried on the inside front cover under the heading: 'Noch unverarbeitet'.

Thus, except for the Kronenberg 88 fragment, all other *Elektra* fragments reflect Strauss's work on the Recognition Scene, and they possibly originate from the same sketchbook.

[28] Personal communication with Stephan Kohler, director of the Richard-Strauss-Institut (July 1987).

We can only hope that over the years to come we shall uncover more information about this missing source through the sale of more folios or by tracking down the entire manuscript itself. The impossibility of examining this sketchbook, or even getting information about it, is especially vexing, for it might help us understand the initial problems Strauss encountered when trying to compose the Recognition Scene.

The Vienna Sketchbook

This preliminary sketchbook, which has been a part of the Theatre Collection of the Austrian National Library since 1947, had belonged to Anna Bahr-Mildenburg since 1909.[29] Dating from around late July until possibly 20 August 1908, it is not only entirely devoted to *Elektra*, but to only one scene: the finale. Yet one wonders why Strauss chose to give the 'brilliant interpreter of Klytämnestra' this particular sketchbook, since by this scene that character has been murdered; the two sisters celebrate her death in a joyful duet. None the less, the fact that the musical material in this sketchbook is focused on one scene offers the scholar an opportunity to examine, in part, how Strauss put the finale together. I say in part, because this sketchbook of 52 folios is largely blank (some 32 empty folios in all); there is sketch material pertaining to the final scene that is lacking. But what does exist is fascinating, revealing some important, preliminary tonal and motivic strategies for scene 7. This important source will be discussed in detail in the next chapter, which is an analysis of the final scene.

What do these surviving *Elektra* sketches tell us about the way in which Strauss approached composing this opera? At the stage of preliminary sketching, Tr. 17 primarily documents Strauss's search for important themes or motives,

[29] See Chapter 5, n. 22.

many of which serve as musical characterizations to be expanded. Strauss is less successful in his attempt at forming a continuity sketch for the last third of the Klytämnestra scene. He also tries to establish promising themes in Tr. 18, but focuses more attention on three sizeable blocs of continuity sketches: scenes 1, 3, and the middle third of scene 4. As in Tr. 17, Strauss experienced significant problems with that fourth scene. In the *Elektra* sketch fragments, whether the excerpts from Tr. 19, the Munich fragment, or the folios reproduced in auction catalogues, we see only hints at the composer's struggle with the Recognition Scene, especially in trying to find a way to characterize the returned Orestes. Strauss no longer searches for new themes in the Vienna sketchbook, but looks for new ways to combine or reinterpret them. This sketchbook covers only the finale, a culminating *tour de force* of motivic integration.

In all of these preliminary sketches we see Strauss's primary concern with establishing a sense of motivic continuity in the orchestral line. This focus on the orchestral role and the manipulation of structural and referential motives that rule various stretches of the opera—as opposed to an initial interest in a lyrical setting of the text—is illustrated time and time again in these sketches. Unfortunately Strauss offers little specific information about his approach, which—at this stage—differs minimally from his compositional approach to the tone poem. Strauss's concern for motivic continuity as evinced in the *Elektra* sketches sheds further light on his statement that he needed to compose an opera in proper dramaturgical sequence 'for the sake of symphonic unity'. We are also reminded of a statement by Strauss's contemporary, Alexander von Zemlinsky, who comments on his compositional method when composing opera.

In order to set a scene to music, he suggests, one must first be clear about which basic motive rules it. The composer should probe beneath the surface of the dialogue and discover the more fundamental motivations and mood out of which the librettist envisioned the scene. Equating mood with the basic motive, Zemlinsky then explains:

> . . . this mood can then—undisturbed by the back and forth of the dialogue—rule the entire scene with only minor modifications . . . Nevertheless, at this level this means a purely musical translation [of the text] . . . The aim is to arrange properly the tempo, rhythm, and motive especially—purely from the musical standpoint. This is one of the most important tasks, and many of the newer, active composers do not know this! . . . One more thing: [aim for] the short, forceful motive that, after two or four bars, leaves no doubt as to its meaning.[30]

Twice Zemlinsky refers to a 'purely musical' interpretation of the text, and in this context he, no doubt, means a purely orchestral rendering of the essential moods, situations, and actions in the libretto at this early level of compositional thought. Although Zemlinsky speaks from his own standpoint as an opera composer, his remarks bolster our understanding of features already observed in the *Elektra* preliminary sketches.

As for the fair sketches, the Tokyo sketchbook is our only source representing this compositional layer, and we should generalize with care and caution. Here we see Strauss's concern with the vocal line, which becomes fully solidified by this stage. His numerous specific and painstaking directions for the troublesome fourth scene exemplify the composer's preoccupation with the final shape of the vocal line, its relationship with the orchestra, and ultimately its audibility.

Strauss once described *Salome* as a 'symphony in the medium of drama', and the description surely applies to *Elektra* as well. In fact, *Elektra* displays a much stronger sense of exposition (scenes 1–3), development (scene 4), and recapitulation (scenes 5–7) than its predecessor. One critic who attended the Dresden première commented that *Elektra* might just as well be performed as a tone poem acted out by

[30] Horst Weber, *Alexander Zemlinsky* (Vienna, 1977), Österreichische Komponisten des 20. Jahrhunderts, vol. 23, p. 49.

stage performers in mime, a remark in response to the loud orchestra that verged on drowning out the singers.[31] But the statement touches upon an issue more important than mere acoustics, for the orchestra is, on the whole, the fundamental vehicle of expression. In much of *Elektra* the voices seem to emerge out of the orchestral continuum. In *The Changing Opera*, Bekker describes the vocal line as the 'final translation of the instrumental action' in early Strauss opera, and the *Elektra* sketches solidly document his observation.[32]

The composer's primary interest in the motivic interplay in the orchestra caused some tension between himself and Ernst von Schuch during rehearsals for the première. Schuch sought to strike a balance between singers and orchestra, but the headstrong Strauss insisted that the motivic complexity of the score be fully audible, whether or not the orchestra drowned the singers. Composer and conductor ultimately compromised on this issue of vocal audibility.[33] Later on, Strauss frankly admitted that the dialogue in *Elektra* was 'still very much handicapped by instrumental polyphony'.[34] In a tongue-in-cheek essay on conducting, he even suggested that the conductor should approach the score to *Elektra* as he would the music of Mendelssohn: 'fairy music'.[35] Strauss's concern for the audibility of the singer increased throughout his life—witness the prefaces to *Intermezzo* and *Capriccio*—yet, despite his well-publicized concern, the primary role of the orchestra basically remained unchanged. In his essay on *Elektra*, he confessed: 'the struggle between word and music has been the problem of my life right from the beginning, which *Capriccio* solves with a question mark.'[36]

[31] August Spanuth, '*Elektra*', *Signale für die Musikalische Welt* [Berlin], 67/4 (Jan. 1909), 122.

[32] Paul Bekker, *The Changing Opera*, trans. Arthur Mendel (New York, 1935), 262.

[33] *Recollections*, 156.

[34] From the composer's preface to *Intermezzo*, which is contained in *Recollections*, 95–102.

[35] Originally written as a piece for a newspaper, Strauss's *Ten Golden Rules* has been reproduced in various sources, including *Recollections*, 38.

[36] *Recollections*, 156.

Taken together these admittedly few sketchbooks, none the less, tell us much about the composer's perception of opera in the first decade of the twentieth century, that the underlying musical basis for musico-dramatic continuity is inherently symphonic. Strauss, no doubt, saw the roots of this perception in Wagner, whose *Tristan* and *Siegfried* he once termed 'great polyphonic symphonies'.[37] It is a pity that more *Elektra* sketchbooks are unavailable. Sketchbooks were little more than souvenirs for friends once the work was completed. Sceptical of studies of his sources, Strauss wished to be judged by the final product of his endeavours. His scepticism brings to mind a statement he made to his one-time librettist, Stefan Zweig, who had urged him to write an autobiography: 'I just . . . provide some signposts and leave it to the scholars to fill in.'[38]

[37] Willi Schuh, *Richard Strauss: A Chronicle of the Early Years*, trans. Mary Whittall (Cambridge, 1982), 232.

[38] Letter to Stephan Zweig, 8 June 1935, in *A Confidential Matter: The Letters of Richard Strauss and Stefan Zweig 1931–35*, trans. Max Knight, ed. Willi Schuh (Berkeley and Los Angeles, 1977), 98.

7 *The Final Scene: Genesis and Structure*

In all of Strauss's fifteen operas, one can hardly imagine a more potent finale than the last scene of *Elektra*. We recall from Chapter 1 that Alfred Kalisch, after hearing the world première, confessed an inability to describe the finale without seeming to exaggerate: 'The mind has to travel back far in a search for anything at all comparable to it in musical mastery and almost elemental emotional power.'[1]

With remarkable thoroughness and élan, Strauss creates a tightly-knit network of returning motives in scene 7. Any attempt to trace all of the motivic reworkings by picking apart this intricate network would risk falling into the quicksand of laborious motive description. Strauss's unqualified success with thematic integration and manipulation in *Elektra* results, to a large extent, from his frequent choice of short, open-ended motives that often seem defined more by rhythmic gesture than by melodic shape. He also shows a predilection for themes that are triadic or that encompass perfect intervals, thus better facilitating simultaneous motivic treatment.

These two observations bring to mind a reproval by Brahms to the young Strauss after the elder composer had heard the early F minor symphony—written some two decades before *Elektra*: 'Your symphony contains too much playing about with themes. This piling up of many themes based on a triad which differ from one another only in rhythm has no value.'[2] Strauss recalled that Brahms's criticism 'always clearly remained in my mind', implying that he paid

[1] Alfred Kalisch, 'Impressions of Strauss's *Elektra*', *Zeitschrift der Internationalen Musikgesellschaft*, 7 (1909), 201.

[2] Ernst Krause, *Richard Strauss: The Man and his Work* (Boston, 1969), 154.

heed to the older composer's suggestion. But this technique—for better or for worse—in fact remained an integral aspect of Strauss's compositional style.

Most of these returning motives in the last scene are related through the anapaestic rhythmic gesture suggested by the name: 'Agamemnon'.

Ex. 7.1

Example 7.1*a* is derived from the motive representing Chrysothemis' virginal beauty and strength that we had first seen in scene 5 (see reh. 25a; Elektra: 'Wie stark du bist!'); it is now raised up a semitone from its original E-flat-major setting at the outset of scene 7 (see 2 bars before reh. 221a). Strauss, indeed, punctuates much of the opening of the finale with just the head motive of the Agamemnon theme (Ex. 7.1*b*). At this moment in the opera it signifies both the returned Orestes ('Orestes lebt!'; reh. 141a) and the death blow that he has just dealt Aegisthus ('Mörder! Sie morden mich!'; 3 bars before reh. 214a). Elektra's cathartic dance theme (Ex. 7.1*c*) is a transformation of her tender theme from

the A-flat-major aria, 'Es rührt sich niemand' (see reh. 149a), and Example 7.1*d* is the so-called childhood theme ('[Agamemnon] zeig dich deinem Kind!'; 6 bars before reh. 46), which reappears at the end of the A-flat-major aria. Although the next example (7.1*e*) is often thought of as the theme of the sisters' duet ('Sie fahren dahin . . .'; reh. 237a), it appeared very briefly in scene 5 as Elektra declared that she would implant her will into her sister's blood ('. . . und mit meinem Willen dir impfen das Blut'; reh. 75a).

Some other, non-anapaestic motives that make an important return are a major-mode version of the motive that originally underlay the text 'Orest ist tot!' (Ex. 7.2*a*), the theme of remembrance of happier times (Ex. 7.2*b*), and the two other Agamemnon motives: Agamemnon as king (Ex. 7.2*c*) and Agamemnon as shadow (Ex. 7.2*d*).

Ex. 7.2

More potent than these linear considerations, however, are the tonal ones, especially the culminating effect of the ultimate movement to C major. The way in which Strauss achieves this compelling final shift, discussed in part in Chapter 4, illustrates the composer's sure-footed sense of harmonic pacing in this opera. In the earlier discussion of the tonal structure in *Elektra* we observed the composer's subtle, yet powerful method of setting up our expectations of C major: in scene 2, he achieved that movement from C minor to C major, undermined by a sudden turn to E major; Elektra had a momentary triumph in C major (albeit in the 6/4 position) in her scene with Klytämnestra, but it was thwarted by a sudden cadence on B♭, and the scene actually ended in B; the movement to C by the end of the Recognition Scene was also not fully resolved and remained in the 6/4 position. Indeed, not until four bars before the end, with the ultimate cadence, do we strongly sense C major in the root position, although there have been occasional instances of it earlier in the scene.

But what are the tonal relationships before that final cadence in scene 7? This final scene represents a culmination of the mediant relationship between C, E, and to a lesser extent, E flat; in this scene the relationship finally comes to a head. The sudden shifts to B flat and B in scene 4 serve as important dominant preparations for E flat and E, respectively, and the semitone relationship between E and E flat is the very essence of the C minor–C major duality.[3] The importance of this mediant relationship becomes clearer as we look at the overall structure of the scene.

The following is a summary of the dramaturgical layout of scene 7:

1. Chrysothemis and chorus rush on stage with the news that Orestes is in the palace.
2. Elektra sings a brief solo that indicates her increasing detachment from the outer world: 'Ob ich nicht höre?'
3. Elektra's and Chrysothemis' duet: 'Wir sind bei den Göttern.'
4. Elektra's dance (two parts):
   (a) extended orchestral passage

[3] At reh. 164 and 200 in scene 4 we see this relationship localized to a blatant alternation of the two keys. The pervasive dotted figure suggests Elektra's victory dance, and it first appears in scene 2. Scene 7 both recalls that figure and alternates E minor and E major.

(b) with voice: 'Schweig und tanze!'

5. Elektra's death

In sum, Strauss transforms Hofmannsthal's ending into a masterful symphonic finale with added voices: a symphonic recapitulation of some of the most important themes in the opera, and it marks the return of a harmonic relationship (that of C and E major) that was foreshadowed in Elektra's expository opening scene. In considering the genesis of this scene—as shown by a preliminary sketchbook devoted to this section of the opera—two initial compositional concerns of Strauss become evident: (1) the laying out of a tonal plan and (2) establishing a network of returning motives. Only after these two plans are solidified does the composer focus on the vocal lines.

The Genesis of the Final Scene

Seven months (October to June 1908) separate Strauss's composition of the end of scene 5 and the beginning of the Recognition Scene. The speed and assurance with which he composed the last two scenes of the opera reflect how important that compositional hiatus actually was. With Strauss's return to composing the opera (*c.*21 June 1908), we find a composer with a firm grasp of the musico-dramaturgical demands of the libretto, and, in a couple of instances, he asks Hofmannsthal for extra text to help realize his musical plans.

Around 6 July 1908, Strauss focused his attention on the final scene, which he finished sketching by 20 August according to a letter to his friend Willy Levin. Thereafter he was preoccupied with finishing the remainder of the Particell and the full score. The undated preliminary sketchbook (Vienna Sketchbook) in the Theatre Collection of the ÖNB documents that period of sketching between *c.*6 July and August.

The Vienna Sketchbook

We recall from the previous chapter that Strauss had given this sketchbook to Anna Bahr-Mildenburg in May 1909, and it remained in her possession until her death in 1947. Devoted entirely to the final scene of *Elektra*, it is our only significant documentation of Strauss's work—at any stage of composition—with scene 7. Strauss's working edition of Hofmannsthal's play is, for all practical purposes, devoid of any musical commentary pertaining to the scene, and no corresponding fair sketchbook survives. Perhaps Strauss wrote out the text to scene 7 by hand and glossed it much like his handwritten copy of the text to the Recognition Scene and following.[4]

Although this source numbers fifty-two folios, only eighteen and a half of them actually contain sketches, which may be divided into two types (kept in separate sections of the sketchbook): section one, which spans folios 2–8, consists mostly of compositional fragments—themes, fragmentary ideas, one-page try-outs, and the like; section two, which spans a dozen folios, comprises two stretches of continuity sketches, based on many of the earlier fragments. These two blocks of sketches overlap in part: from reh. 230a to reh. 241a (Elektra: 'Die Tausende, die Fackeln tragen' to '. . . und meine Flamme verbrennt die Finsternis der Welt').

The Sketch Fragments

The most important fragments for this scene are found near the opening of the sketchbook; they are the two thematic fragments pertaining to Elektra's dance on fols. 2^v and 3. On fol. 2^v Strauss writes, 'Elektras Tanz zuerst', a thirteen-bar sketch for reh. 247a and following; it is the first part of her dance, which is set in E major. On the next page, Strauss composes a four-bar sketch—consisting of material for reh.

[4] See the discussion of this document on pp. 137–49 of Chapter 5.

259a—for the end of the second part of her dance (labelled 'Tanz am Schluss nach Elektras leztem Gesang'); the sketch is in C major.

The remainder of that page is a fifteen-bar sketch for Elektra's 'Ob ich nicht höre?' (continued for another six bars on fol. 4^v). In an unlabelled and untexted sketch on fol. 3^v, Strauss tries to compose a little bit of what appears to be the opening of the final scene (around 2 bars before reh. 221a), and on folio 5 the composer comes up with a preliminary idea for the opening of the duet, 'Sie fahren dahin . . .'; he makes another try on the verso side of the folio. Except for fols. 2 and 3, all of this fragmentary material is worked out in the continuity sketches at the end of this sketchbook.

Of the sketches at the beginning of the book, fols. 6–7^v are exceptional, for they comprise a short continuity draft for the end of the opera, beginning with 'Ich trage die Last des Glückes', continuing through to the final bar. The last two pages of that draft show Strauss focusing on two important harmonic events: (1) E flat minor to symbolize Elektra's death (he writes 'Sie stürzt zusammen' above the first entrance of the E-flat-minor chord) as well as the alternation of E flat and C minor (the key of the dead Agamemnon) and (2) the final juxtaposition of E and C by way of V/V of E and V of C (see last two bars of fol. 7^v, first system, resolving to C major (see Ex. 7.3).

The Continuity Drafts

Folios 21 to 29^v comprise a continuity draft that covers a sizeable portion of scene 7: from 3 bars before reh. 221a ('Es ist der Bruder drin im Haus!') to 5 bars after reh. 255a ('Schweig und tanze!'). Five folios earlier Strauss jots down a shorter continuity sketch that predates corresponding material in the later draft. It is a rough sketch pertaining to material spanning around reh. 230a to reh. 241a in the score; there are numerous empty bars with nothing but text written above the staves. Indeed only the uninterrupted flow of text

Ex. 7.3 Vienna sketchbook, fols. 7 and 7v

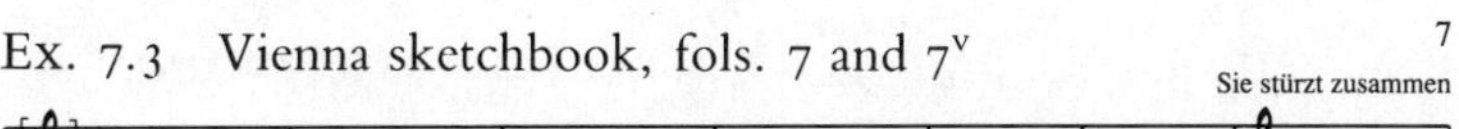

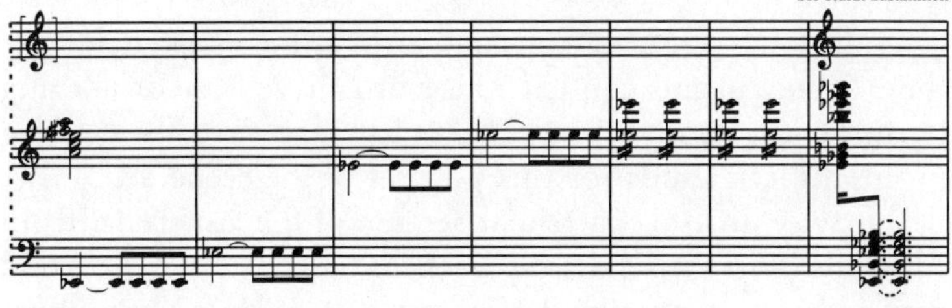

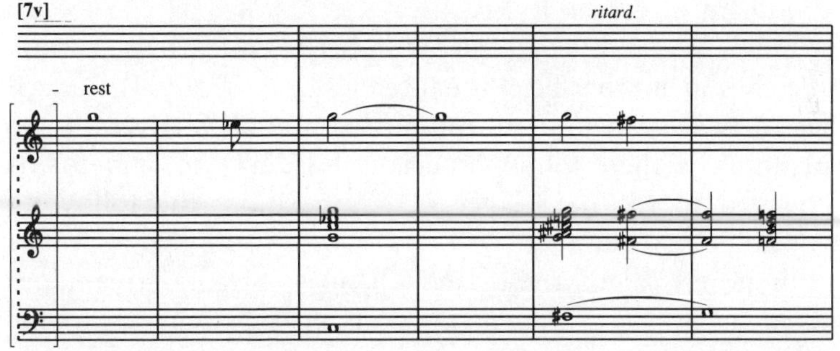

provides any sense of continuity to Strauss's sketching in these folios. In this context, the words have little or nothing to do with vocal setting, but rather serve as a detailed programmatic guide for this portion of the scene.

But why just this particular section of the last scene (from Elektra's 'Die Tausende, die Fackeln tragen' to her '. . . und meine Flamme verbrennt die Finsternis der Welt')? Musically, it marks a critical point in the scene: the movement from E major (which opens the scene with Chrysothemis and chorus and then Elektra's 'Ob ich nicht höre?') towards C (which opens the duet for the sisters). Furthermore, with the duet Strauss is presented with the problem of deciding how to lay out the two simultaneous texts. His purpose in these five folios is not only to map out a tonal strategy, marking the important points of tonal articulation, but to tackle the problem of arranging the text for the only traditional vocal duo in the opera.

A look at some of these important tonal junctures illuminates Strauss's preoccupation with the mediant relationship. For example, on fol. 18^{v} (within the context of E major), the composer jots down a localized shift to the dominant of C (see Ex. 7.4).

Likewise, on fol. 19, after a number of empty bars, Strauss sketches in another brief tonal reference to V of C ('. . . weil ich den Reigen führen muss'). Some of Strauss's tonal planning in these folios, especially fols. 19^{v}, 20, and 20^{v}, is changed in the next layer of composition: the following continuity sketch.

In nearly all of these later changes, Strauss streamlines tonal events by doing away with keys extraneous to the relationship between C and E major. Thus, on fol. 19^{v}, Strauss maps out three important points of articulation: C^6_4 ('. . . sie tragen ihn auf ihren Händen!'), $E\flat^6_4$ ('Wir sind bei den Göttern'), and C ('. . . wir vollbringenden . . . Sie fahren dahin'). The first articulation marks the end of part II (see above dramaturgical layout) of scene 7, the second articulation begins part III, and 'Sie fahren dahin' marks the beginning of

Ex. 7.4 Vienna sketchbook, fol. 18^v

the actual simultaneous duet between Elektra and her sister. Thus fol. 19^v (see Ex. 7.5*a*) shows Strauss delaying the cadence on C until the duet; the opening of part III is not articulated by its tonic, but by an E$\flat^6_4$ chord. In the next layer (fols. 25 and 25^v) Strauss strengthens our perception of the important shift from E to C major by dispensing with the reference to E flat altogether. Thus, the end of part II is on the dominant of E, part III begins on C^6_4, leading to the duet in root position C (see Ex. 7.5 *a* and *b*).

In the short continuity draft preceding the longer one, Strauss shows little concern for the vocal setting of Hofmannsthal's text; text in this instance serves as a dramaturgical *aide mémoire*. Strauss is preoccupied with tonal—and to a lesser extent motivic—planning, as well as the arrangement of the duet text. In the later continuity draft, which essentially begins with the opening of scene 7 and ends with

Ex. 7.5*a* Vienna sketchbook, fol. 19v

the opening of the second section of Elektra's dance (65 bars before the end of the opera), Strauss not only solidifies the orchestral part of the finale, but formulates much of the vocal setting as well.[5] Evidence from the Vienna sketchbook strengthens our understanding of Strauss's musico-dramatic structure in scene 7; it helps confirm observations that might otherwise have remained speculation.

[5] The only significant exception to this latter observation is that part of the sketch relating to the vocal duet. In that instance Strauss has not yet come up with a definitive layout for the simultaneous texts.

Ex. 7.5*b* Vienna sketchbook, fol. 25

Structure of the Final Scene

For Paul Bekker, Strauss's technical brilliance—especially with motivic manipulation—should not command our sole attention in scene 7; the composer's greater strength was in the broad musical layout and pacing of musical ideas in that scene.[6] In overall design, the last scene of *Elektra* is like no

[6] Paul Bekker, '*Elektra*', *Neue Musik-Zeitung*, 14 (1909), 391.

Ex. 7.5b (cont.)

other in Strauss's operatic output, where we may categorize three fundamental types of endings: the grand monologue or solo (*Guntram*, *Feuersnot*, *Salome*, *Die schweigsame Frau*, *Daphne*, and *Capriccio*); the duet-finale (*Ariadne auf Naxos*, *Der Rosenkavalier*, *Intermezzo*, *Die ägyptische Helena*, *Arabella*, and *Die Liebe der Danae*); and the ensemble-finale (*Die Frau ohne Schatten* and *Der Friedenstag*). Scene 7 of *Elektra* stands apart in that it is, paradoxically, none of the above and all of the above at the same time. On the one hand it, indeed, includes an important monologue for Elektra ('Ob ich nicht höre?'), an extended duo ('Wir sind bei den Göttern'), and a chorus hailing the return of Orestes. But on the other hand, these apparent operatic conventions are treated in a way that is entirely unconventional. The chorus does nothing more than exclaim the name 'Orest!', and Elektra's final monologue is as brief as it is powerful. The duet, the text of which was added for the libretto, comes the closest to a traditional operatic number, but it is relatively brief as well.

Much of the uniqueness in the textual layout of this scene results from Hofmannsthal's original plan—fully at odds with any traditional type of operatic close of the time. The dialectic of word and deed, which is so vividly expressed in the Klytämnestra scene and which threads its way through the play with increasing tension, reaches a climactic moment with the murders. The gestural overcomes the verbal by then ('Be silent and dance!'), and—according to Hofmannsthal's original intentions—Elektra should say as little as possible following the deed. After the murder of Aegisthus, the play moves swiftly to her dance; shortly thereafter she falls lifeless on the stage. From the moment of Aegisthus' death only thirty-nine lines of text remain, and the abruptness of Hofmannsthal's original ending must have been part of the reason that Strauss was so vexed, early on, about the end of the opera.

The problem of Hofmannsthal's abrupt finale was, no doubt, one of many that contributed to Strauss's break in composition between scenes 5 and 6. During that period he undoubtedly had given the ending much thought, and when he returned to composing he resolved to enlarge Hofmannsthal's ending. Starting with scene 6 we find Strauss turning towards more traditional operatic conventions such as aria, chorus, duo, and dance, although the last-mentioned element is admittedly the central part of Hofmannsthal's initial plan.

Before the Recognition Scene Strauss sought to make the text more concise, and he made extensive cuts. Yet after that pivotal scene Strauss sought just the opposite; he required more text from Hofmannsthal in order to compose Elektra's aria, as well as the duet of the two sisters. The playwright, unusually deferential in this early period of their collaboration, quickly obliged the composer in each instance. Hofmannsthal's textual additions, representing his first real collaborative work with Strauss, exemplify his amazing instincts for what would be effective with music—all the more amazing since he had never collaborated with an opera composer before. After receiving the added verses for the aria, Strauss, indeed, called Hofmannsthal a 'born librettist, in my eyes the greatest compliment, because I believe that it is much harder to write a good libretto than a good play'.[7] In short, Strauss needed more text because he required more musical space for the last two scenes; Hofmannsthal supplied him with the text that would help him fill out his symphonic vision, especially in this final scene.

Elektra's dance is the highlight of the finale in both play and libretto, but these texts differ significantly in the pace of events leading to her final ritual. In order to move swiftly to the dance, Hofmmansthal has Chrysothemis exit right after she asks Elektra:

> Don't you hear, they carry him,
> they carry him on their hands, their faces
> are quite changed, their eyes are glistening
> and their old cheeks, with tears! They are
> all weeping, can you not hear it? Ah!

But in the libretto Chrysothemis remains to sing a duet with her sister before she exits; thereafter Elektra's dance begins.

> *Elektra*
> We are with the gods, we who accomplish.
> They go through us like the blade of a sword,
> the gods, but their
> splendour is not too much for us!
> I have sown the seeds of adversity and reaped
> joy upon joy!

[7] *Correspondence*, 18.

I was a blackened corpse
among the living, and in this hour
I am the fire of life
and my flame burns up
the darkness in the world.
My face must be whiter
than the glowing white face of the moon.
If anyone looks at me
he must embrace death or
waste away with joy.
Do you see my face?
Do you see the light that shines out of me?
Ah! Love kills!
But no one dies
without having known love!

Chrysothemis

Don't you hear, they carry him,
they carry him on their hands, their faces
are quite changed, their eyes are glistening
and their old cheeks, with tears! They are
all weeping, can you not hear it? Ah!
The gods are good! Good!
Life is beginning for you and me
and for all mankind.
Goodness has poured from the gods
and brought it about.
Who has ever loved us?
Who has ever loved us?
Now our brother is here and love
flows over us like oil and myrrh:
love is everything!
Who can live without love?
Elektra!
I must be with my brother!

(Translation—with certain changes—taken from Decca Records 1986: G. M. Holland and K. Chalmers)

This text exemplifies Hofmannsthal's faithfulness to Strauss's request (6 July 1908) for 'nothing new, just the same contents, repeated and working towards a climax'.[8] There is, indeed, little new in these additional words, which allow the composer to pace better the musical build-up, to slow the cascade of events leading to the dance. These textual additions are not significant to the original structure of the play, but are structurally important to Strauss's music. Perhaps Hofmannsthal sensed how important the music could be at this moment in the drama, more important than words, for he offered Strauss the extra text—text that might have ruined the final scene of the play—without protest. In a letter (16 August 1908) to Strauss, Hofmannsthal predicted that the conclusion would be 'far more impressive and important in the opera than in the play'.[9]

In the added duet, Hofmannsthal reinforces the dark–light imagery that he had emphasized to Strauss, by letter, earlier in their collaboration.[10] Elektra declares that she has sown the seeds of darkness, yet has reaped great joy; she was a blackened corpse among the living, but now burns with the flame of life, a flame that burns through the darkness of the world; her face is now as white as the face of the moon, and she asks her sister whether she sees this light that shines from her. These lines also reinforce the fact that she has, once again, become a sexual being.

The return of moon imagery is reminiscent of the Recognition Scene, when she recalls her beauty in particularly narcissistic terms.

> I think I was beautiful: when I blew out
> the lamp in front of my mirror, I felt
> with chaste wonder how my naked body
> gleamed immaculate through the sultry night
> like something divine. I felt how the thin beam
> of the moon bathed in its white nakedness
> as in a pond, and my hair was such hair
> as makes men tremble . . .

[8] Ibid.

[9] Ibid., 22.

[10] Ibid. 4.

The lamp in front of the mirror and the reflected light of the moon are strong symbols for Elektra's self-reflection. A line cut from this scene foreshadows part of Hofmannsthal's added text for the duet. After Agamemnon was murdered Elektra says her that her body 'was as cold as ice and yet was charred, consumed with fire inwardly'.

Just after the final lines, 'Ah! Love kills, but no one dies without having known love', Chrysothemis rushes off stage, and Elektra begins her dance. Strauss divides the dance into two sections: the first section, which is entirely orchestral, and the second section, which begins with the lines, 'Be silent and dance! All must approach!' The dance culminates in her collapse and death.

Tonal Structure

Strauss's musico-dramaturgical plan becomes especially clear when one focuses on his tonal layout, which is, simply put, an extended juxtaposition of E and C major (E flat does not assume an important role until the end of the scene when Elektra dies). Although the final scene is clearly in C major, E major serves as a vital secondary key; these two keys serve as equally potent forces throughout this scene. And, as stated in Chapter 4, Strauss prepares us for this duality between C and E as early as Elektra's opening monologue, which suddenly shifts to E after an apparent final cadence on C (see reh. 63).[11]

To make this tonal relationship absolutely clear to the listener, Strauss composes a scene that is unremittingly diatonic and consonant—an effective counterbalance to

[11] In Strauss's *Daphne* we find a structural parallel. Daphne's opening monologue (sc. 2) begins in G and ends in F sharp major. Not only does this scene foreshadow a similar tonal event at the end of *Daphne* (the end of her final monologue and the beginning of the ensuing transformation [see 5 after reh. 249, etc.]), but it serves as a kind of tonal microcosm for the entire opera, which, too, begins in G and ends in F sharp. Through G major, Strauss depicts Daphne in all her bucolic simplicity. The movement down a semitone ultimately signifies her magical transformation into the laurel tree.

previous moments of extended chromaticism in the opera, especially the Klytämnestra scene where the E–C tension also operates (E is represented by its dominant), but in a more obscure way.[12]

Strauss paces this dual tonal relationship in scene 7 with remarkable skill. Parts I and II of the scene are set in E, while part III—the additional duet—is in C. This process of going from E to C is then repeated, but over a shorter span, in Elektra's dance: section 1 is in E and section 2 ('Schweig und tanze') is in C. The overall effect is that of an increasingly concentrated tension betwen these two keys. After Elektra dies, the conflict is played out one last time (with the secondary dominant of E and the dominant of C) within a span of merely two bars: the sixth and fifth bars before the end (Ex. 7.6).

Ex. 7.6 5 bars after reh. 262a

Therefore, by the end of the opera the previous tonal conflict has boiled down to this 'double tonic' of scene 7.[13] Strauss reinforces, indeed intensifies, the strong relationship between these two tonal spheres by inserting, in a localized way, reminders of E or C in a section of its opposite key. The overall effect is that of a brief incursion by the sphere of the

[12] See pp. 90–2, Chapter 4.

[13] Robert Bailey, among others, has demonstrated the prevalence of the double tonic principle in numerous late 19th- and early 20th-century works. His cogent argument for the double tonic in *Tristan und Isolde* is exemplary. See 'An Analytical Study of the Sketches and Drafts', *Wagner: Prelude and Transformation from Tristan und Isolde*, Norton Critical Scores (New York, 1985).

other key. The first part of the scene is exemplary (the incursion is in bold face):

Part I

E	Chrysothemis: 'Es ist der Bruder drin im Haus!' + Chorus: 'Orest!'
(V^7/C)	[Chrysothemis: 'Alle, die Aegisth von Herzen hassten . . .'] **Chorus: 'Orest!'**
E	Chrysothemis: 'Tausend Fackeln sind angezündet' + Chorus: 'Orest!'

Thus, of the three choral exclamations ('Orest!') the middle one touches upon the dominant of C; that dominant (in root position) is sustained for six bars before sliding down by a semitone to the second-inversion dominant of E at reh. 227a. The brief, six-bar appearance of C—by way of its dominant—is too fleeting to be considered a true secondary tonal area in part 1, but it none the less acts as subtle, yet effective, preparation for what is to come. Part 2 ('Ob ich nicht höre?'), which is also set in E, likewise exhibits a temporary shift to the realm of C by way of its dominant (reh. 231a to 4 bars after reh. 232a). Similarly, the C major duet between Elektra and Chrysothemis has its share of local intrusions of E major as well: either on E (which highlights Elektra's phrase, 'und diese Stunde bin ich das Feuer des Lebens') or by way of its dominant, when Chrysothemis sings, 'Wer hat uns geliebt?'

Elektra's Dance

The significance of this E–C duality cannot be fully appreciated without understanding the overall importance of dance in the final scene. Dance is the most forceful gesture in the opera; it is referred to in Elektra's opening monologue and carried out in the final scene. It is the ultimate physical release after the murders of Klytämnestra and Aegisthus.[14] But neither

[14] Dance also plays a role in Elektra's brief encounter with Aegisthus just before she leads him to his murder:

Hofmannsthal nor Strauss specifies what type of dance Elektra actually carries out, and the ambiguity is probably deliberate.

In a study of dance in the *Elektra* play, Reinhold Schlötterer reminds us of two basic types of dance in ancient Greece—the round dance and the maenadic dance rituals—and Hofmannsthal was keenly aware of this distinction.[15] The former dance was a social rite; the participants joined hands, generally in a circle, and a community took part. The latter was a solo dionysian dance of ecstatic release—a transcendence from the present world.[16]

Although Hofmannsthal's text for the final scene refers to both types, it is only in the opera that these contrasting rituals are vividly articulated. The triumphant round dance symbolizes restored social harmony after the socially dissonant elements—Klytämnestra and Aegisthus—have been removed. After the murders, the solitary Elektra wishes to join the group and the community at large. Her dissolution as an individual is achieved through the social gesture of the round dance. We recall that she tells her sister: 'Be silent and dance. All must approach!' In her opening monologue, she prophesied the moment when she would be able to join hands with her siblings and dance on their father's grave.

But an equally vital impulse for Elektra is her maenadic dance of transcendence in the final scene; it is the primary vehicle for her catharsis. In undertaking this awkward, nameless dance, she separates herself from her immediate

---

Aegisthus
What are you dancing for?
Watch the way.

She circles around him in a kind of weird dance, suddenly bowing very low.

In this instance, it seems to serve as a type of *Totentanz*.

[15] Reinhold Schlötterer, 'Elektras Tanz in der Tragödie Hugo von Hofmannsthals', *Hofmannsthal Blätter* 33 (1986), 47–9.

[16] The maenads were women who celebrated the rites of Dionysos in the form of uninhibited, furious dance. There were no specific or organized gestures to this frenzied dance, although leaping is said to have been an important aspect of the ritual. Homer describes Andromache as leaping about the palace like a maenad when she intuitively learned of Hector's death. See Marcel Dentienne, *Dionysos at Large*, trans. Arthur Goldhammer (Cambridge, Mass., 1989), 57.

surroundings at this moment of personal ecstasy. Hofmannsthal deliberately obscures these two apparently opposing states, for Elektra is never joined by the group, and Agamemnon's children never join hands. In the final scene the poet, once again, exploits the dialectic of word and deed. As Elektra dances in maenadic gesture, she can only speak of the round dance; the latter ritual only takes place in her mind.[17]

Strauss symbolizes and intensifies these impulses through the juxtaposition of E and C major. The former key symbolizes the bacchic or maenadic state of being. Elsewhere in this study we have already seen how Strauss uses E major to suggest passionate or even erotic states.[18] C major not only represents Elektra's victory over Klytämnestra and her accomplice, but in a broader sense symbolizes the restoration of order and the hope for reconciliation. Here, too, we can trace various examples of C major used in this manner throughout the works of Strauss: evoking the ultimate restoration of the soul in the coda of *Tod und Verklärung*; the perfection of nature in *Also Sprach Zarathustra*; the restoration of sexual harmony at the end of *Die Frau ohne Schatten*; and the final chorus of *Der Friedenstag*, where opposing armies are reconciled at the end of the Thirty Years War.

The sketch fragments (fols. 2^{v} and 3) of the Vienna sketchbook leave no doubt that Strauss not only perceived the two types of dances, but wanted to delineate them musically. We recall that the sketch fragment on fol. 2^{v} ('Elektras Tanz zuerst') was in E major and the fragment on the next page ('Tanz am Schluss nach Elektras letztem Gesang') was in C major. On these two pages we see the kernel of Strauss's musical thought concerning dance in *Elektra*: that the cathartic dance should be in E and the round dance should be in C. The tonal planning seen in fols. 18^{v}–20^{v} (the short continuity sketch) further illuminates

[17] Elektra only spoke of murdering Klytämnestra and Aegisthus; Orestes actually executed the deed.

[18] See Chapter 4, pp. 68–9.

Strauss's concern for the expressive duality of E and C. After a number of empty bars on fol. 19, for example, he places a V/C chord directly under the word 'Reigen'—strengthening our understanding of the connection between C major and the round dance (*Reigen*) ritual.

In sum, through the interplay of E and C, we better understand this important polarity between individual expression and the harmonious social gesture; these opposing states operate simultaneously in Elektra's mind. We also better understand those brief 'incursions' of E or C in a section of its opposite key; it is an essential element of this intentional ambiguity. Thus, as Chrysothemis and chorus ecstatically rush on stage—in E major—with the news of Orestes' return, the brief reference to C (as they exclaim 'Orest!') underscores the sense of incipient reunification; it hints at the possibility of restoration.

Likewise in part II (also in E), where Elektra becomes increasingly lost in her state of cathartic transport, Strauss touches upon C just as she envisions the others gathering around her ('alle warten auf mich'). Strauss ultimately modulates to C as the two siblings are, indeed, joined together in part III, but creates tension in this third part with brief references to E. With those incursions of E, Strauss makes us aware that although Elektra sings with her sister she alone is transported to a different world. Like a meteor, she burns brightly but will soon burn out. The first brief shift to E accompanies Elektra's text: '. . . diese Stunde bin ich das Feuer des Lebens' ('this hour I am the fire of life'). Finally, in the dance, which goes from E to C, we witness the ultimate process of the dissolution of the individual, and there is nothing left but her death.

Table 7.1 gives a summary of the tonal layout for scene 7. In part III (see Table 7.1), the central section of the scene, Strauss creates three distinctly parallel passages at reh. 241a, 242a, and 244a, which are in E flat, E, and C major, respectively. The composer links them together with the so-called childhood theme (Ex. 7.7).

TABLE 7.1 Summary of tonal layout (Scene 7)

Part	Key	Rehearsal no.	Text
I Chry. + chorus	E	3 before 221a	Chrysothemis: 'Es ist der Bruder' Chorus: 'Orest!'
	(V/C)	226a	Chorus: 'Orest!'
	E	227a	Chorus: 'Orest!' /Chrysothemis: 'Tausende Fackeln sind angezündet.'
II Elektra's entrance	E	2 before 229a	Elektra: 'Ob ich nicht höre?'
	(V/C)	231a	Elektra: '. . . die Erde dumpf dröhnen machen . . .'
	(F m)	2 before 233a	Elektra: 'Und ich kann nicht . . .'
	V/E	235a	Chrysothemis: 'Hörst du denn nicht?'
III Sisters' duet	C	236a	Elektra: 'Wir sind bei den Göttern . . .'
	(E)	3 after 240a	Elektra: 'Diese Stunde bin ich das Feuer des Lebens . . .'
	(E♭)	241a	Chrysothemis: 'Die überschwänglich guten Götter . . .'
	(V/E)	242a	Chrysothemis: 'Wer hat uns geliebt
	C	244a	Elektra: 'Seht ihr denn mein Gesicht?'
IV*a* Elektra's dance	E	247a	
IV*b*	V/C	5 after 255a	Elektra: 'Schweig und tanze!'
	(V/E)	5 after 258a	Elektra: '. . . schweigen und tanzen . . .'
	V/C	259a	
V Elektra's death	(E♭ m)	261a	
	C	7 after 262a	

Ex. 7.7

Thus, as the sisters join together in a duet, Strauss presents Chrysothemis' life-affirming E flat major, as well as the duality of E and C. But the relationship is more complex, for it both foreshadows the final relationship of these three keys at the end of the opera (Elektra's last line [V/E], Elektra's death [E flat minor], and the final cadence on C) and looks back to the tonal tension of the Klytämnestra scene. In that scene, which is in three parts, C clashes with the dominants of E and E flat.

Scene 4 (Klytämnestra and Elektra)

I	II	III
Klytämnestra and Attendants	Klytämnestra and Elektra	Elektra
reh. 132–177	reh. 177–229	10 before reh. 229–273
Bm (V/Cm)	Bm	Cm (C) B♭ B

In the third section, Elektra has a type of double cadence (first on C, then on B flat), but the scene itself climaxes on B in the orchestral postlude, for Klytämnestra is temporarily triumphant with the news of Orestes' supposed death. We sense the importance of the B flat, when, in the next scene, Chrysothemis rushes in (E flat minor) to tell Elektra the news.

Table 7.1 part IV illustrates another important parallel, for five bars after both reh. 255a and 258a Strauss juxtaposes the dominants of C and E with Elektra's declaration that all should be quiet and dance. A closer look at part IV shows that although it is, itself, in two sections (E and C), the second section juxtaposes these two keys one last time. And, as a preparation for the final cadence, part 4*b* is defined as being in C major only by its dominant, which, indeed, frames that section.

Elektra's Death

The sketches to scene 7 shed light on the fact that Strauss delineates—through tonal symbolism—two modes of dance implicit in Hofmannsthal's play. But what do the sketches offer as an indication of how Strauss interpreted her death, which immediately follows her dance? Two surviving sketches—one from Tr. 17 and the other from the Vienna Sketchbook—reveal profoundly different interpretations of Elektra's death and the way in which the opera should end.

Tr. 17 is the earliest surviving *Elektra* sketchbook; material contained therein dates from around spring 1906 to possibly as late as early September 1907. On fol. 49 of the sketchbook Strauss sketches a one-page fragment labelled 'Schluss'; it is a sketch of the last twenty bars of the opera (see Ex. 7.8).

In this early one-page version of the close, sketched a year or more before Strauss began composing the end of the opera in earnest, *Elektra* ends not in C major, but in E flat minor. In Tr. 17 the work does not end with those sharply profiled triumphant utterances of the Agememnon motive, but rather with a sustained E flat in the tubas. The final gesture is an open octave articulated by trombones and pizzicato strings. C major plays a role in this earlier sketch, as Chrysothemis exclaims her final 'Orest', but it quickly shifts to C minor and upward by step from D minor to E flat minor.

This fragment from Tr. 17 suggests Strauss's misunderstanding of the meaning of Elektra's death (and, more generally, of her role in the play) in the early stages of the opera's genesis. In *Elektra*, E flat minor symbolizes Orestes' supposed death, and it comes to signify Elektra's actual death, negating Chrysothemis' life-affirming E flat major.

Ex. 7.8 Tr. 17, fol. 49

Thus, Strauss's early sketch is concerned with the death of Elektra the individual—a far cry from Hofmannsthal's intent, which centres not so much on the death of the individual, but the dissolution of the individual. He observed:

In Elektra the individual is dissolved in the empirical way, in which the content of her life explodes outwards from inside like water that becomes ice in an earthen jug. Elektra is no more Elektra, because she has dedicated herself entirely to being only Elektra. The individual can only remain to endure where a compromise has been struck between the community and the individual.[19]

Elektra embodies the polarization of the past and future; she lives entirely without concern for the present. With Elektra's dissolution, Hofmannsthal endorses Chrysothemis, for ultimately the play's values—and those of nearly every play or libretto of Hofmannsthal—are anchored in vitalism.[20] His concern—indeed, preoccupation—with the continuity of life is well evident in Chrysothemis' monologue in scene 3 when she declares:

> With knives each passing day carves his mark
> on your face and mine, and outside, the sun rises
> and sets, and women whom I have known slender
> are heavy with blessing, and toil on their way
> to the well and scarcely lift the pail, and all
> at once they are delivered of their weight
> and come to the well again and they themselves
> flow with sweet drink, and, suckling, a new life
> clings to them, and the children grow—

In her Act I monologue in *Der Rosenkavalier* the Marschallin considers this theme within the context of time and mutability; she likens the passing of time not to knives that 'carve [their] mark on your face and mine', but to the sand in an hour-glass: 'It trickles away in our faces, it trickles in the mirror, in my temples it flows away.' In *Die Frau ohne Schatten*, Hofmannsthal focuses upon the threads that bind generations. At the end of Act I, the Watchmen sing:

[19] 'In der Elektra wird das Individuum in der empirischen Weise aufgelöst, indem eben der Inhalt seines Lebens es von innen her zerspringt wie das sich zu Eis umbildende Wasser einen irdenen Krug. Elektra ist nicht mehr Elektra, weil sie eben ganz und gar Elektra zu sein sich weihte. Das Individuum kann nur scheinhaft dort bestehen bleiben, wo ein Kompromiss zwischen dem Gemeinen und dem Individuellen geschlossen wird.' Taken from 'Zwei bisher unveröffentlichte Aufzeichnungen von Hugo von Hofmannsthal', *Programmheft 2: Salome und Elektra* (Frankfurter Oper: 1974), 28.

[20] Lorna Martens, 'The Theme of the Repressed Memory in Hofmannsthal's *Elektra*', *German Quarterly*, 60 (1987), 48.

Married folk under the roofs of this town,
love one another more than your own lives,
and recall: it is not for your own lives' sake
that the seed of life is given to you,
but for the sake of your love alone . . .
you are the bridges spanning the chasm
over which the dead find their way back to life![21]

Without the present to bridge the past and the future, Elektra is a socially dissonant element at odds with Hofmannsthal's world view. She threatens to upset the continuity that connects society and ultimately links civilizations.

As the sketches seem to suggest, it was not until after that moment of creative impasse that caused the seven-month break in composition between early October and late June 1908 that the composer began to understand this important element of Hofmannsthal's work. Letters show that during this time and shortly thereafter Strauss became more and more preoccupied with matters of characterization and dramaturgy, and he probably voiced some of his concerns to Hofmannsthal in person as well. The composer's later sketch (August 1908) for the ending in the Vienna Sketchbook interprets Elektra's death in a more positive way. Her death allows for a restoration of harmony, and the final, emphatic cadence on C major is as much a reflection of that sense of restoration as it is a symbol of triumph. The composer signals the beginning of her dissolution at the opening of the second part of her dance, as she sings 'Be silent and dance!' over an extended G pedal (5 after reh. 255a). From then on E major no longer plays a significant role in the opera, for Elektra's cathartic dance has finally resulted in her transcendence. Indeed, Hofmannsthal seems to suggest that, at that moment, Elektra is already in a trance-like state: 'Elektra remains motionless, gazing at [Chrysothemis].'

In that later sketch, and in the final version as well, Strauss juxtaposes E flat minor and C minor (Elektra's death and

[21] Trans. (1988) Mary Whittall for EMI Records Ltd.

Agamemnon's death, respectively) after Elektra falls lifeless to the ground. This blatant alternation between the quiet, static E-flat-minor chord and the vociferous C-minor Agamemnon motive is one of the most gripping juxtapositions in the score. It leads to one final interplay between catharsis and triumph: between the secondary dominant of E and the dominant of C (six bars before the end, see Ex. 7.6). The powerful cadence on C major celebrates the avengement of Agamemnon's death and the preservation of the status quo. The penultimate and ultimate chords (E flat minor and C major) signal that, with the death of Elektra, the individual is finally dissolved, for only after the deaths of Klytämnestra, Aegisthus, and Elektra can social harmony be restored.

Appendix I: Elektra *Chronicle*

ABBREVIATIONS

Erken	Günter Erken, *Hofmannsthal Chronik: Beitrag zu einer Biographie*. Unpublished (ca. 1963). Willi Schuh Estate.
von Schuch	Friedrich von Schuch, *Richard Strauss, Ernst von Schuch, und Dresdens Oper*. Leipzig: Breitkopf und Härtel, 1953.
Hofmannsthal–Nostitz	*Hugo von Hofmannsthal–Helene von Nostitz: Briefwechsel*. Ed. O. Nostitz. Frankfurt: Fischer, 1965.
Huesmann	Heinrich Huesmann, *Welttheater Reinhardt*. Munich: Prestel, 1983.

1905

21 Oct. 1st performance of the 2nd production of Hofmannsthal's *Elektra* in Berlin, now at the *Deutsches Theater*. Willi Schuh claims Strauss saw it that day, although '*Barbier von Bagdad*' is written in his *Schreibkalender*. [RSA]

7 Nov. 3rd and last performance of the *Elektra* production at the *Deutsches Theater*. [Huesmann]

1906

2 Feb. Hofmannsthal in Berlin for première of his *Oedipus und der Sphinx* at the *Deutsches Theater*. According to Günther Erken, Strauss and Hofmannsthal met that day and discussed the possibility of an *Elektra* opera. [Huesmann and Erken]

7 Mar. Hofmannsthal wants to know whether Strauss is still interested in the *Elektra* project. [*Briefwechsel/Correspondence*]

11 Mar. Strauss is still interested and has made cuts in the text for his own use. He expresses some worry that *Elektra* and

	Salome might share too many similarities. [*Briefwechsel/ Correspondence*]
8 May	Strauss wants to meet Hofmannsthal in Vienna (Südbahnhof) during a two-hour stopover in Vienna on his way to Graz. [*Briefwechsel*]
5 June	'I would like to begin with *Elektra* . . .' (Strauss to Hofmannsthal) [*Briefwechsel*]
13 June	'I steadily occupy myself with *Elektra* and will be very happy when all of the business worries are soon put in order.' (Strauss to Hofmannsthal) [*Briefwechsel*]
16 June	Strauss is busy on the first scene of *Elektra*, is 'still making rather heavy weather of it'. (Strauss to Hofmannsthal) [*Briefwechsel/Correspondence*]
16 July	'The first two scenes of *Elektra* are already done.' (Strauss to Levin) [BSt]
7 Aug.	'I am [working] diligently on Elektra . . .' (Strauss to his mother) [BSt]
11 Dec.	'Strauss played and sang' parts of *Elektra* for Hofmannsthal (Hofmannsthal to Helene von Nostitz on 12 December) [Hofmannsthal–Nostitz]

1907

23 Jan.	'. . . I work diligently on Elektra . . .' (Strauss to his sister) [BSt]
24 Aug.	'I don't want to exert myself too much this winter and would like to work steadily on *Elektra*.' (Strauss to Schuch) [von Schuch]
12 Sept.	'*Elektra* progresses steadily.' (Strauss to his sister) [BSt]
13 Sept.	'*Elektra* has progressed as far as page 60 [midway through scene 5] in the textbook.' (Strauss to his wife) [RSA]
17 Sept.	'I am doing well: have unfortunately too much to do: official duties, correspondence, building the house, *Elektra*, you must please excuse my belated writing!' (Strauss to his mother) [BSt]
23 Sept.	'I shall play for you *Elektra* which has progressed quite far.' (Strauss to Schuch) [von Schuch]
7 Oct.	Begins scoring *Elektra*. (date inscribed on first page of autograph score) [RSA]

13 Oct. 'I am also doing well, despite the fact that I am again deeply involved in my work (*Elektra*).' (Strauss to his mother) [BSt]

25 Oct. 'I work diligently on *Elektra* and also take advantage of the beautiful weather for vigorous walks.' (Strauss to his mother) [BSt]

17 Nov. [Sunday] Strauss states that after the problematic *Salome* première in Amsterdam, he feels peacefully at home (Willem Mengelberg's home) and is orchestrating *Elektra*—which he has already resumed on Friday—at Mengelberg's desk. (Strauss to his wife) [RSA]

7 Dec. *Elektra* orchestrated up to p. 44 (2nd scene, 1 before reh. 64). [RSA]

8 Dec. 'Fifty pages of the score are already written.' (to Schuch) [von Schuch]

14 Dec. *Elektra* orchestrated up to p. 58 (3 after reh. 90) [RSA]

late Dec. Strauss and Hofmannsthal meet in Berlin, among other things—such as a discussion of *Semiramis*—they probably discussed the Aegisthus scene: Hofmannsthal appears to have suggested that the scene might be dispensed with entirely. [*Briefwechsel/Correspondence*]

22 Dec. Strauss writes to Hofmannsthal that Aegisthus cannot be cut out altogether; he must be killed with the rest ('preferably before the eyes of the audience') and as soon after Klytämnestra's murder as possible. [*Briefwechsel/Correspondence*]

25 Dec. *Elektra* orchestrated up to p. 78 (2 after reh. 128) [RSA]

1908

3 Jan. Hofmannsthal suggests they cut the serving maids' scene, segueing to Aegisthus just after 'Triff noch einmal!', etc. [*Briefwechsel/Correspondence*]

8 Jan. 'I work day and night: *Elektra* progresses further, but one must give a quarter of one's life to such a work.' (Strauss to his mother) [BSt]

19 Jan. *Elektra* scored up to p. 128 (2 after reh. 127) [RSA]

20 Feb. Strauss asks for 'those small additions to *Elektra* (chorus and final scene) . . . *Elektra* is making vigorous headway. I could play it to you in Vienna.' Strauss wants to meet with Hofmannsthal *c.*7 March in Vienna. [*Briefwechsel/Correspondence*]

26 Feb. 'This morning Hofmannsthal was here [in Berlin], I played *Elektra* for him.' Hofmannsthal also discussed the three-act Casanova comedy. [RSA]

28 Feb. 'Yesterday [Ernst von] Schuch was here [in Berlin], I played *Elektra* for him, [Willy] Levin, and [Friedrich] Rösch. All were very impressed.' (Strauss to his wife) [RSA]

12 Mar. *Elektra* scored up to p. 160 (4 after reh. 269) [RSA]

18 Mar. *Elektra* scored up to p. 176 (5 after reh. 23a) [RSA]

30 Mar. 'I have recently returned to *Elektra*.' (Strauss to his wife) [RSA]

1 Apr. Strauss explores a business deal (re: *Elektra*) with Schott. [RSA]

4 Apr. 'I sit diligently working on *Elektra*.' (Strauss to his wife) [RSA]

4 Apr. *Elektra* scored up to p. 182 (6 after reh 38a) [RSA]

8 Apr. '*Elektra* progresses heartily forwards.' (Strauss to his wife) [RSA]

9 Apr. Strauss is busy finishing *Elektra*. (Strauss to his mother) [BSt]

11 Apr. Strauss makes deal to sell *Elektra* to Fürstner for 100,000 DM [RSA]

14 Apr. '. . . Just now I've had to stop the hard work on *Elektra*, if I'm to spare any time for the tour. I still have three rehearsals this week.' (Strauss to his wife) [RSA]

16 Apr. '. . . [working on] *Elektra* is no fun.' (Strauss to his wife) [RSA]

22 Apr. Strauss mentions the Fürstner contract in his *Schreibkalender*. [RSA]

30 Apr. 'Yesterday afternoon I worked very peacefully on my *Elektra* score.' (Strauss to his wife) [RSA]

24 May 'With Rösch I can also discuss everything necessary until lunch, and I will also be with Sieger in the hotel around two o'clock. I *must* speak with him about *Elektra*.' (Strauss to his wife) [RSA]

21 June — Strauss resumes sketching Recognition Scene, etc. [*Briefwechsel/Correspondence*]

22 June — Strauss asks for more text to fill out a 'great moment for repose at recognitions scene'. Is not quite sure about the stage layout at end. Full score done up until Orestes' entry. 'I made a start yesterday on composing from there onwards.' [*Briefwechsel/Correspondence*]

25 June — Hofmannsthal sends textual additions and explains layout in a diagram. [*Briefwechsel/Correspondence*]

25 June — Schuch visits Strauss. [RSA]

4 July — Hofmannsthal asks Strauss for list of corrections so that he 'can get it [textual additions?] all done'. [*Briefwechsel/Correspondence*]

6 July — Strauss requests more text for 'simultaneous duet' between Elektra and Chrysothemis. He says he has already set Recognition Scene to music. [*Briefwechsel/Correspondence*]

8 July — 'I work diligently with *Elektra* and hope to have completed it by September.' (Strauss to his mother) [BSt]

8 July — Hofmannsthal promises to send *Elektra* changes by tomorrow or the next day. [*Briefwechsel/Correspondence*]

9 July — Hofmannsthal encloses expansions that Strauss requested on the 6th [*Briefwechsel/Correspondence*]

12 July — 'Scene between Elektra and Orestes is finished.' [RSA]

13 July — 'Particell [to] *Elektra* finished to the entrance of Orestes' tutor.' [RSA]

[The two dates above (12 and 13 July) could all be a single entry for 12 July; the alignment is not clear in Strauss's diary.]

14 July — 'Continuation of the *Elektra* score from page 218.' (6 after reh. 111a) [RSA]

17 July — Strauss finishes p. 228 of full score. (7 after reh. 129) [RSA]

11 Sept. — '*Elektra* is finished and the close is quite juicy.' (Strauss to Schuch) [von Schuch]

1908

22 Sept. Strauss finishes orchestrating final page of full score. [RSA]

23 Sept. Letter to Felix Mottl re: Munich première—gives schedule for publication of score, parts, etc. [BSt]

1944

? July Gertrude Eysoldt, in a belated birthday greeting to Strauss, reminds him of the performance of the *Elektra* play (at the *Kleines Theater*, according to her) that he attended. Strauss corrects her with a memo at bottom of the letter: 'Berlin, Deutsches Theater. Schumannstr[asse].' [RSA]

Appendix II: Sketchbook Inventories

TRENNER 17

Date : ?1906–18
Size: 12.5 × 16.5 cm.
No. of fols.: 50
Sketchbook type: Preliminary
Sketchbook make: Jos. Eberle, Vienna
Implements used: Pencil and ink
Contents: Contains material pertaining to *Elektra*; *Der Rosenkavalier*; Lieder Op. 56, No. 6; Op. 69, No. 3; *Deutsche Motette*; *Eine Alpensinfonie*.

Inside front cover: 'VII | Elektra Themen | Die heiligen 3 Könige | Reinheit C dur 4/4 | Heroisches Thema Es dur 4/4 (3/2) | Lied von L. v. Arnim: O du liebes Einerlei | E dur.' All other annotations concern plans for the house and garden in Garmisch; there are also some numerical calculations probably concerning royalties.

Inside back cover: The text (in ink) to *Deutsche Motette* in Pauline Strauss's hand. There are musical *Randnotizen* (in pencil) by Richard. At the bottom of the page (in Strauss's hand): 'Kaiser Wilhelm Mittelfrühe Bohnen.'

Score pp. *Fol. no.*

*1: 'Largo | das Schicksal der Atriden | Agamemnon | Tuben | Elektras Hass! | das Geschick der Atriden | die Katze'
*1v: 'Steigerung für Elektras Tanz 4 Taktig | Anfang | Siegestanz | E dur'
*2: 'Anfang | Andante 1 "Wo bleibt Elektra? . . ."'
*2v: 'Coda | oder Quartett'
*3: 'Elektra | [illegible] | dann | g moll'

★3^{v}: 'Agamemnon | Ägisth trage u. gemein | Agamemnon d moll | Elektra A moll—c moll (im Trauergesang)'
★4: 'Agamemnon'
★4^{v}: 'Reinheit. für St. Helena'
★5: 'Elektra kauernd vor Klytämnestra | Schmerz u. Klage (weich) | die Jüngere mitleidig'
★5^{v}: 'Elektrathemen: stolz königlich, die alte Elektra | schmerz gebeugt | aggressif | Vater! | "Lass mich heute nicht mehr"[?]' [The word should be 'allein', but it doesn't appear to be.]
★6: 'Elektra | unerwartet Des moll oder C moll | "Vater dein Tag wird kommen" '
27, 32–3 ★6^{v}: 'und der mit ihr in einem königlichen Bette schläft . . . nur so wie gestern . . .'
29–31 ★7: '*Orest*. Ernst u. feierlich unter dem Druck des Schicksals | bis | "lass mich heute nicht allein . . ." '
★7^{v}: [unlabelled *Elektra* sketch: A flat maj. ('Kindheit' motive?)]
★8: '[illegible] | Coda | tan- | zen'
8^{v}: '3 Könige'
9: [cont.]
9^{v}: 'Heroisches Thema'
10: 'als Hochsatzfugen schwungvoll siehe Skizzenbuch VI' [2 poems are pasted in on this page: *Wiegenlied* (Wilhelm Raabe) and *Sonnett* (Friedrich Hebbel)]
10^{v}: [sketch for '3 Könige']
11: [cont.]
11^{v}: [cont.]
12: 'Anfang des Liedes | Celesta . . .'
12^{v}: 'Allegro vivace'
13: 'männliche Kraft u. Trotz'
13^{v}: 'Arnim'
14: [cont.]
14^{v}: [cont.]
15: [cont.]
15^{v}: 'Fröhlich | Sinfonieanfang | 'andere erste Fortführung D dur bleiben'
16: [cont.] 'Cantilene in F dur'
16^{v}: [cont.]

17: 'Elegie' [E flat maj.—*Alpensinfonie*?]
17v: 'Codathema: | innig' [*Alpensinfonie*?]
18: 'Seele | Hauptsatz Es dur die Schläferin, Mittelsatz G moll Vision des Marthyriums . . .'
18v: 'Coda | St. Helena | Schluss . . .'
19: 'Hymne von Rückert: a capella . . .'
19v: [cont.]
20: [cont.]
20^{v}: 'feierliche Marsch für Blech u. Pauken'
21: [cont.]
21^{v}: 'Einleitung' [see fol. 20^{v}]
22: 'Marsch' [see fol. 20^{v}]
22^{v}: [unlabelled sketch for 'Marsch']
23: 'Quartett | breit | schneller . . .'
23^{v}: 'Adagio'
24: 'Nachsatz'
*24^{v}: 'Orest' [also *Deutsche Motette* sketches?]
25: 'Mailied v. Göthe'
25^{v}: [*Deutsche Motette*?]
26: [cont.]
26^{v}: 'Beginn.' [for 'Quartett'?]
*27: [unlabelled sketch (*Elektra*?)]

146	*27^{v}: 'Elektra | Wie?' [Kl.] 'Es heisst, er stammelt . . .'
146–7	*28: '[Ich] schickte viel Gold . . .'
147–9	*28^{v}: '[bei Tag] an nichts als an ihr . . .'
149–50	*28*a*: '[die To-] re zu bewachen . . .'
150–2	*28a^{v}: '[die] Bräuche, die mir nützen . . .'
153–5	*29: 'ist nur ein Narr . . .'
156–8	*29^{v}: '[der Jäger] abgefangen hat . . .'
159–61	*30: 'Willst du nach rechts . . .'
162–3	*30^{v}: 'und ich bin wie ein Hund an deiner Ferse . . .'
163–5	*31: '(das Beil hängt in der Luft) und dort im tiefsten dunkel . . .'
164–6	*31^{v}: 'drücken wir dich hin | Du möchtest schreien . . .'
167	*32: 'Diese Zeit sie dehnt sich . . .'
167–9	*32^{v}: 'ahnen wie es Scheiternden zumute ist . . .'
170	*33: 'Und so wie jetzt kannst du nicht schrein!'
170, 155–6	*33^{v}: 'das ungeheure Wort | El. Was bluten muß'
156–8	*34: 'Ich hör' ihn durch die Zimmer gehn'
158–60	*34^{v}: '[er ist] hinterdrein'

160–2	*35: '[Gewöl-]be hin, Gewölbe und Gewölbe . . .'
162–4	*35^{v}: '[in eine] Höhle spring' ich dich von seitwärts . . .'
164–6	*36: '[der] Vater, er achtet's nicht . . .'
166	*36^{v}: 'Wie von Sinnen hältst du den Nacken hin . . .'
166–8	*37: 'alles schweigt, du hörst dein eignes Herz . . .'
168–70	*37^{v}: '[und des] Todes zerfrisst . . .'
170	*38: '[so] eingekehrt als wär's der glühende Bauch . . .'
171–2	*38^{v}: 'erhängt ist dir die Seele . . .'
172–5	*39: '[brauche] ich nicht mehr zu [träumen . . .]'
175–6	*39^{v}: [orchestral passage for servants' entry]
176	*40: 'Lichter!/Lichter!'
176–7	*40^{v}: [cont.]
196 f.	*41: 'Citat | "Tot, Elektra, Tot, gestorben in der Fremde!"'
	*41^{v}: *Elektra* sketch [cont.?]
188–91	*42: 'Sei still. Orest ist Tot . . .'
191–2	*42^{v}: 'Elektra | "Niemand weiss [es] . . ."'
193	*43: 'Es ist nicht wahr . . .'
	*43^{v}: 'weicher worden'
	44: 'Zum heroischen Thema Es dur Coda'
	44^{v}: [cont.?]
	45: 'Zu Göthes Wanderlied . . .'
	*45^{v}: 'Elektra die dich zum Opfer bringt'
	*46: [unlabelled sketch (*Elektra*?)]
	46^{v}: [unlabelled sketch]
	47: [related to above]
	47^{v}: 'Lady Hamilton: Portrait | nach Casanovas C.C. Band III, Schluss . . .'
	48: 'aufsteigend' [*Alpensinfonie*?]
	48^{v}: 'elegisch'
	*49: 'Schluss | "Orest!"'
	*49^{v}: [*Deutsche Motette* sketches,] 'Elektras Hass'
	[50: torn out]

***Elektra* sketch

Trenner 18

Date: ?1906–7
Size: 12.5 × 16.5 cm.
No. of fols.: 50

Sketchbook type: Preliminary
Sketchbook make: Jos. Eberle, Vienna
Implements: Pencil and ink
Contents: *Elektra, Parademarsch für Cavallerie, Vier Frauengestalten der National Gallery*

Inside front cover: 'IX | enthält gute Elektraskizzen | u. Porträtskizzen | der National Gallery'

Front cover page [recto]: 'Eigentum des Herrn Willy Levin | zum andenken an den Eibsee | Juli–August 1906 | Richard Strauss

Front cover page [verso]: blank

Inside back cover: '4 Frauengestalten der National Gallery: Lady Hamilton | Veroneses Schläferin | Hogarths Crevetten Girl | (Reynolds 5 facher Kinderkopf.)' [Written upside-down is a formula (in Pauline's hand) for taking care of wounds.]

Back cover page [recto]: Building details for the Garmisch villa.

Back cover page [verso]: Text for part of the Elektra–Klytämnestra scene 'Kl. Die Bräuche sag! | Wie brächt ich's dar? ich selber muss— | El. Nein. Diesmal | gehst du nicht auf die Jagd mit Netz und mit Beil . . .' [through] 'El. Das Kind war ganz gesund.'

Score pp.	*Fol. no.*
	★1: 'Anruf des Agamemnons	Parsifal!	Anfang . . .'
	1^{v}: 'Paul Veronese'
	★2: 'Agitato	Elektra beschwört Chrysothemis'
5–6	★2^{v}: 'Elektra	"Wo bleibt Elektra?" . . .'
7–8	★3: 'Habt ihr gesehn . . .'
7	★3^{v}: 'Habt ihr gesehn . . .'
7–8	★4:'[wie sie uns] ansah?'
9–10	★4^{v}: '[wie eine] Katze . . .'
10–12	★5: 'sollt nicht schmatzen . . .'
12–13	★5^{v}: 'so isst du auch . . .'
14	★6: 'in ihren Winkel . . .'
14–15	★6^{v}: 'bei Gott [!] sie unter Schloss und Riegel . . .'
15–16	★7: 'Habt ihr den Herrn nie . . .'

16–17	*7^{v}: 'Ich will die Füsse ihr salben . . .'
17–19	*8: '[Nie-]mand, Niemand ist hier im Haus . . .'
19–20	*8^{v}: '[um] dessen willen, was ihr an Elektra . . .'
20–1	*9: '[kann man er-] niedern, wozu man uns hat . . .'
21–2	*9^{v}: 'Tag und Nacht erneut in Winkel fegen . . .'
22–3	*10: '[und ge-] boren haben . . .'
	*10^{v}: 'Beschwörung des Agamemnon | langsam Elektra allein | Klytämnestra' [various thematic fragments]
25	*11: '[illegible] des [illegible] | Elektra tritt hervor | Elektra langsam'
26–7	*11^{v}: [E.] 'Wo bist du Vater? Hast du nicht die Kraft . . .?'
27–8	*12: '[die Stun-] de wo sie dich ge[schlachtet haben.]'
27–8	*12^{v}: 'dein Weib und der mit ihr . . .'
29, 36, 39	*13: 'Kopf voraus die Beine schleifend . . .' [in 3rd system:] 'u. wir schlachten dir die Rosse | As dur | Rosse | u. wir schlachten dir die Hunde | H dur | Hunde | u. wir dein Blut Orest' [thematic fragments for these various lines of text]
	*13^{v}: [unlabelled: pertaining to E.'s monologue?]
	*14: 'Chrysot.'
61–2	*14^{v}: 'Lebhaft' [from 'Kinder will ich haben']
55–6	*15: 'Ich hab's wie Feuer in der Brust . . .'
56–7	*15^{v}: '[trepp]ab, mir ist als rief' es mich . . .'
57–8	*16: '[bei] Tag und Nacht. Mir ist die Kehle . . .'
58–9	*16^{v}: '[mit Eisen-]klammern mich an den Boden . . .'
59–61	*17: '[sie zittern,] ah! so liessen sie . . .'
61	*18: '(*a*) bis an den Tod . . .'
61–2	*17^{v}: '(*b*) Kinder will ich haben . . .'
62	*18: [continued on third system: 'in kalten] Nächten wenn der Sturm . . .'
62–3	*18^{v}: 'Hörst du mich an? . . .'
63–4	*19: 'Der Vater der ist Tot . . .'
64–5	*19^{v}: 'wenden links und rechts den Kopf . . .'
65–6	*20: '[kein] Bote von dem Bruder . . .'
66–7	*20^{v}: '[die] Sonne auf und ab . . .'
67–8	*21: '[kom-] men [zum] Brunnen wieder . . .'
69–71	*21^{v}: '[und] säugend hängt ein Leben . . .'
71–2	*22: '[Weiber-]schicksal! Viel lieber . . .'
73–4	*22^{v}: '[und] nicht Leben— | Elektra Was heulst du?'

	*23: 'Orest' [motivic fragment]
75–7	*23^{v}: 'Sechszehnter | "Es geht ein Lärm los! . . ."'
77, 91	*24: '"drauf zu schlafen . . ." | Klytämnestra erscheint'
77–9	*25: 'dass sie dich nicht sieht! . . .'
78	*24^{v}: 'Sie schickt den Tod aus [jedem Blick]' [5-bar working of this musical phrase.]
79–81	*25^{v}: 'ich weiss nicht was, ich hab es . . .'
81–3	*26: 'Sie kommen schon . . .'
83–5	*26^{v}: 'diese Stunde geh' aus ihrem Weg! . . .'
	*27: [sketch for orchestral interlude before Klytämnestra scene]
97	*27^{v}: 'Halt | "Sie meint es tückisch"'
122	*28: '"es kriecht ein Hauch" | Klytäm.' [various thematic fragments]
113	*28^{v}: 'abends ihre | Beulen | abends ihre Beulen u. all ihr Eiterndes der kühlen'
113–15	*29: '[der kühlen] Luft preisgeben, abends . . . | ein halbes Ton höher | "lasst mich allein"'
	*29^{v}: [unlabelled sketch: Orestes material?]
	*30: 'Elektra fährt auf!'
117	*30^{v}: 'Klytämnestra Schlagzeug. Juwelenbehängt | oder | oder | "Träumst du | Mutter"'
117–8	*31: [K1.] '"Wer älter wird" | Bräuche | immer Dominant | H moll dann d moll | beim Eintritt der Klytämnestra'
117	*31^{v}: 'Klytämn | mit Steinen behängt | "Ich habe keine gute Nächte . . ." | Bräuche'
117–18	*32: 'B moll | "Wer älter wird der träumt"'
118–20	*32^{v}: 'Allein es lässt sich vertreiben . . .'
120–1	*33: 'man muss nur wissen wie man sie nützen kann . . .'
121–2	*33^{v}: '"[Du könntest] vieles sagen . . ." | immer länger im Bass'
	*34: [unlabelled sketch: report of Orestes' alleged death?]
122	*34^{v}: 'und doch kriecht zwischen Tag und Nacht . . .'
122–3	*35: 'nichts ist es, nicht einmal ein Alp und'
123–5	*35^{v}: 'dennoch, es ist so fürchterlich . . .'
125–6	*36: '[Kann man] denn vergehn, lebend . . .'
126–7	*36^{v}: '[wenn man] gar nicht krank ist? . . .'

128–31 *37: 'und täumle wieder auf . . .'
131–3 *37^{v}: '[meinen Schlaf] belauert . . .'
133–4 *38: 'jedes Tier, das kriecht . . .'
135–6 *38^{v}: '[des letzten] Thule im blutroten Nebel . . .'
136–7 *39: '[län-]ger! Also wüsstest du . . .'
137–8 *39^{v}: 'Und was für Bräuche? . . .'
139–41 *40: 'Ein Weib . . .'
*40^{v}: 'H moll'
*41: 'E dur | triumphierend pp'
*41^{v}: 'visionär | feierliche Triumph Elektras'
*?42: 'Reigen' [crossed out]
*42^{v}: 'agitato | agitato'
43: 'Parademarsch für Cavallerie | Maestoso'
43^{v}: [cont.]
44: [cont.?]
44^{v}: [cont.?]
45: 'Lady Hamilton | Thema con Variazioni . . .'
45^{v}: 'Thema'
46: 'Thema'
46^{v}: unlabelled [another 'Thema'?]
47: 'Schnell'
47^{v}: 'Crevetten Girl . . .'
48: 'Schlendernd | Auf der Gasse schlendernd . . .'
*48^{v}: 'Elektra auf der Fersen der Kl. | Klytämnestra | langsam'
49: 'Schnell | Crevetten Girl . . . | [*] Klytämnestra erschlagen | Becken gültig' [?]
49^{v}: 'Quartett | stürmisch'
*50: 'Schmerzen um den Tod Orests | also Unterbrechung dann den 'Elektraruf der Chrysot. | Elek-tra!'
*50^{v}: 'elegisch' [*Elektra* sketch?]

**Elektra* sketch

Trenner 19

Date: ?1906–26
Size: 10.5 × 16 cm.
Make of sketchbook: Hans Licht, Leipzig
No. of folios: 72 (1 fol. torn out?) Paginated in a different hand.
Sketchbook type: Preliminary

Implements used: Pencil and ink

Contents: Contains material relating to *Elektra*; *Die Frau ohne Schatten*; Lied Op. 69, No. 5; *Eine Alpensinfonie*; *Der Rosenkavalier*; *Parergon zur Symphonia Domestica*; *Fanfare für die Wiener Philharmoniker*; *Die ägyptische Helena*; *Militärmarsch* o.O p. 112. Also sketches to unrealized projects: *Sonatine für Klavier an Bubi*, *Semiramis*, *Casanova*, 'Volkslied'.

Score pp. *Fol. no.*

1: 'Sonatine für Klavier an Bubi'
1^{v}: [cont.]
2: [unlabelled F maj. sketch (AV 112—'Militärmarsch' for *Rosenkavalier* film music)]
2^{v}: 'Codathema' [for 'Sonatine'?]
3: [cont.]
3^{v}: [cont.]
4: 'Trio | Canon' [*Die ägyptische Helena*?]
4^{v}: [Unlabelled sketch]
5: [cont.]
5^{v}: [F maj. sketch, see fol. 2]
6: [cont.]
6^{v}: [cont.]
7: 'Melodie umbrische'
7^{v}: 'Semiramis | Bachtrompeten | Kriegerisch'
8: [expansion of fol. 7 sketch]
8^{v}: [cont.]
9: [alternate opening of fol. 7 sketch]
9^{v}: 'breit' [follows mood of fol. 7 sketch although in different key (E flat major)]
10: [cont.]
10^{v}: [unlabelled F sharp major fragment]
11: [unlabelled D maj. fragment]
*11^{v}: 'Orest' [4-bar theme] | 'Elektra' [4-bar theme]
12: [another version of fol. 10^{v} fragment]
12^{v}: [expansion of 'Melodie umbrische' sketch]
13: [cont.]
*13^{v}: unlabelled *Elektra* sketch
*14: 'Orest | grollend'

★14^{v} 'Orest | Bass Kl. | Bassethrn. | Poss. | Cbasse'
★15: 'für verbreiteten | Schluss | doppelt so langsam' [*Elektra* sketch?]
★15^{v}: [cont.?]
★16: 'Coda | moderato' [cont. of above?]
★16^{v}: 'Elektra | innig zärtlich'
★17: 'ruhig | Oktave tiefer' [*Elektra* sketch?]
★17^{v}: [cont.]
312 ★18: 'Ägisth. gemächlich | Holz | "He Lichter! Lichter!"'
312, 315 ★18^{v}: '"Ist Niemand da . . ." | Elektra gleitet herab | "O Herr, sie melden's nicht mit Worten bloss"'
★19: 'lebhaft' [*Elektra* sketch?]
19^{v}: unlabelled sketch ['Melodie umbrische'?]
20: unlabelled sketch
20^{v}: unlabelled sketch [related to 'Baraks Verzeihung']
21: 'Baraks Verzeihung'
21^{v}: 'grazioso'
22: ['grazioso']
22^{v}: unlabelled sketch ['Melodie umbrische'?]
23: 'Schnell | Orchester Einleitung zu Casanova . . .'
23^{v}: 3 unlabelled sketch entries
24: [cont.]
24^{v}: unlabelled E-maj. sketch
25: 'Steigerung' [see fol. 24^{v}]
25^{v}: 'Menuett'
26: 'Volkslied'
26^{v}: 'Heine: "Das ist ein schlechtes Wetter"'
27: 'Nachspiel | Coda' [to 'Schlechtes Wetter']
27^{v}: [cont.?]
28: [cont.?]
28^{v}: 'Allegro grazioso'
29: 'gemütlich'
29^{v}: 'Ländler | Alpensinfonie | Coda'
30: '2. Trio rasche Oberpfälzer Dreher . . .' [cont.]
30^{v}: [blank]
31: 'Abgang des | Baron'
31^{v}: 'Marschallin Anfang'
32: 'Moderato | Deutsches Volk deutsches' [o.Op. 101?]
32^{v}: [sketch to o.Op. 101?]
33: [cont.]

33^{v}: [blank]
34: [sketch to o.Op. 101?]
34^{v}: 'Orgel | getragen'
35: [cont.]
35^{v}: [another attempt at 'Orgel getragen']
36: [cont.]
36^{v}: 'Klavierconzert' [*Parergon zur Symphonia Domestica*]
37: 'Der verlorne Sohn | Weihnachten 1923' [*Parergon*]
37^{v}: ['Klavierconzert', cont.]
38: [cont.]
38^{v}: [cont.?]
39: [cont.?]
39^{v}: [cont.]
40: [cont.]
40^{v}: [cont.]
41: [cont.]
41^{v}: [cont.]
42: [end of sketch with the instructions at end:] 'F dur idylle Trost in der Natur. | zuerst Bläser allein | dann umspielt vom Klavier | als Coda das Sommerlied | als Duett'
42^{v}: 'Allegro | hierauf das D dur thema: wieder normal als Ruf zu einem Leben u. schönes Finale | G dur' [still 'Klavierconzert'?]
43: 'als tutti' [cont.]
43^{v}: [cont.]
44: 'Coda' [cont.]
44^{v}: 'Seitensatz [?]'
45: [cont.]
45^{v}: 'Modulationen'
46: [cont.]
46^{v}: [unlabelled sketch for *Vienna Philharmonic Fanfare*]
47: [cont.]
47^{v}: [cont.]
48: [cont.]
48^{v}: [cont.]
49: [cont.]
49^{v}: [cont.]
50: [cont.]
50^{v}: [cont.]

51: [cont.]
51^{v}: 'der kranke Sohn u. die Mutter . . .' [*Parergon*?]
52: 'Klavier' [cont.]
52^{v}: 'Mein lieber armer Bubi . . .'
53: [illegible]
53^{v}: 'zuerst auf Fis moll'
54: [illegible]
54^{v}: 'Steigerung [illegible]'
55: [cont.]
55^{v}: 'Cadenz | Schluss erheben vom Krankenlager . . .'
56: [unlabelled]
56^{v}: [cont.]
57: 'Gebet'
57^{v}: [cont.]
58: [cont.]
58^{v}: 'langsamer [illegible]'
59: [cont.]
59^{v}: [cont. from fol. 58]
60: 'nach der Krise, beruhigen—Hoffnung! | zaghaft, schwach.'
60^{v}: [mostly illegible; last word: 'Steigerung'.]
61: [cont.?]
61^{v}: [unlabelled sketch for AV 112 ('Militärmarsch')]
62: [cont.]
62^{v}: 'Trio' [to o.O p. 112?]
63: [cont.]
63^{v}: [cont.]
64: [another o.O p. 112 sketch]
64^{v}: 'Trio | Coda' [to o.O p. 112]
65: [blank]
65^{v}: [blank]
66: [conclusion of *Parergon*; then] 'Der Scheich blickt auf zu Helena'
66^{v}: [unlabelled F maj. sketch (*Parergon*?)]
67: [*Parergon*]
67^{v}: [cont.]
68: [cont.]
68^{v}: [cont.]
69: [cont.]
69^{v}: [cont.]

70: [cont.]
70^{v}: [cont.]
71: [cont.]
71^{v}: [cont.]
72: [cont.]
72^{v}: [cont.—the conclusion of this sketch is on fol. 66]
Inside back 'Vorsatzblatt' torn out.
**Elektra* sketch

Vienna Sketchbook

Date: 1908
Size 12.5 × 16.5 cm.
Make: Jos. Eberle, Vienna
No. of folios: 52
Type of Sketchbook: Preliminary sketch
Implements used: Mostly pencil, some ink
Comments: Inside cover page foliated as no 1, first page of staff paper thus begins as no. 2
Contents: *Elektra* sketches for the last scene

Score pp. *Folio no.*

1: 'Der genialen Darstellerin / der Klytämnestra in Wien / Frl. von Mildenburg / zu freundlicher Erinnerung / an ihren grössten Bewunderer. / Der dankbare Componist der Elektra. / Dr Richard Strauss / Garmisch, 7. Mai 1909.'
1^{v}: blank
2: 'Lebhaft' [sketch in B flat major; reminiscent of music for 'Wie stark du bist!' from scene 5]
2^{v}: 'Elektras Tanz zuerst' [E-major sketch corresponds to reh. 230a and 247a]
3: 'Tanz am Schluss nach Elektras letztem Gesang' [C-major sketch; this label pertains to the first system only]
[2nd and 3rd systems: E-major sketch for the passage, 'Ob ich nicht höre?' Continuation on fol. 4^{v}]
3^{v}: [E-major sketch for the opening of the final scene]
4: [cont.]
4^{v}: [continuation of fol. 3]

344–5 5: [one-page try-out for reh. 237a: 'Sie fahren dahin . . .']

344–5 5^{v}: [another try-out for reh. 237a]

364–5 6: [beginning of a 4-page continuity sketch for the end of the opera beginning with: 'Ich trage die Last des Glückes']

366–7 6^{v}: [cont.] '[schweigen und tan-]zen'

368–70 7: [cont.] 'Sie stürzt zusammen' | ' "Orest" '

370 7^{v}: [cont.] '[O-]rest' | ritard.' | breit' | 'Schluss'.

8: 'siehe hinten[?]' [sketch for Elektra's E-major dance; *c.*reh. 250a?, etc.]

8^{v}–18: [blank]

336–8 18^{v}: [beginning of continuity sketch, which begins with reh. 230a and goes to 5 after reh. 255a] 'Die Tausende, die Fakkeln tragen . . .'

339–41 19: 'Reigen führen muss . . .'

342–5 19^{v}: 'Hörst du denn nicht? . . .'

345–6 20: '[Wan-]gen vor Tränen' | 'sind die Götter'

346–7 20^{v}: 'Gut sind die Götter—gut!'

326–8 21: 'Chrysot. "[Es ist der] Bruder drin im [Haus!]" '

328–9 21^{v}: 'Kommt! Er steht im [Vorsaal]' [text for chorus ('Orest!') omitted]

329–30 22: 'alle sind um ihn . . .'

330–1 22^{v}: '[ge-]worfen auf die andern . . .'

332–3 23: 'und haben selbst Wunden'

334–5 23^{v}: 'hörst du denn nicht? . . .'

335–7 24: 'ob ich die Musik nicht höre? . . .'

337–40 24^{v}: '[Myria-]den Tritte überall die Erde dumpf . . .'

340–3 25: '[zwangzig-]fache Ozean begräbt mir jedes Glied . . .'

343–5 25^{v}: '[Göt-]tern. Wir Vollbringenden. Sie fahren dahin . . .'

345–7 26: 'uns | alle weinen | Ich habe Finsternis . . .'

347–8 26^{v}: '[Flam-]me verbrennt die Finsternis der Welt . . .'

349–51 27: 'mich sieht muss er den Tod empfangen . . .'

351–3 27^{v}: '[Bru-]der [da] u. Liebe fliesst . . .'

353–6 28: ' "[ge-]kannt | muss bei meinem Bruder stehen" ' | 'Tanz breiter und schwer'

356–8 28^{v}: [continuation of dance]

358–61 29: [ditto]

361–2 29^{v}: '"Elektra!"' | "Schweig und [tanze!]"'
30–51^{v}: blank

Tokyo Sketchbook

Date: July 1906–September (?) 1907
Size: 12.5 × 16.5 cm.
Make: Max Lieber, Freiburg
No. of pages: 98 (96 are paginated)
Sketchbook type: Fair
Implements used: Pencil
Contents: *Elektra*, scenes 1 to part of scene 4 (to 4 after reh. 217)
Scene 1: pp. 1–15
Scene 2: pp. 15–29
Scene 3: pp. 29–49
Scene 4: pp. 49–95 (actually the 97th page of the sketchbook, see comment 1)
Comments:

1. Pages [90] and [91] are not paginated; the former is a rejected page and the latter consists of a handful of sketch fragments (for sc. 2?). Page [92] is, thus, paginated as 90.
2. Page 96 is a rejected one-page sketch labelled 'Fackeltanz'. It was possibly intended as material for the instrumental passage at the end of scene four.
3. On the recto side of the inside front cover page Strauss writes: 'Elektra Reinschrift'. On the verso side he writes: 'Electra allein. B moll, der Welt gegenüber gesteigert H moll. | Agamemnon C moll, Siegestanz C dur.'
4. On the recto side of the inside back cover page Strauss writes an excerpt from Klytämnestra's text in scene 4:

    will ich von meiner Seele alle Hüllen
    abstreifen und das Fächeln sanfter Luft,
    von wo es kommen mag, einlassen wie
    die Kranken tun, wenn sie der kühlen Luft,
    am Teiche sitzend, abends ihre Beulen
    und all ihr Eiterndes der kühlen Luft
    preisgeben abends u. nichts andres denken
    als Lindrung zu schaffen.
    Lasst mich allein mit ihr.

5. On the verso side of the page Strauss has jotted down some details concerning furnishings for his new house in Garmisch.

Works Cited

Adorno, Theodor, 'Richard Strauss. Born June 11, 1864', trans. Samuel and Shierry Weber, *Perspectives of New Music*, 1 (1965), 14–32; *Perspectives*, 2 (1966), 113–29.

Altmann, Wilhelm, '*Elektra* von Richard Strauss', *Velhagen und Klasings Monatshefte*, 23/8 (1909), 573–9.

Asow, E.H. Mueller von, ed. *Richard Strauss: Thematisches Verzeichnis*, 3 vols. (Vienna, 1955–74).

Bailey, Robert, *Wagner: Prelude and Transfiguration from Tristan und Isolde*, Norton Critical Scores (New York, 1985).

Bales, Suzanne, 'Elektra: From Hofmannsthal to Strauss', Ph.D. Dissertation (Stanford University, 1984).

Beecham, Sir Thomas, *A Mingled Chime* (London, 1944).

Bekker, Paul, *Wandlungen der Oper* (Zurich, 1934). See also *The Changing Opera*, trans. Arthur Mendel (New York, 1935).

—— '*Elektra* Studie', *Neue Musik-Zeitung*, 14, 16, 18 (1909), 293–8, 333–7, 387–91.

Bie, Oskar, '*Elektra*', *Die neue Rundschau* [Berlin], 4 (1909), 589–93.

The Bodley Head Bernard Shaw: Shaw's Music, vol. iii, ed. Dan H. Laurence (London, 1981).

Brosche, Günter, and Dachs, Karl, eds., *Richard Strauss: Autographen in München und Wien*, Veröffentlichungen der Richard-Strauss-Gesellschaft, München, vol. iii (Tutzing, 1979).

Catalogue of Valuable Printed Books and Some Manuscripts, Christie, Manson, and Woods, Ltd. (London, 1955).

Del Mar, Norman, *Richard Strauss: A Critical Commentary on his Life and Work*, 3 vols. (London, 1962–72).

Dentienne, Marcel, *Dionysos at Large*, trans. Arthur Goldhammer (Cambridge, Mass., 1989).

Erken, Günther, 'Hofmannsthal Chronik: Beitrag zu einer Biographie' (unpublished, *c.*1963, Willi Schuh Estate).

Erwin, Charlotte. 'Richard Strauss's Presketch Planning for *Ariadne auf Naxos*', *The Musical Quarterly*, 67 (1981), 348–65.

Ewen, David, ed., *Book of Modern Composers* (New York, 1942).

Geissler, F. A., '*Elektra* von Richard Strauss', *Die Musik*, 8/10 (1909), 243–6.

Gilliam, Bryan, 'Richard Strauss's Daphne: Opera and Symphonic Continuity', Ph.D. Dissertation (Harvard University, 1984).

—— 'Strauss's Preliminary Opera Sketches: Thematic Fragments and Symphonic Continuity', *19th-Century Music*, 9 (1986), 176–88.

Gould, Glenn, 'Strauss and the Electronic Future', *Saturday Review*, 30 May 1964, 58–9.

Gräner, Georg, *Elektra: Tragödie in einem Aufzug von Hugo von Hofmannsthal und Richard Strauss*, Schlesinger'sche Musik-Bibiothek Opernführer Nr. 122 (Berlin, 1909).

Gregor, Joseph, *Richard Strauss: Der Meister der Oper* (Munich, 1939).

Hamburger, Michael, ed., Introduction to *Hugo von Hofmannsthal: Selected Plays and Libretti*, Bollingen Series 33, no. 3 (New York, 1963). Reprinted in Hamburger, *Hofmannsthal: Three Essays* (Princeton, NJ, 1972).

Hofmannsthal, Hugo von, *Aufzeichnungen*, Hugo von Hofmannsthal: Gesammelte Werke in Einzelausgaben, ed. Herbert Steiner (Frankfurt a.M., 1959), 131–2.

—— 'Ein Brief', *Prosa II*, Hugo von Hofmannsthal: Gesammelte Werke in Einzelausgaben, ed. Herbert Steiner (Frankfurt a.M., 1951), 7–22. See also *Selected Prose*, trans. Mary Hottinger and Tania and James Stern, Bollingen Series 33, no. 1 (New York, 1952), 129–41.

—— *Elektra*, trans. Alfred Schwartz, in *Hugo von Hofmannsthal: Selected Plays and Libretti*, ed. Michael Hamburger, Bollingen Series 33, no. 3 (New York, 1963).

—— *Hugo von Hofmannsthal: Briefe 1900–09* (Vienna, 1937).

—— 'Über Pantomime', *Prosa III*, Hugo von Hofmannsthal: Gesammelte Werke in Einzelausgaben, ed. Herbert Steiner (Frankfurt a.M., 1952), 46–50.

Huesmann, Heinrich, *Welttheater Reinhardt* (Munich, 1983).

Hutcheson, Ernest, *Elektra by Richard Strauss: A Guide to the Opera* (New York, 1910).

Kalisch, Alfred, 'Impressions of Strauss's *Elektra*', *Zeitschrift der Internationalen Musikgesellschaft* 7 (1909), 198–202.

Kennedy, Michael, *Richard Strauss*, The Master Musician Series (London, 1976).

—— 'Richard Strauss', *Turn of the Century Masters*, The New Grove Composer Biography Series (New York, 1985), 185–267.

Kohler, Stephan, 'Richard Strauss in Marquartstein: Eine Chronik', *Richard-Strauss Blätter*, 2 (1979), 29–48.

Krause, Ernst, *Richard Strauss: Dokumente* (Leipzig, 1980).

—— *Richard Strauss: Gestalt und Werk* (Leipzig, 1955). See also *Richard Strauss: The Man and his Work* (Boston, 1969).

Louis, Robert, *Die deutsche Musik der Gegenwart* (Munich, 1909).

Litterae Rarae Liber Primus (Tokyo: Biblioteca Musashino Academia Musicae, 1962).

Mann, William, *Richard Strauss: A Critical Study of the Operas* (London, 1964).

Marek, George, *Richard Strauss: The Life of a Non-Hero* (New York, 1967).

Martens, Lorna, 'The Theme of the Repressed Memory in Hofmannsthal's *Elektra*', *German Quarterly*, 1 (1987), 38–51.

Mayer, Hans, 'Hugo von Hofmannsthal und Richard Strauss', *Sinn und Form* 13 (1961), 888–915.

Mennicke, Carl, 'Über Richard Strauss' *Elektra*', *Riemann-Festschrift: Gesammelte Studien* (Leipzig, 1909).

Newcomb, Anthony, 'The Birth of Music out of the Spirit of Drama', *19th-Century Music*, 5 (1981), 38–66.

Newman, Ernest, *Richard Strauss*, Living Masters of Music (London, 1908).

Newman, Vera, *Ernest Newman: A Memoir by his Wife* (London, 1963).

Nostitz, O., ed., *Hugo von Hofmannsthal-Helene von Nostitz: Briefwechsel* (Frankfurt a.M., 1965).

Overhoff, Kurt, *Die Elektra-Partitur von Richard Strauss* (Salzburg, 1978).

Platzenbecker, Heinrich, 'Uraufführung der *Elektra* und Rich[ard] Strauss-Woche in Dresden', *Neue Musik-Zeitung* 10, (1909), 205–8.

Reiss, Hans, 'Hugo von Hofmannsthal', *The Writer's Task from Nietzsche to Brecht* (Totowa, NJ, 1978).

Röse, Otto, and Prüwer, Julius, *Richard Strauss: Elektra. Ein Musikführer durch das Werk* (Berlin, 1909).

Rosen, Charles, *Arnold Schoenberg* (Princeton, NJ, 1975).

Sayler, Oliver, ed., *Max Reinhardt and his Theater* (New York, 1924).

Schlötterer, Reinhold, 'Elektras Tanz in der Tragödie Hugo von Hofmannsthals', *Hofmannsthal Blätter*, 33 (1986), 47–58.

Schneider, Hans, ed., *Richard Strauss: Manuskripte und Briefe*, Catalogue No. 194 (part 1).

Schuch, Friedrich von, *Richard Strauss, Ernst von Schuch, und Dresdens Oper* (Leipzig, 1953).

Schuh, Willi, 'Hugo von Hofmannsthal und Richard Strauss: Legende und Wirklichkeit', *Umgang mit Musik* (Zürich, 1970), 173–202.

—— *Richard Strauss: Jugend und Meisterjahre, Lebenschronik 1864–98* (Zurich, 1980). See also *Richard Strauss: A Chronicle of the Early Years*, trans. Mary Whittall (Cambridge, 1982).

—— ed., *Richard Strauss-Stefan Zweig: Briefwechsel* (Frankfurt a.M., 1957). See also *A Working Friendship: The Letters of Richard Strauss and Stefan Zweig 1931–1935*, trans. Max Knight (Berkeley and Los Angeles, 1977).

Spanuth, August, '*Elektra*', *Signale für die Musikalische Welt* [Berlin], 67/4 (1909), 121–4.

—— 'Nachträge zur *Elektra*', *Signale für die Musikalische Welt*, 67/5 (1909), 165–8.

Steinitzer, Max, *Richard Strauss* (Stuttgart, 1927).

Sternfeld, Richard, '*Elektra*', *März* [Munich], 3/8 (1909), 135–41.

Storck, Karl, 'Richard Strauss's *Elektra*', *Der Türmer* [Stuttgart] 11/6 (1909), 877–84.

Strauss, Richard, *Betrachtungen und Erinnerungen*, ed. Willi Schuh, 3rd edn. (Zurich, 1981). See also *Recollections and Reflections*, trans. L. J. Lawrence (London, 1953).

Tenschert, Roland, ed., *Richard Strauss und Joseph Gregor: Briefwechsel (1934–1949)* (Salzburg, 1955).

Trenner, Franz, *Richard Strauss: Dokumente seines Lebens und Schaffens* (Munich, 1954).

—— ed., *Richard Strauss: Werkverzeichnis* (Vienna, 1985).

—— ed., *Die Skizzenbücher von Richard Strauss aus dem Richard-Strauss-Archiv in Garmisch*, Veröffentlichungen der Richard-Strauss-Gesellschaft, München, vol. 1 (Tutzing, 1977).

Wachten, Edmund, 'Das Formproblem in der sinfonischen Dichtungen von Richard Strauss' (Ph.D. Dissertation, University of Berlin, 1933).

Weber, Horst, *Alexander Zemlinsky* (Vienna, 1977).

'Zwei bisher unveröffentliche Aufzeichnungen von Hugo von

Hofmannsthal', *Programheft 2: Salome und Elektra*, Frankfurt Opera (Frankfurt a.M., 1974).

Zweig, Stefan, *Die Welt von Gestern: Erinnerungen eines Europäers* (Stockholm, 1947). See also *The World of Yesterday* (Lincoln, Nebr., 1964).

Index